Also by Nina Atwood

Be Your Own Dating Service

Date Lines

♥ ♥ ♥

NINA ATWOOD

Date Lines

♥ ♥ ♥

COMMUNICATION FROM
"HELLO" TO "I DO"
AND EVERYTHING
IN BETWEEN

♥

An Owl Book
Henry Holt and Company
New York

Henry Holt and Company, Inc. / *Publishers since 1866*
115 West 18th Street / New York, New York 10011

Henry Holt® is a registered trademark
of Henry Holt and Company, Inc.

Published in Canada by Fitzhenry & Whiteside Ltd.,
195 Allstate Parkway, Markham, Ontario L3R 4T8.

Library of Congress Cataloging-in-Publication Data

Atwood, Nina.
Date lines: communication from "hello" to "I do"
and everything in between / Nina Atwood.
p.   cm.
"An Owl book."
ISBN 0-8050-5537-1 (pbk.: alk. paper)
1. Dating (Social customs).   2. Man-woman relationships.
3. Conversation.   4. Couples.   I. Title.
HQ801.A8256   1998   97-28247
646.7'7—dc21   CIP

Henry Holt books are available for special promotions and
premiums. For details contact: Director, Special Markets.

First Edition 1998

Designed by Victoria Hartman

Printed in the United States of America
All first editions are printed on acid-free paper. ∞

1   3   5   7   9   10   8   6   4   2

To my father, who had the courage
to initiate a single conversation, out of which
we are in each other's lives today.
And to the memory of my "Grandma,"
Pauline, for all the happy times.

♥

Contents

♥   ♥   ♥

Acknowledgments

♥   ♥   ♥

My thanks and acknowledgment, first and foremost, to Denise Marcil (the World's Greatest Agent!), for believing in me and what I do, and for continuing to support my vision.

A very special acknowledgment to my good friend (and world-renowned consultant/entrepreneur), Peggy Pepper, for sparking the concept of this book.

A very warm acknowledgment to Suzan Oran, for creating many of the powerful distinctions and communication processes that are the foundation of this book.

Thanks and much appreciation to Russ Martin, for inviting me to be a regular part of the Sunday Night Talk Show, 97.1 KEGL in Dallas, and for being a terrific on-air conversation partner.

Much gratitude to my support system (you know who you are), for believing in me and for cheering me on.

Most of all, thanks, love, and appreciation to my sweetheart, for all of the powerful conversations that have touched my heart and transformed my life.

Introduction: Author's Story

♥   ♥   ♥

When *Be Your Own Dating Service: A Step-by-Step Guide to Finding and Maintaining Healthy Relationships* was published, I began traveling around the country, doing workshops and interviewing with members of the media. One of the first questions I am usually asked is, "What motivated you to write this book?" I'm always tempted to answer something such as, "Well, I have this expertise as a therapist, and I wanted to contribute something to humanity by sharing my insights,". . . and so on.

But the real answer is, for myself! I developed the ideas that went into the book and that I share in my seminars because years ago, before my marriage, I was truly puzzled about the whole dating scene. Finally, I admitted that I didn't know everything I needed to know, so I began looking around for resources to help me.

In the self-help section of the bookstore I found basically two kinds of books. The first kind explained how to improve an established relationship with communication skills and provided information about how romantic love works. I found these books very helpful, and thought to myself, "Well, if I can ever find a partner who's willing to work on a relationship together, this will be great!"

The second kind of book, targeted to singles, was essentially a compilation of tips and techniques offered with the promise that if I learned to do this, do that, and have the right line to say, I could attract and win over the object of my desire. I didn't find this kind of information very helpful, as I am uncomfortable with the implication that I, as a single person, have to sell myself to someone in order to have a relationship. I was far more interested in *being myself and attracting a good partner.*

No one was addressing what I wanted to know: how to go through this whole process of meeting people, choosing whom to go out with and whom to go on and become involved with, in a way that would help me get into a healthy, loving relationship. Since the information wasn't out there, I began formulating my own ideas, sharing them with friends and clients, and using them myself. As a result of what I developed, I met and married my husband, and eventually wrote *Be Your Own Dating Service.*

Five and a half years into our marriage, when my husband let me know that he no longer wished to be married, I was painfully reminded that in relationships, as in life, there are no guarantees. Over the months that we were separated and divorced, we talked and listened to each other a lot. One painful truth emerged: Our marriage wasn't working, and he didn't want to do what it would take to make it better.

Something else became clear thanks to those conversations, a deeper truth about how we had interacted as a couple. Eventually we traced the breakdown of our relationship back to the *third month we dated*, to a significant conversation that took place one evening. Looking back, we both realized that we had failed to express ourselves and to listen to each other as fully as we could have at a critical time. In short, our communication wasn't all it should have been, and, as a result, in our unfolding relationship, we were building on a faulty foundation.

After our divorce, as I began exploring life again as a single person, I was struck by one fundamental truth: At any given moment, whether meeting someone for the first time, or discussing long-term commitment, or any of the ground in between, the potential of these budding relationships hinges on the quality of our communication. *Date Lines* was written with this in mind, and therefore specifically addresses the communication process in dating. As I did in *Be Your Own Dating Service*, I take the topic and progress from the time prior to the first encounter with a possible romantic partner all the way through to deciding about marriage. As it was in that book, here also the basic goal is to set the stage for a healthy, loving relationship, realizing that there are no guarantees, and focusing on the process of learning and growth along the way. Thus, I hope each bit of information I offer in this book will add to men's and women's deeper understanding of each other and of romantic love, now and in the future. Practice the exercises offered here, and you'll develop the emotional muscle needed to be in a good relationship and to maximize the chances that you'll find and maintain a lasting love.

If you're already in a relationship, reading this book will help you uncover what you may have overlooked in building the foundation for your connection. It's never too late to backtrack and have the critical conversations that will help move your romance into a more healthy direction. Most importantly, this book contains powerful communication tools that will benefit any relationship, romantic or platonic, dating or married. My hope is that with this material, you will find your life enriched by a deeper, more rewarding connection with those whom you love now, and with those whom you have yet to meet and love.

Date Lines

♥   ♥   ♥

1

Setting the Stage

♥   ♥   ♥

You're pushing your shopping cart through the grocery store. You stop, look up from perusing the vegetables, and you see . . . her. She's attractive and she's not wearing a ring. You want to approach her, but how? What do you say? How do you ask for her phone number? How do you connect?

♥

It's your fourth date with Mr. Right. Everything seems to be clicking for you both, but you've felt this way before. This time, you don't want to find yourself empty-handed in a few weeks or months. How can you be sure he's ready for a real relationship, before you risk your heart? How do you talk about this without scaring him off?

♥

You've been dating for six weeks, and so far, it's been perfection. All of a sudden, you're arguing about things that you were totally in sync about just last week. How do you make the transition from blissful love to the harsh reality that your needs may clash from time to time? How do you talk about these difficult issues?

♥

You're in a two-year relationship, and it's time to make a commitment: You either move forward or you break up. How do you talk about this without issuing ultimatums or sweeping everything under the rug?

♥

From the very first encounter, today's relationships present us all with incredible challenges, and at the heart of every one of them is the *quality of our connection*. Sometimes we click, and then suddenly we clash.

How it all happens seems to be a great mystery. What we know is that it all comes to light through the magic of conversation. Perpetually, we struggle with finding the right words. About virtually every circumstance we wonder

- What to say
- How to say it
- When to say it

We worry that we'll

- Hurt someone's feelings
- Hurt ourselves
- Damage the relationship

These concerns we have are realistic, because the truth is,

The heart and soul of relationships is COMMUNICATION.

When we communicate effectively, love thrives and grows and knows no bounds. Listening to each other, talking about our cares and pains, desires and dreams, we are transported to a place that is far more fulfilling than simply talking in our own heads. Sharing feelings with a loving partner is one of life's deepest satisfactions. In fact, it is so wonderful that we are motivated to do almost anything in order to find someone with whom to share this experience.

When communication breaks down, the relationship itself deteriorates, and if the trend isn't reversed quickly, heartache is inevitable. The problems can begin with the *very first encounter*. Witness Tom and Mona on their first date:

TOM: I'm really glad to finally meet you, after hearing about you from my friend Nancy for so long.

MONA: Yeah, well, it's amazing how you can live in this town and never meet anyone new for months at a time.

TOM: That's true, but I've found that if you make an effort, it's not that difficult. After all, here we are!

MONA: And then there's the kind of people you meet in this city. Even when I do meet someone new, it's usually someone who's either out of work or unstable. The last guy I went out with still lives with his mother, and he's forty-two years old!

TOM: That's too bad. Uh, maybe we could decide what to order. This is one of my favorite restaurants, and the food's always great.

MONA: Well, I'm starving. As usual, my boss threw a pile of work on my desk just as I was getting ready to leave for lunch and announced that I had to finish it before the end of the day, so I missed lunch. What a jerk.

As you can imagine, the date went downhill from there. Mona's negative conversation didn't stop, and the result was uncomfortable feelings that grew as the date went on. Tom's efforts to distract her from negativity went nowhere, and any romantic sparks that might have been ignited were lost forever.

Setting the Stage

From the very first encounter with a potential romantic partner, the stage for your future relationship is being set, and you are the set designer! The kind and quality of communication that occurs at the outset determines everything. You are either headed for an unhappy, draining relationship, or you are paving the way for a joyful, fulfilling one.

Let's replay Tom and Mona's first-date conversation:

TOM: I'm really glad to meet you, after hearing about you from my friend Nancy for so long.

MONA: You know, I've noticed that if I'm not really careful, I can fall into the same old dull routine and not meet anyone new for months at a time.

TOM: Me, too. But with some effort, it's not too difficult. After all, here we are!

MONA: Yes, and it's so refreshing to meet someone I like. I've had a few dates that didn't exactly go the way I wanted them to go (smiles and laughs a little, catching Tom's eye).

TOM: Yeah, dating can be a challenge (smiling in return). Are you ready to order? This is one of my favorite restaurants, and the food's always terrific.

MONA: The sooner the better—I'm starving! My work kind of piled up today, so I didn't get a chance to eat lunch. I hope you like someone with a healthy appetite!

TOM: Absolutely. In fact, why don't we begin right away with this wonderful appetizer. . . .

And they're off and running. A connection is made, and rapport naturally builds. Notice that this conversation contains essentially the same information as the first one. Mona doesn't have to lie about her past experiences, nor does she have to lie about not eating lunch. The difference is in her attitude and the way she chooses her words. By being positive and speaking effectively, Mona is setting the stage for a spark and a connection to occur with Tom. Regular practice of open and honest, yet uplifting, conversation like this will give them the opportunity to develop and maintain a fulfilling romance.

Communication: The Essentials

Communication is made up of two main parts:

- Listening (the most important)
- Speaking

In Chapter Four we'll go into much greater detail about these two all-important aspects of communication. Throughout the book, we'll look at both the listening and the speaking parts of each new level of conversation between you and your partner, from the first encounter all the way through discussing marriage. Always, the focus will be on setting the stage for a loving, lasting relationship.

Listening is at the top of this section for a very good reason: It's the most vitally important part of communication, and the most often overlooked. Listening is much more than just having your ears open and not being distracted by television or the newspaper. Listening is

- Being fully focused on your partner
- Working to understand him/her

and much more that we'll discuss later.

Listening begins long before someone begins speaking. It begins with an *attitude* and a *focus*, even before you have someone with whom to talk! In the search for a partner, meeting effectively has everything to do with setting the stage for a great relationship. Bringing the right *vision* and *focus* into the meeting game can make all the difference in determining who you come across and notice. Think of the rest of this chapter as a guide to *tuning in your ears to listen* for the partner you will soon meet, which will prime you for your opening conversations.

A New Vision and a Shift in Focus

The other day I was walking into a restaurant, when I almost collided with an attractive man coming out of the same door. We dodged each other, smiled, laughed, and made eye contact. A few minutes later I left the restaurant to get something from my car and the same guy was coming back. I looked up in surprise, and he said, a bit self-consciously, "I came back because I really wanted to meet you. You look like an interesting person, and I was wondering: Are you married? Are you engaged? Are you available? And would you like to go to lunch sometime?"

I was flattered, but my answer was a disappointment to him. "No, I'm not married or engaged, but I am in a relationship, so I'm not available." He looked deflated, and I said to him, "But, you know what? Congratulations to you for doing what most people only think about doing! You saw an opportunity and you took a chance, and I think that's wonderful."

In my workshops, I tell this story, as well as the one about the man I saw one day at the gas station. We were standing about six feet apart, and I kept waiting for him to look up. He was so intent on putting the gas in his car that he never even saw me. And I'll bet he tells people in his life that he never meets anyone great to date, never knowing that he was standing just a few feet away from someone who might have been a potential partner!

Everywhere I go, the complaint from singles is the same: "Where, oh where, are all the great people to date?"

The answer is obvious: They're everywhere! The problem isn't lack of people, it's our own difficulty with being open and actually seeing them. It's easy to realize how this happens.

Most singles I know have experienced what I did a number of years ago. I was stuck in what I call "The Singles Rut": You know, your life! You get up each day, go to work, after work you go to the grocery store and buy your dinner, go home, watch a little TV while eating dinner, maybe read a book, walk the dog, and go to bed. Get up the next day and do what? The same thing, of course! And the next day? Why, the exact same thing.

Many of us do this, day after day, week after week, month after month. In my workshops, I say "Day after . . ." with a pause, and someone usually yells out, "Year!"

After a few months of this rut, I eventually got tired of it and resolved to take some action. So, I would call up a friend and we'd go to the next big singles dance or party that we could find, even though our belief was that those events usually did not work.

As I tell this story in my workshops, I get lots of heads nodding and sheepish grins. Back in those days, I chose the most strategically comfortable place in the room to stand. Yes, you guessed it— that happened to be in the back, along a wall, preferably in the dark! From this vantage point, my friend and I would check out the other people and quickly conclude that most of them just weren't our kind of folks!

However, there was usually one guy that we would spot, who looked very attractive and interesting, but it didn't take long to see that he was—you guessed it again—*already taken!* Of course.

Eventually, we became offended, because no one was coming up to us to make us feel warm and welcome. What kind of people were these singles anyway?! I guess we thought we were the only ones who were shy and needed an extra smile and friendly hello. As you can imagine, we soon left the party and said to ourselves, "See, once again, we have proven it. *There just aren't any great people to date out there!"* Of course, our next step was to go right back into The Singles Rut.

I ask my workshop participants what the problems are with this scenario, figuring they're a lot smarter than I was back then, and I get these answers:

• Our attitude going into the event was negative ("We just know this won't work—these things never do!"), so of course that's what happened. It is what is known as a self-fulfilling prophecy. We got exactly what we expected.

• We made ourselves unavailable by standing in the back in the dark. Our body language screamed "stay away!", so of course people did just that.

• We judged people from afar, not realizing that from across the room we weren't seeing people, we were seeing

1. Bodies
2. Clothing
3. Hairstyles
4. Shoes

Eventually, I discovered that people aren't people until I approach them and talk to them. I discovered that even if I found myself in a room full of two hundred strangers, I could walk up, introduce myself, and chat with just a handful of them, and my experience of that gathering was transformed! This enabled me to make the huge leap from Stranger to Acquaintance with a number of people. Suddenly, I was no longer looking at bodies, clothing, hairstyles, and shoes. I was connecting with *real people*, most of whom, I discovered, *were my kind of folks!*

• We were being completely passive, waiting and hoping for someone to talk to us, leaving us with a powerless feeling that culminated in a huge sense of disappointment at the end of the evening.

• We were entirely too focused on finding Prince Charming, right then and there!

As you can see, our vision was narrow and limited, and the inevitable outcome drove us right back into The Singles Rut. After analyzing the scene, it's understandable that our focus became so off base, as well. The pressure of trying to find Prince Charming was just too difficult and made us feel way too anxious to mingle. We fell into that trap, like so many singles do, because we live in a society that pressures us to focus on the bottom line: Did we meet someone new, did we get a date, was it a "love connection," are we going to fall head over heels, get married, have 2.5 children, and live happily ever after?

How often have we had friends and family ask us, "Well, have you met anyone new lately?" If we dare to answer in the positive, and say good things about the new romance, the next thing we hear is something along the lines of: "Oh, this sounds like a good one! You'd better hang on and don't let him/her get away!" As if you are so desperate that you had better grab onto the first warm body that comes along and hang on for dear life! As if being single is some dreaded affliction that you must be cured of as quickly as possible by finding a partner.

To all of this is added the pressure we put on ourselves. A long time ago, on my good days, I said things to myself and to my friends like: "Well, I don't need a relationship! After all, I have my career, my friends, and my cat. What else do I need?" For me, this was partly true, but it was also my defense against the pain of being without an intimate love relationship.

I knew this to be the case because on my bad days, I said things like, "What's wrong with me? Why can't I connect with someone in a healthy relationship?" With all this pressure, from without and from within, it's no wonder that we search desperately for Prince or Princess Charming, often overlooking the perfectly wonderful *real people* standing right in front of us!

As you can see from my story, that is what I was doing. I desperately needed a new vision and a drastic shift in focus. I eventually did look at my situation and my mind-set and came to understand the true purpose of those evenings with other singles: *to expand my social circle and to practice my relationship skills.* Once I came to that new realization my attitude and experience changed remarkably.

Expanded Vision and a New Focus

Trying to find the perfect partner is a goal that is far too limiting, and isn't likely to yield results. If I'm scanning the room looking for Prince Charming, the odds are I won't see him. After all, most really good people don't fit the images of idealized partners we carry around in our heads. Thus, when I look out into a room full of available men, I see ordinary guys who are not carrying glass slippers and I'm disappointed and frustrated. Plus, I remain separate and apart, since the purpose of my being there is to find *him*.

After years of searching in this way, I took a few steps back, did some introspection, and came up with the following:

• *I can't control this process.* Contrary to popular belief, you can't make someone like you, you can't force someone to fall in love with you, and even if you do meet someone and have a great relationship, there's no guarantee that it will last forever. The sobering reality is that *love can't be forced*—it either happens or it doesn't, and it lasts as long as it lasts.

• *Love is an energy that occurs between two people.* We have influence over that energy, either positively or negatively, but we have no direct control over the nature of the energy itself.

• Given that the first two conclusions are true, it seems I'm stuck with the process for the time being. So, since I'm here anyway, maybe I can use my time of being single in a positive way. Maybe I can use it to make some discoveries about myself, about men and women and relationships, about communication, and about healthy love.

• Instead of focusing on the end result of finding Prince Charming, I can *focus on my own process of learning and growth.* In so doing, I can develop the kind of skills I need to learn to have a great relationship, such as the art of rapport and communication. It is not a science. No matter how many books I read, I can only really learn about communication by doing it.

• I compared this process to that of working out to build the muscle in my body—which I do in order to be stronger, to breathe better, to move around with more ease, and to feel better about myself. In the same way, I began to practice relationship skills (rapport, connection, communication) to build *emotional muscle,* which enhances the overall quality of my life, and is valuable in and of itself.

With these realizations came an *expanded vision* of being single and dating, and with it an *entirely new focus.* No longer did I attend parties and dances looking for Mr. Right, being passive and standing in the back. I saw the value of *enlarging my social circle*, inviting lots and lots of new people into my life. I attended these events in order to meet new people.

I made the shift from a narrow, *I have to find Prince Charming* vision to an expanded *who looks like an interesting person* view. I shifted from a restricted, *I have to meet "the one" today* to a much larger *what am I learning in this process* focus. I realized:

• Being open to lots of different people expands my world and gives me lots of opportunity to practice my relationship skills. It fills me with a sense of abundance, which empowers me to stay in the meeting and dating game, rather than retreating in frustration because I can't find the right man now.

• I never know where my connection with a new man will lead. Maybe we'll do some kind of business together, maybe we'll have a date and it won't go anywhere, maybe we'll become buddies, maybe we'll be friends for life. Perhaps one day he'll invite me to his house for a party and I'll meet the love of my life through his social circle!

Bill, one of my workshop participants, expressed it this way:

"You're really asking us to make a 'paradigm shift,' Nina, a whole new way of looking at being single. I've been able to make that shift, and since I did, wow, have things changed! I'm a lot more relaxed, having a lot more fun, and the women are attracted to me like crazy! I think it's because I'm no longer the desperate, anxious person I used to be. I now know that I will naturally find Ms. Right, and that I don't have to try so hard."

Making the Most
of Everyday Opportunities

So, what does all of this have to do with communication? Everything! In order to have someone with whom to talk, you must meet someone, and how you go about it determines your future success. With an expanded vision, you are open to all kinds of opportunities, and with a correct focus, you are more relaxed and able to create and maintain rapport with lots of different kinds of people.

In one of my workshops, I take singles through an exercise to bring into focus the abundance of opportunities to meet others that we naturally encounter. We take several different areas of life (i.e., work, home, recreation, organizations, religious, and so on) and generate ideas about how and where to meet other singles and potential dating partners. This is the list that one workshop generated:

Home
- Play an instrument on your front porch/patio/front yard
- Hang out at your neighborhood or apartment pool
- Attend crime-watch meetings
- Do some kind of outdoor hobby
- Do yard work and talk to passersby
- Wash your car and make it a point to talk to passersby
- Go introduce yourself to your neighbors
- Throw a party; invite singles and couples, and ask them all to bring single people with them

Work
- Join volunteer groups
- Participate in social groups or happy hour meetings after work
- Introduce yourself to one person outside your immediate work group each day
- Talk to people in the elevator
- Join a Toastmasters group (speakers club)
- Start your own club
- Hang around the copier/coffee machine/break room
- Talk to people on the way in from the parking lot

- Go to office parties
- Invite others to lunch/happy hour with customers or coworkers

Shopping
- Grocery store: ask or offer advice about certain foods
- Clothing stores: ask or offer advice about choosing colors, etc.
- Larger bookstores: hang out in coffee shops
- Video stores: ask about movies you haven't seen
- In general, look for opportunities to chat with people in public places

Errands: Talk to people
- At the car wash
- In bank-teller lines
- On driver's-license lines
- At the dry cleaners
- In the laundry room (take extra change/detergent/fabric softener)
- On post office lines

Recreation
- Get involved in volunteer work
- Join special interest groups (i.e., skiing, boating, cycling, tennis, softball, in-line skating, book-of-the-month clubs, and so on)
- Join bowling/pool leagues
- Take dance classes
- Go to a park
- Go to sporting events
- Attend concerts
- Attend plays and mingle during the intermissions
- Go to festivals, street fairs, flea markets
- Check out the clubs that feature your hobby

Health/exercise
- Talk to people at your gym/health club
- Chat in the waiting room of your doctor/chiropractor/acupuncturist/nutritionist

- Indulge in any sports you love (i.e., sky diving, bungee cord jumping, running in marathons, power walking in parks, and so on)

Education
- Take adult education classes
- Attend craft classes at craft fairs
- Go to wine tastings
- Sign up for professional continuing education
- Check out offerings at public libraries
- Attend lectures at large bookstores
- Look for how-to seminars featured by retail stores
- Start training for a specific sport (i.e., scuba diving, tennis)
- Go to personal growth workshops

Organizations: Join and show up early, help out, become a part of the leadership, and invite others to attend
- E-Quest
- Sierra Club
- Habitat for Humanity
- Big Brothers/Big Sisters
- ASPCA

Religious: Attend
- Church/synagogue
- Singles parties
- Dinners and luncheons
- Singles Sunday school classes

Travel
- Go on Club Med singles trips
- Take singles cruises
- Attend traveling classes sponsored by adult education facilities

**Singles Watering Holes and Functions: Find the
newspaper in your town with a listing of local events,
including those for singles and seek out**
- Wine tastings
- Jazz and rock clubs
- Dance clubs
- Charity events that cater to singles
- For Jewish singles, join Profiles, a singles dating service provided by the community centers

Other Opportunities
- Network with friends (See *Be Your Own Dating Service*, Chapter Six)
- Go to your high school reunion
- Create your own!

I encourage you to type or write up these lists, adding your own ideas, and using colored pens, make an eye-catching display that you can then place somewhere you see everyday (such as your bathroom mirror, your closet door, your refrigerator door). This primes your unconscious mind each time you see it to be aware and alert and constantly creating new opportunities to meet people.

With expanded awareness day to day, you now begin each morning *looking for opportunities* to meet interesting others. Like my clients and workshop participants, you are *primed for interaction and conversation*, which will naturally lead you into a great relationship. Instead of casting head and eyes down, nose to the grindstone, rushing through your errands just to get to the next item on your "to do" list, you are

- Slowing down so that there's time to meet people throughout your day
- Open, aware, and noticing people and events around you
- Looking for natural opportunities to connect with others
- Practicing your communication skills at every opportunity, regardless of whether this is a potential Prince/Princess Charming, remembering that you never know where that connection will lead!
- Optimistic and expecting good things to happen

Sam was waiting in line at the post office when a woman walked by and accidentally bumped into him. He saw an opportunity, so he feigned injury saying "Ow!" to which she responded with surprised laughter. "You made my day," she said, and they stood in line and chatted.

Pete got on a crowded, silent elevator and when the doors closed, said to no one in particular, "Isn't it funny how no one talks in the elevator?" Everyone laughed, and he ended up walking off the elevator chatting with one woman.

Anna and Lisa got tired of waiting for the party to pick up, so they took markers and added the letter *a* on the end of everyone's name tags, causing lots of laughter and conversation.

Patsy, in conversation with the manager of her health club one day, revealed that she wasn't having much luck lately meeting men. Immediately, he told her about Jason, who called Patsy within a couple of days and asked her out. They're now engaged and building their dream house together.

Rachel told her computer consultant, Janet, one day that she was looking for a forty-to-fifty-something guy who's into personal growth. Less than a week later, Janet introduced her to Jerry. They're now in love and planning a future together.

The moral of these stories: *Look for opportunities to interact with lots of people, on a day-to-day basis, and in every situation imaginable.* Practice the skills of connection and communication every chance you get, realizing that the person you're having a casual conversation with today may be, or introduce you to, the love of your life tomorrow. With practice you can't fail, and with practice there's always progress!

Getting to the First Conversation

Now that you're looking for these opportunities to meet people, let's suppose that you're eating lunch by yourself, or you're in the video store, or waiting in line at the post office, and you notice across the room *an interesting other, whom you would like to meet.* If you're like most singles, at this point you do what? Naturally, you do absolutely nothing! Why? Very simply: FEAR.

In every workshop I teach, this comes up. Singles want to know, How do I overcome the fear of approaching this stranger? We list the most common fears on the blackboard, and it looks something like this:

1. Fear of rejection.
2. I don't know what to say.
3. I'm not good at "the close"; getting a phone number or date.
4. They might be unavailable.
5. I can't read their body language.
6. I'm afraid of what observers might think.
7. I'm afraid of what my friends will think/say.
8. I'm afraid of what his/her friends will think/say.
9. I'm feeling awkward.
10. I'm afraid of looking desperate.
11. I don't look good enough today.
12. I'd rather just check them out.
13. What if I can't keep their interest?
14. I worry they'll be uncomfortable.
15. What if they're psycho?
16. I'm afraid of success: What if I succeed? Then what?

Given the sheer numbers and magnitude of our fear, it's a wonder anyone ever meets anyone new!

Someone once said that fear stands for *False Evidence Appearing Real*, and nowhere is this more true than in the singles scene. Because we've all had negative experiences, we tend to shy away from anything that has the potential to hurt or embarrass us like it has in the past. Approaching strangers with the hopes of getting a date ranks at the top of anxiety-provoking situations in life, no doubt right behind the fear of public speaking.

The false evidence is that what we fear is usually not the case, and what we think and surmise on our own is almost always totally off base, blown out of proportion by our fear and anxiety. Are these fears justifiable? Given our past history and the risk we're taking, yes. Are the conclusions we draw accurate? (If I do this, such and such is bound to happen.) Almost always, no. Let's tackle the number one fear, first of all.

How to Overcome the Fear of Rejection

From infancy, we crave attention and love, both of which validate our existence and our value. If we were hungry, tired, or frightened, and someone came, picked us up, held us, and nurtured us, then we felt noticed, cared for, loved, and valued as a worthy being. If not, we felt the rejection at the very core of our selves. Incapable of rational thought ("Mom's just busy right now. She'll be here shortly and I'll be okay."), there was only raw emotion. The terror of being abandoned and rejected translated itself into escalating wails. For most babies, this brought immediate relief as a caretaker or parent came running in response.

But parents and caretakers aren't perfect, so there were times when we didn't get the response we craved, leaving us to experience the emotions of abandonment and/or rejection. Therefore, to some degree, we all carry the pain of not feeling important enough to rate the desired response in another person. As adults, this becomes the fear of rejection, and it is one of our greatest as human beings. If you don't like me or love me, our internal voice says, what does that say about me? Rational or not, the conclusion is that I'm not worthy. As was the case for many of us, these fears were reinforced in adolescence, by not being the prettiest/most handsome one in school, and not always being included in social activities.

In social encounters, we take the risk of rejection each time we approach someone new, not knowing if he will like and accept us, or if we will be left standing there with the echoes of those old emotions from childhood and adolescence resonating within us. How do we separate those old feelings from today's situation so that we can assume the risk of approaching unknown but interesting people?

First of all, take a moment and assume an adult mind-set. You're not at the high school dance with a bad case of acne or new glasses that you think make you look nerdy. Take a brief inventory of your assets and remind yourself that you are, inherently, a worthy and attractive human being.

Second, realize that *attraction is a fluke of nature*! We've been brainwashed in our culture to believe that attraction is determined by hairstyle, clothes, perfume and aftershave, height, weight, body shape, income, and the kind of car you drive! This belief sells a lot of makeup, blue jeans, and new cars, but it's not grounded in true psychological principle.

The reality is that *attraction comes from internal factors that are beyond our conscious control.* You can't make it happen, nor can you stop it from happening. True attraction, the energy that draws two people together, is caused by a combination of *psychology* (how we think and our perceptions about the world), *personality* (who we are), *emotionality* (how we process emotions), and *personal history* (family of origin, past relationships).

All of these things form what we might think of as a little radar on the inside. We all have one, and when we meet a person, one of three possibilities exists:

1. *Their little radar goes off and ours doesn't.* We have a tendency to believe that if we're not attracted to them, it's because something's wrong with them. They're too tall, too short, too fat, too thin, too old, too young, not pretty/handsome enough. The truth is that we are simply not attracted to this person! If I don't like you, this is no reflection of your value and worth, or your attractiveness, as a human being. You are just *not for me*, and that's all. This is why we sometimes see couples and don't understand what they see in each other. "What is she doing with him?" we wonder. Well, guess what. We don't have to know! They know how they feel about each other, and that's all that matters. Learn to avoid making these judgments about others, and there will be less likelihood of making the same judgment of yourself. Remember that one person's "not for me" is another person's dream come true.

2. *Both of our little radars go off.* Whether it happens instantaneously, as in "love at first sight" or slowly, this is mutual attraction, and, assuming that both people are available and all goes well, a romance is in the making.

3. *My little radar goes off and yours doesn't.* Ouch! This one hurts, but as in the number one scenario (in reverse), it's truly not personal, so learn not to take it as such. The fact that someone else's radar didn't go off with you is no reflection on your value and worth as an individual, or on your attractiveness. You are simply *not for them*, and that's all there is to it.

Remember these principles about attraction, and you will be able to approach interesting others with less fear. Knowing and remembering that whether or not the connection happens is not personal helps you take the steps to get to know someone new, realizing that the attraction will either happen or it won't, and there's very little you can do to influence that. If it doesn't happen, you simply move on! There are lots and lots of other wonderful people to meet, and you don't want to waste your time on someone who doesn't return your feelings.

Now that we've handled the number one fear, we'll move on to the second, third, and fourth fears in our list above. With a plan for initiating conversation, maintaining the connection, and getting to a phone number or date, most singles find that the other fears take care of themselves. Empowered with a plan of action, you are able to approach those people who look interesting to you, and rather than stopping you as it has in the past, fear is merely a passing blip on your emotional screen.

2

Opening Lines

♥　　♥　　♥

Many years ago, I recall being in a group of singles and noticing a very attractive man whom I wanted to meet. As I stood there considering approaching him, I imagined what he was like. I pictured him smiling and being very receptive to me, and then I imagined that he would ask me out and soon after that I pictured our first date. Of course, that would go very well and very soon we would be dating and would fall in love. In my own mind, before ever meeting him, I built this man up into Prince Charming, my knight on a white horse, and the answer to my prayers.

Of course, my palms began to sweat and my anxiety level skyrocketed. Now I was truly faced with a dilemma. If he was my Prince, then I had to meet him. What if he left the party and got away? He was so busy talking to other people that he surely didn't know I was there, and the only way I could make him notice me was to walk up to him.

On the other hand, how could I approach him feeling the way I did? I was just too nervous about meeting him and was sure I would stumble as I walked over or say something stupid once I arrived in front of him. I decided to act quickly before I talked myself out of it. I walked over to this man and caught his eye, introducing myself.

He was pleasant enough and spoke to me, but I could tell that his interest level was nowhere near mine. Shortly thereafter, he excused himself and left. I was crushed. I was so sure that he was "the one"! I felt as though I had failed. Of course, I had set myself up to experience that failure by

- Placing far too much expectation on that one meeting
- Projecting into the future, visualizing him as my Prince Charming
- Not preparing myself for an outcome other than the one I wanted
- Having a focus on the result, rather than valuing the process itself
- Not understanding that his rejection wasn't about me

How to Win Every Time

Years later, I learned to set myself up for success in situations just like this one. I discovered that *there is no failure in practice*, and that's how I began to approach meeting and dating. Rather than looking for that one right man, I attended social events for two primary purposes:

- To expand my social circle (meet new people, make acquaintances and potential friendships)
- To *practice* my relationship skills

What was I practicing? The *art of rapport and communication*: Speaking and listening, endeavoring to understand someone else, creating sparks of interest, and connecting with them as a person. These are things that only improve with practice, and I became determined to *practice, practice, practice*. With that as my goal, I discovered, *I couldn't fail*. I could only get better.

Years later, with my newfound focus, I was able to approach a very attractive man at a party and practice my relationship skills. I thought he looked like an interesting person, but didn't allow myself to project any further than that. We talked, exchanged information about ourselves, and then a couple of other people joined our group. Later, I left the party with a number of new acquaintances made and a couple of friendships strengthened. I was proud of myself for having the guts to interact with several new people. *I felt great success*, even though I never saw or heard from that particular man again.

You, too, can experience success in every single social situation you experience in the future by

Dealing with the rejection factor. Realize that attraction is not in your control; it will either happen mutually, in one direction, or not at all.

Focusing on social situations as a vehicle for practice. Rapport and communication, making acquaintances and friendships, and improving your relationship skills are your primary goals.

No matter the outcome of the interaction, you will always have the accomplishment of knowing that you did it: You approached new people, practiced your relationship skills, became a better communicator, and reinforced your winning attitude.

Getting Past the Fear

Remember that list of fears in the first chapter? After getting them written on the blackboard in my workshop, I ask the class: "Even though you've all experienced one or more of these fears in social situations, somehow you've managed at one time or other in the past to go ahead and approach someone. How did you do it? What enabled you to overcome the fear?" Some of the solutions we came up with, in addition to the two above, are:

Remember past successes. Actually visualizing times in the past when a social situation went well can be effective in helping you to summon up the courage to approach someone.

Imagine a successful ending. In this case, visualizing a good outcome is the strategy. Of course, the key to this solution is not to become attached to the outcome, which is unpredictable, but merely visualize and draw on the positive feelings generated by that image.

Be genuinely interested in the other person. Rather than having an agenda ("I'm going to get a date with you or else!"), just get to know the person in front of you, trusting that the appropriate level of connection will happen naturally and that you don't have to force it. Be open to friendship, dating, or only just this one conversation.

Realize that they're afraid, too. We sometimes think that we're the only ones with social anxiety. The truth is that most people are fearful to some degree when meeting strangers. Keeping that in mind puts you on the same level with others, creating a more comfortable atmosphere as you reach out to them.

Imagine the worst and that you could survive it. If you know that the worst thing that could happen is that the person isn't interested or rejects you with a look or by walking away, then you can picture yourself living through your worst fear.

Plan a retreat. Decide ahead of time how you'll get out of the encounter if it doesn't go well. Some common exit lines are:

1. "Oh, would you look at the time. I've just got to run and get some other things done."
2. "It was nice meeting you. I think I'll go get a bite to eat over at the buffet."
3. "I think I see my friend, and I'd like to go say hello. Nice meeting you."
4. "Great party, isn't it? I hope you have an enjoyable evening. Thanks for the conversation."

Of course, use an exit line that is sincere and reflects the reality of your situation. Plan and rehearse a variety of these lines ahead of time so you have a quick way out of awkward situations.

When all of the above ideas haven't helped you overcome the fear of approaching someone, maybe you'll remember this story of mine during your next moment of panic at the thought of meeting someone new.

Nina's Day on the Mountain: Just Do It

Many years ago, I was a participant in a personal growth workshop that incorporated experiential training in mountain-climbing. This particular day, we hiked up a small mountain and were told that we would be doing something called the Zip Line. The Zip Line was a rope suspended between the top of our mountain and the ground below, so that it followed a huge downhill angle. We were supposed to stand on a small wooden plank (about three feet by one foot) that jutted out from the side of the mountain, reach up and grab a T-shaped bar attached to the rope, and step off of the plank. The force of gravity would pull us rapidly down the hill to the ground below.

Never mind the fact that we were connected by numerous straps and ropes to a pulley that was firmly hooked to the T-bar, so that even if we completely let go of the bar we couldn't possibly fall. The logical reality was that we were never unsafe. The psychological reality was that we were stepping off the side of a mountain into space!

Human beings aren't made to do that. In fact, studies have been done with infants in which they were placed on clear Plexiglas set over two tables with a space in between. The babies were content when placed on the part of the glass that had the tabletop underneath but cried when placed on the part that extended over the space between the two tables. Even though they were on a solid surface each time, psychologically they could sense the depth underneath and became fearful. It makes sense that humans have a fear of heights since falling from a cliff or a building can be fatal!

As in the case of those infants, our rational knowledge didn't matter. We could see the height to which we were climbing, and our fear mounted with every step. As I progressed upward, I was having my own internal dialogue, trying to find some way to become okay with this exercise. I finally came to the realization that the one thing that would definitely not work would be my stopping on that plank and thinking about the plunge to come. *I knew that if I hesitated at that point, the fear would overwhelm me and I would never step off of that plank, not ever.* They would have to pry me off the mountain after that, because I knew that I would never budge.

Thus I resolved that when my turn came, I would step onto the plank, reach up and grab the bar and just step off, without thinking about it. And that's exactly what I did.

As I flew down the Zip Line, at first I closed my eyes and sort of screamed silently. Then, I opened them, began breathing, and noticed the beauty of the hills and the valley. I felt the wind rushing past my face and body, and I heard the cheering from the people above and below me. I saw the endless blue sky above, and I became exhilarated. I felt truly alive in that moment, in a way I never had before. Because, for once, I had done something without hesitation, without thinking it to death, even though I was truly terrified. In so doing, I broke through to the other side of fear: excitement. I felt the power of *going for it*. Fear, though it was present, had not stopped me nor killed me. This was a great discovery.

After that experience, I found that I had more willingness to go for it in social situations. Compared to falling off of a mountain, the risks of social rejection seemed smaller. Instead of standing around, hesitating, thinking of all the reasons not to walk up to someone, I just put my body in motion, walked over, and introduced myself, sweaty palms and all. By taking the steps I knew were good for me, without hesitation, I had learned to transform fear into excitement.

Never again should you have to go home at the end of the evening regretting that someone really interesting got away because you didn't have the courage to go up and meet them. Like me on the mountain, you can step up, reach out, and grab that opportunity without hesitation. Stop thinking about it so much; *just do it*. Some of the greatest magic in life happens when we simply step out into space, taking a risk and not knowing the outcome.

Now that you're primed for success, let's look at those critical first few moments in a relationship: establishing rapport.

Body Language First

Someone once said that there's no such thing as *not communicating*. The fact is that even if we don't consciously mean to, we're continually sending and receiving messages through body positioning and facial expression. We're also being constantly bombarded by silent messages from others. In the singles social scene, the ability to read body language and to interpret signals from others is vital.

Body language, including facial expression and the look in someone's eyes, is communication without words and often happens in those moments before the words are spoken. You might think of it as the message preceding the message. When interpreted correctly, body language tells a story about the other person, which enables you to prepare yourself for the language and behavior that will follow. It also enables you to choose your own responses accordingly.

• Sam was talking to Jenna, an attractive woman he had just met at the party. As he talked, attempting to engage her attention, she avoided direct eye contact with him. She continually looked past him or down at her watch. Her arms were crossed and she was turned slightly away from Sam. Her responses to him verbally were minimal at best, but she did occasionally give him a polite smile and nod her head. Not understanding her signals, Sam "went for the close," asking for her phone number and mentioning dinner some night. Jenna, looking surprised and a little offended, answered, "No, that's not possible. You see, I'm dating someone. In fact, he's supposed to be here and I'm waiting for him." Sam was shocked and crushed. Not understanding body language, he thought the fact that Jenna stayed near him for that long, smiled, and made small talk meant that she was interested.

• Susan was introduced to her friend Helen's brother, Eric, after hearing wonderful things about him for weeks. Left alone to chat, Susan found that she was carrying most of the conversation. Eric looked uncomfortable and Susan, reading his signals as those of someone uninterested in her, finally asked if he was okay. "I'm sorry," he apologized. "I guess I'm not good company tonight. The truth is that Helen's always inviting me to these parties and introducing me to her friends when she knows that my divorce isn't even final yet. I'm not ready to date and she's trying to find a new wife for me! It has nothing to do with you, believe me." After that, they were both able to connect as possible friends with no romantic expectations. Susan was glad that she had noticed Eric's signals and not opened herself up to the rejection and discomfort they would both have felt if she had mentioned going out.

What do you see when you look at another person? We usually focus first on appearance:

• Body (height, weight, proportions, fitness, etc.)
• Clothes (trendy or not, colors, fit, how flattering to the person, etc.)
• Hairstyle (short, long, stylish or not)

Actually, those things are usually registered somewhat in the background of our awareness, because our main focus is on the face and, particularly, the eyes. We look into another person's eyes to answer our questions without having to ask them directly:

• Who are you?
• How are you feeling right now? (happy, sad, energetic, tired, etc.)

- How interested are you in me?
- If I ask you out, will you reject me?

Inclusive facial expressions that suggest an opportunity to connect are

- Eye contact
- Smiling
- Head nodding
- Warmth coming from the eyes
- Interest in the eyes
- Pupils slightly dilated
- Eyebrows slightly lifted
- Face turned toward you attentively

If someone is flirting with you, her eyes may not look at you all the time. In that case, her eyes will be somewhat downcast and then look at you, accompanied by a smile, which may be mischievous or shy. While all of these signals don't have to be present, generally at least some of them will be if there's genuine interest.

After facial expression, body language tells the rest of the story. Generally speaking, a person is either uncomfortable or uninterested if they display

- Crossed arms
- A body turned away from you

How do you know the difference? You don't, always. Either way, the signal is, more or less, "Stay away." Respect the message you're getting and move on to someone more open and interested.

What about Shyness?

With shy people, body language can be confusing. Maybe she's interested, but feeling self-conscious and unsure about your interest in her; so her eyes are downcast most of the time and her responses are short. Perhaps he'd really like to ask you out, but he's not making much eye contact and you've been standing here talking forever without any indication that the conversation is going anywhere. What can you do?

You will notice that shy people aren't any better with anyone else than they are with you. It's not as if they are open and enthusiastic with everyone else and then quiet and withdrawn with you; their response is universal. They're shy with everyone, and social situations bring out their fear of being noticed and appraised negatively.

If you're attracted to a shy person, you might try

- Not looking directly at them as much as you would someone else
- Keeping the focus of the conversation on yourself more than on her
- Taking the initiative to ask for or offer a phone number rather than waiting for him to do so
- Accepting him for the way he is and never expecting him to be different!

Rapport: Making the Connection

When eyes connect, an energy passes between two people that has the potential to spark a relationship. You've probably heard it said many times that the eyes are the windows of the soul, and maybe that is why eye contact is so special. Perhaps in that split second of eye contact our souls meet and begin to understand each other. Until then, other forms of connection seem inappropriate and unlikely. After eye contact, all other forms of connection are possible, even if all do not necessarily occur in a given relationship.

Rapport is that indefinable energy that passes between people when they connect and know one another. It is laughing together at a joke; commiserating with each other over a common experience; empathizing with feelings that we've each had; understanding and liking each other. We call it *being in sync, or on the same wavelength*. It makes us feel less alone, less vulnerable: There's someone else who understands what we're going through.

Rapport is one of life's most positive experiences, and feels so good that it leads to friendship and even love. Eye contact and rapport pave the road to intimacy, the lifeblood of romantic love. The word *inti-*

macy can be broken down phonetically to read *into me see*. As we gaze into each other's eyes, feeling the energy of our connection, looking into each other's souls, we create intimacy. We literally see each other and connect with one another on an energy level that requires no verbal explanation in order for it to work. It is the sum and substance of human relationship.

Intimacy is what we seek when we mingle socially, put ourselves at emotional risk, reach out to others for friendship and for dates. It all begins with eye contact and rapport. How do we do this? How do we *create this connection* with an interesting other?

Sending/Receiving Signals

Signals must be both sent and received in order to strike up a rapport with someone. Observing body language carefully, and *receiving signals* from another, you can begin to notice those who are

- Interested, available
  versus those who are
- Not interested, not available

When someone is signaling lack of interest or availability (closed body positioning, lack of eye contact, minimal responses to attempts at conversation, etc.), you have a couple of choices. Like Susan, you can gently make a statement or inquiry in order to find out what's going on. Here are some examples:

- "Well, you seem to be very occupied so I won't trouble you any longer."
- "Am I really striking out here or is there something else going on?"
- "I'll let you get back to what you were doing."

Sometimes if the person is really interested but distracted for some reason, and you sound like you're leaving, you'll get a protest. Then there is an opportunity for the conversation to take a new direction. If you have the kind of personality that can carry off a joke, you might make light of the situation or yourself:

- "It's okay if you feel like taking a nap after talking to me. I've been told that I'm better than Sominex."
- "I never know what to say at these things, do you?"

Your other choice is to just take the hint and politely disengage. On the other hand, when you read signals that someone is interested/available (eye contact, smiling, open body posture, lots of verbal response, etc.), you know that establishing rapport will be much easier. The choice is yours. You can exhaust yourself trying to get a response from someone who's not interested/available, or you can move on to someone who is.

What about the person who sends interested/available signals but who says no when you ask for more contact? Realize that *interested/ available signals aren't a guarantee that you'll get what you want.* Some people universally bestow these positive signs, being inviting and inclusive of almost everyone, and then decide later with whom they really wish to make a connection. Some are just trained to do this in social situations, regardless of how they actually feel about individual people. Therefore, it's a waste of your energy to make assumptions and then become offended or hurt because they don't pan out. Take positive signals with a grain of salt, knowing that the communication has only just begun and you really have no idea where it will lead.

Sending signals means paying attention to your own body language and making sure that you communicate "I'm interested and available!" Do this by

- Making eye contact
- Having an open body posture—no crossed arms!
- Nodding your head
- Giving flirty looks
- Leaning slightly toward someone
- Facing the person you're talking to as opposed to turning away
- Responding to their attempts to converse with you

- Keeping your focus on the person in front of you rather than on everyone else in the room
- Striking up a conversation
- Standing close, but not too close!
- Gently touching the other person's hand or arm while talking to them, if it seems appropriate

You may not remember all of these things the first time you go out to practice, but the goal is to bring gradually more and more *inclusive, inviting behaviors* into your repertoire of signals. Of course, if you find yourself standing in front of someone in whom you're not interested, keep this behavior to a minimum. Be polite, but find a way to disengage quickly. Remember to create and practice your exit lines ahead of time so that you'll be prepared.

Getting to the First Conversation

Great opening lines aren't just what you say but *how you're being*. Contrary to popular belief, it isn't enough to just memorize some clever phrases. There must be something of substance behind your words in order for them to be effective:

- Personality
- Positive attitude
- Warmth
- Ability to connect with others
- Genuine interest in the other person
- Wit and a sense of humor
- Life experience to share
- Comfort with self
- Physical, emotional, and spiritual well-being

These things are so important that even if you read a hundred books on great opening lines and use them all, they will have little or no impact if you are not present and possessing these attributes. By present, I mean *emotionally present*, in your body. "The lights are on and someone is home," as the old saying goes. When you feel good from the inside out, you are able to exude a certain presence, an energy that attracts people and gives you a definite social advantage.

Use the list above to take a brief personal inventory:

- In which areas are you lacking?
- Which need more development?

If you're like me, you're developing all of these areas and that process will last a lifetime. For this exercise, make some sort of determination about how you're doing now in each of these areas, and set goals to further your process of becoming the best possible you. Be as honest with yourself as you possibly can. This is for your benefit; no one else ever has to look at your inventory. If you want to really stretch yourself, ask a close friend to give you honest feedback about where they see you within these areas of your life.

So, does this mean you have to wait until you're fully developed as a person before you can be successful in social situations? Absolutely not! In fact, *interaction with lots and lots of people is necessary for self-development as well as social development.* Face-to-face with other people, connecting (or trying to) with them, we have the opportunity to understand them, and all humans, better, and to know ourselves more fully. *Relationships offer us a mirror of who we are.* This is a concept we'll return to again and again because it's so important.

What does this mean? It means that

- We are primarily social beings; we derive our greatest satisfaction in life from our relationships, both with friends and family, and with a significant partner.
- The quest for intimacy eventually brings us into contact with ourselves: discovering who we are, what our lives are about, and what our personal challenges are.
- It is through our interactions with others that we have our greatest opportunity to understand ourselves better.
- It is through our relationships, especially those that are closest, that we have our greatest opportunity to grow and heal ourselves.

Again, the real opportunity from social interaction is not getting a particular result, but *making self-discoveries and becoming a better you*. If you've done your personal inventory with some genuine self-reflection and honesty, you know that it's important to engage yourself in these opportunities as much and as often as possible, and to use them as a vehicle for your personal growth.

Breaking the Ice

Remember that list of fears from Chapter One? The number two fear was "I don't know what to say." Everyone wants to know *what to say first*. It seems that if we could only get past those first few words, everything else would fall into place. Actually, there's some truth to this. We call it "breaking the ice," and it means that we literally "break through" the initial barrier of distance and not knowing one another, creating more psychological comfort. An exercise that I do in my seminars illustrates how this works.

First, I ask everyone not to talk or interact for this part. The instructions are to slowly look around the room and make eye contact with the other people present, until I tell them to stop. As they do so, silence fills the room. The discomfort is palpable, and I say only four things, each statement spaced apart from the next by about ten seconds: (1) Notice how awkward you may feel. (2) Notice the curiosity you may have about some of the other people here today. (Long pause here, people are getting tired of this exercise.) (3) Notice how much you wish I would stop this exercise. (Nervous laughter here, followed by another long pause; I actually count this one out to make sure I stretch it as far as I can.) (4) Okay, stop the exercise.

This first part of the exercise only takes about two minutes, but it seems more like two hours. Everyone breathes a sigh of relief. Then, I prepare them for the next part, which does include talking and interacting. The instructions are to stand up, move around the room, and introduce themselves to as many people as possible, in a particular way.

Traditionally, we've been taught that the way to break the ice is to get the other person talking immediately about himself, and that the way to do this is to ask questions. Thus, icebreaking conversations in the singles social scene typically look something like this:

HE: Hello, my name is Mark. And you are?
SHE: Jill.
HE: Nice to meet you, Jill. So, are you new to this club?
SHE: No, I've been a member for several months.
HE: Really. Are you from this city?
SHE: No, I grew up in a small town about a hundred miles from here.
HE: That's nice. Where did you go to school?
(And that leads to . . .)
HE: What is your degree? What kind of work do you do? Have you ever been married? Do you have any kids? What company do you work for? (And so on . . .)

The conversation is launched, but there's a problem. What if Jill doesn't want to answer one of his questions? Perhaps she just got laid off and is feeling anxious about looking for a new job. She may not feel comfortable getting into that conversation with a total stranger. Maybe she's going through a divorce and doesn't want to burst into tears, so any questions about marriage are also a problem. She may react to his questions in a defensive manner, and he may be tempted to draw the wrong conclusions: "She's obviously a secretive person and not someone I would like to be around," or "She's got something to hide."

The problem with the Twenty Questions approach to breaking the ice is that it's intrusive and tends to put people on the defensive. It basically says that I have the right to drill you about your life while I stand here not opening up about mine. This is not conducive to emotional safety and makes it more difficult for you to strike up a connection with another. *Remember that your main goal at this point is to establish rapport.* The answers to these questions will naturally flow between you once you have a connection.

What I've found to be infinitely more effective is to *begin by sharing about myself.*

The following is the example I use in my workshop: (I ask someone to stand up and be my guinea pig.)

"Hello, my name is Nina." (Pause for them to say their name.)

"It's nice to meet you. One thing I can tell you about me is that I have a cat named Biscuit. How about you?" (The other person will then say whether or not they have a pet, what it is, and their pet's name.)

I've been told that my example is a little silly, and it certainly gets laughs in the workshop. I guess most people wouldn't start a conversation that way. The point is that it gives an example of what an opening statement that shares something about me can do: It opens the door for the other person to give me some personal information as well. I don't have to pry that door open; it happens automatically because this is the way relationships work. I talk a little about me, and the other person feels like he understands and knows me better. This helps him feel a little safer to reveal something about himself, so he does. I then talk a little more about me, he talks about himself, and before we know it, a connection is made and rapport is established. It happens naturally and is much more relaxed and positive than forcing someone else to do all the sharing first with a line of questions.

After I've illustrated how this works, I then instruct the members of the class to stand up, move around the room, and practice introducing themselves and making a connection with as many people as possible, using the share first, then listen method. We usually take about five minutes for this exercise, and the time flies. Everyone is up and moving around, talking and laughing. The energy rises, and everyone feels so good that I sometimes have trouble getting the group to stop! As people take their seats, I look around the room and notice eyes sparkling and big smiles. Rapport feels good.

For the last part of the exercise, I ask my workshop attendees once again just to look around the room and make eye contact. Then I ask how that feels and whether it is any different from the first time. Universally, they acknowledge that they feel much more comfortable with the other people there now that a connection has been made. At this point I tell them: "Congratulations! You've just made the huge leap from *stranger to acquaintance* with a number of people in this room. Notice what a difference it makes."

This is the magic of rapport and connection. I discovered in my own process that I could enter into a room of 150 strangers, and by simply walking up to, introducing myself, and making a connection using the above technique with five or six of them, I transformed my experience there. Instead of being filled with anxiety and fear, I was relaxed, confident, and enjoying myself thoroughly. No longer surrounded by strangers, I was a part of a group of really great people, like me, who were interesting and worth knowing.

In similar situations, you can begin to develop and practice your own unique icebreaking lines. After you've introduced yourself by name you could try one of the following examples I've run across:

- "I couldn't help but notice you from across the room, and I really wanted to meet you. You look like someone interesting to get to know."
- "Sometimes I don't know exactly what to say when I meet someone new, but I thought I'd give it a try!"
- "This is my first time at this club, but I love to dance. I've been taking lessons for the last couple of weeks and we're learning how to do the swing. How about you?"
- "I'm new to this group and am trying to meet new people. What about you?"

These lines can be used repeatedly with each visit to a particular group:

- "This is only my second time here and I'm trying to meet people and learn what goes on here."
- "I'm relatively new to this group and trying to get to know everyone."

You can talk about yourself in general:

- "I just moved to _____ (fill in your city) a couple of months ago and I'm still trying to find my way around town and meet new people. My company transferred me here. So far, I like it a lot."
- "I go to school at night, so it's rare for me to have the time to get out and socialize. I like to make the most of it by meeting new people when I can, and you seem like someone I'd like to meet. I'm

working on my MBA. What about you? Did you ever go to night school?"

You can talk about the circumstances of your meeting:

• "I almost didn't come to this party tonight. I was so tired after working all week—we had some pretty tight deadlines on a project we just finished. I'm really glad I came, though; otherwise I wouldn't have had the chance to meet you!"
• "My friend Dave says I should come over here and meet you, that you're one of his best friends."
• "You know, I stood over there for the last fifteen minutes working up the nerve to come over here to meet you, and now I'm glad I did!"
• "My relationship coach says I have to introduce myself to at least two new people tonight, so you're my first guinea pig. How am I doing?" (My clients and readers use this one a lot!)

When you find yourself in social settings in which you're expected to introduce yourself and meet people, this icebreaking method works really well. Sometimes, though, life presents us with opportunities that aren't so obvious. Standing in the checkout line at the grocery store, waiting to get the oil changed in your car, walking through your office building, making copies at the office supply—these are the everyday activities that bring us into contact with other people, some of whom we may wish to meet.

I was sitting recently with a friend of mine and her teenager, and we were talking about how, as single people, we tend to overlook or even avoid opportunities to meet others. Her daughter, with the wisdom of youth, said, "Yeah. It's like opportunity knocks on the front door, and they go running out the back door! Then, they peer around the corner, saying, 'Is it gone yet?'" We laughed, but it was with the recognition of having been there at one time, and with the understanding of how much fear can grip us in even the most seemingly unimportant situations.

I hope this book will help you overcome the irrational fear that keeps all of us from reaching out in everyday life to others. It's about focusing on the mental and emotional preparation that empowers us to take those scary steps. In so doing, opportunity becomes our friend, not something frightening from which we feel compelled to run. Next, we'll look at how to step boldly into these chances to meet and connect with others, and how to get from the first encounter to the first date.

Exercise

If you want to reduce your anxiety about meeting others significantly, spend time crafting some good opening lines that you can use in almost any situation, then practice them in front of a mirror. Keep working until the lines come naturally and easily, and you feel that you are being genuine and sincere. Be the best possible you. Keep practicing until you can look at yourself in the mirror and feel, "There's someone I'd like to meet!"

3

Getting to the Date

♥　♥　♥

Anumber of years ago, I was sitting through yet another boring professional meeting, when a man sat down across the table from me. He could have simply introduced himself and listened to the program, as I could have, but instead, we struck up a conversation. Later, I attended a workshop he was presenting, which led to an association that spanned a couple of years. Through him, I met a number of people who became very good acquaintances and dear friends, and through me, he met a number of people who became associates of his. That chance meeting led to a network of friendships and opportunities that continues to have an impact on my life even today, ten years later.

You never know where a connection will lead, and it always begins with a *single conversation*. Rather than going through life with blinders on, oblivious to the opportunities that surround you, you can actually open yourself up to events and people in everyday life. *You can seek conversational opportunities virtually everywhere you go*, thus expanding your world in ways that you might not even be able to imagine while sitting and reading this book today.

Seeking Conversational Opportunities

Being open to and aware of other people as we move through life gives us the chance to develop and practice our opening lines. Sometimes, the best icebreakers are presented to us by the circumstances themselves, if we're observant and looking for them:

• Susan, while waiting for a teller at her bank, noticed the cute guy in front of her and whispered conspiratorially, "It's really quiet in here. It's as if we're not supposed to talk, like in the library!" He laughed and a conversation was launched. The cute guy asked for her phone number and later asked her out.

• Tom was about to leave the dance club one night, when the attractive redhead he'd shared a number of dances with asked a simple question: "Why are you leaving so soon?" This sparked a conversation, which led to a date, which led to a great relationship. Tom and the redhead are now married.

• Joe wandered into a toy store at the mall one day and began asking questions about a game he was thinking of buying for his nephew. He and the salesperson hit it off, he asked for her number, and that led to a two-year relationship.

If you're aware and paying attention, opportunities abound for conversation-starters in everyday life. In any given situation, be observant and notice the following:

• Who looks like an interesting person?
• What does the situation offer the two of you to have in common? (the aggravation of waiting in line for some reason; a common interest; a common friend; you're both new to the club/group/class; one of you is selling/teaching/offering something the other wants; something humorous in the current surroundings; etc.)
• How can you use this situation to make a connection with this person?

It's easy to get caught up in the flow of life and overstep these chances to meet others. Rushing here and there, giving ourselves a limited amount of time to accomplish a hundred tasks, it's no wonder that we don't see all the wonderful people around us, nor do we take the time to try to connect with them.

If you want to meet more people, make more friends, and have more choices of dating partners, *practice*

- Slowing down
- Giving yourself more time for your errands, and
- Being acutely aware of people around you and the opportunities there are to meet them.

How can you remember on a day-to-day basis to do this? Take the list of ways/places to meet people from Chapter One, add your own ideas to the list, and remember to put the complete list someplace you'll see it every day. Be aware enough to take advantage of the abundance of opportunities to meet new people. Begin moving through the world awake, aware, and ready to practice your opening lines.

Remember, the goal is *practice* and *self-development*. Be willing to feel awkward at first, be willing to stumble a little, even feel a little foolish. Actually, as you might have noticed on the receiving end of them, a little clumsiness with opening lines is much more endearing than coming across slick and polished. By practicing, you build awareness of the people around you and of the opportunities that abound in everyday life. You grow more comfortable with being yourself, available and ready to connect in a variety of relationships.

Continue the Conversation

Now that you've started the conversation, what comes next? Once you've launched the beginnings of a connection, the goal is to *establish a dialogue*. The way to do that is simply by balancing these three things:

- Sharing something about yourself (I tell you a little about me)
- Really listening to what the other person says
- Asking open-ended questions

Remember that too much questioning can be intrusive. However, some questioning can help the other person open up, especially if he's feeling shy. Gentle, open-ended questions can accomplish this. What does this mean?

Closed-ended questions always lead to a response of either yes or no, for example:

- "Is this your first time to this group?"
- "Do you live in this area?"
- "Do you like Chinese food?"
- "Do you like to dance?"

Sometimes a person will answer yes, and then take the initiative to elaborate: "I love to dance. I used to have two left feet and thought I could never be a good dancer, but then I started taking lessons and now I do all right. It's really fun knowing what to do and really being able to move to the music." But, more often than not, especially if the answer is no, the conversation dies at that point.

Open-ended questions such as these, however, encourage more discussion:

- "How often do you come here?"
- "What kind of movies do you enjoy?"
- "What are some of your favorite restaurants in this area?"
- "How did you happen to join this club?"

To encourage even more discussion, make a personal statement before you ask the question. Notice how sharing opens the door and creates safety for the other person to share:

- "This is the second time I've come here and I really like it. How often do you come?"
- "Last night I rented *Casablanca* again, it's one of my favorite movies. What kind of films do you enjoy?"
- "I'm new to this area and I love dining out when the food is really good. What are some of your favorite restaurants in this area?"
- "I've been checking out a number of clubs and this is the first time I've visited this one. How did you find it and decide to join?"

The more self-disclosing you are with your statements, the more conversation you are likely to receive from the other person: "Last night I rented *Casablanca* again; it's one of my favorite movies. I love those old, classic films, when the relationships were more subtly portrayed. I guess I'm a sucker for romance anyway. What kind of films do you enjoy?"

This is not a soul-baring revelation but just tells a little something about you, which helps the other person open up as well. Since it is your first encounter, you generally want to keep the topic of conversation light and nonthreatening.

As you continue the dialogue, practice your rapport-maintaining skills, which are the same ones we've discussed previously: maintain eye contact, lean slightly toward the other person you're talking with, have an open body posture, smile, and so on. Try not to focus too much on whether or not you have something clever to say, but rather on the other person and getting to know him/her. Be genuinely curious, but not intrusive. This is a difficult balance to maintain, especially if you're accustomed to the Twenty Questions routine. Practice makes it easier, so the more social situations you can place yourself in the better.

As your dialogue unfolds with an interested/available person, you will begin to get a sense of whom you're dealing with, but you, of course, will have only indications of who he/she is at this point. Many singles make the mistake of trying to draw too many conclusions from a first encounter. Realize that you don't know the circumstances of this person's life. Maybe she's having a bad day, maybe his dog ran away that morning, perhaps you're talking to someone who had two flat tires on the way to work that day. Any number of circumstances can bring a person's energy down, so that even if someone is interested/available he may not be at his best at that moment.

Develop realistic expectations. For the first encounter, basically look for

A spark of interest. Does she seem genuinely interested in what you have to say? Is her body language inclusive? Does he carry his end of the conversation? Is there a positive energy flowing between you?

A desire on your part to know the person better. You don't have to feel mad, passionate love at this point, or even infatuation. Contrary to popular belief, you don't have to know that this is the love of your life. All you really need now is curiosity about this person; the sense that this is someone worth taking the time and energy to get to know.

If neither of these is present, then you're probably better off moving on and meeting someone else. If you're feeling one or both of the above, then at some point in the conversation you will want to do something to make sure the connection isn't broken.

Maintain the Connection

Many a potential relationship has been lost because someone didn't take the initiative to exchange phone numbers or ask for a date in the first encounter. In sales, this is called "making the close" or "asking for the sale," and, as in the business world, in the singles world, the same thing is true: If you don't ask, the opportunity may be irretrievably lost. So, why many times don't we go for it? It's that old fear of rejection once again.

When you find yourself hesitating to get a number or set the next meeting, bring your training into focus and realize that if you ask, the worst that can happen is that you might be told no. The only risk you take is that you will momentarily feel the sting of not getting what you want. The potential reward is that this could be the first step in getting to know the love of your life! And, even if you are told no, take from that experience the satisfaction of knowing that *you went for it*, thus building your confidence to make more of these assertive moves in the future. Because, of course, you aren't taking the rejection personally!

What do you say at this point? How do you continue the connection? Because men and women tend to respond differently in these situations, I like to make a distinction in my coaching for the two genders.

MEN

No matter how great the rapport in your dialogue, it usually doesn't work to ask for a date at this point. This brings too much pressure to bear on the woman. She may be interested in you but feel that she doesn't yet know enough about you to accept a date, especially if she has visions of a long evening encounter. Therefore, offer only to exchange telephone numbers now, and ask her out later when you call her back.

Because she doesn't know you, she may be uncomfortable giving you her number, so offer to give her yours. A good way to say this is the following:

"I've really enjoyed talking with you and would love to continue our conversation at a later time, if you're open to that. If you'd like, I'll give you my phone number and if you feel like calling we can discuss meeting for lunch or coffee sometime. If you are comfortable giving me your number, I'll be glad to call you, whichever way feels most comfortable to you."

Put this in your own words, and practice saying it alone so that you're ready with your "close" anytime the situation calls for it. You should get a good response with this approach. There's no pressure on her. If she's not sure about continuing the connection, she can take your number and decide later what to do. If she's more certain, she can give you her number or take yours and it's okay either way. This communicates that you understand that being a woman in today's world is risky and that she may feel vulnerable in social settings trying to make connections with strangers because of that fact.

WOMEN

If you're doing well in a conversation with a man and he asks you out, you may not want to make that commitment at this point. You can then steer the conversation in a more comfortable direction for you. One way to handle this is to say, "I've really enjoyed our conversation also, and I'd love to continue it later. However, I'm not sure of my schedule and don't want to commit to anything right now. I'd like to give you my number and if you'll call in a couple of days we can discuss it." Or, you can end with, "How about if I take your number and call you later to discuss it?"

This response gives you the opportunity to change your mind if you decide later that you'd rather not go out with this man, and also the chance to protect yourself by not giving out your number to a stranger.

What if you want to go out with him and he's making no moves to continue the connection? A word of caution: Be careful of coming on too strong. Generally speaking, relationships work better if the man has to put energy into seeing you in the beginning. This may sound antiquated, but social studies bear out this premise. Female-driven relationships generally end up less satisfying for both the man and the woman. The best relationships are *balanced*, with both wanting the connection very much, and both putting energy into being together. In the beginning, however, men can be put off easily or become lazy in the relationship if the woman does too much.

At the same time, you don't want to let an opportunity to connect slip by just because he's suffering from the fear of rejection. One way you can handle this is by taking your conversation in this direction: "It's been really great meeting you, and I would enjoy the opportunity to talk more at another time. If you'd like, I'll give you my number, and if you want to perhaps meet for coffee or lunch one day, you can call."

This way, if he's interested, he'll be grateful that you took the initiative. The burden will be on him to make the next move, which allows you to discover if he's really interested in going out with you. If he's not, he'll simply never call, and no harm has been done.

When to Skip the Close

Sometimes, you'll find yourself trying to strike up a dialogue with a person who is not interested/not available, yet who continues to stand there and converse with you in a limited manner. In that case, you will not get the responses you want no matter how your dialogue sparkles. If you're paying attention, and the signals are telling you "I'm not interested!" then don't bother trying to maintain the connection. Your "close" will either offend or fall on deaf ears, and you'll set yourself up for certain rejection. If you've double-checked your perceptions, as we discussed earlier, with a humorous line or an attempt to walk away, and there's still no interest, the next step is to disengage politely and *just walk away*.

What If I Don't Want to Connect?

Sometimes you'll find yourself the recipient of someone else's efforts to connect when you're not interested/not available to him. You may exhibit disinterested body language, respond with monosyllabic an-swers, and generally ignore this person, yet still he persists. In that case, be prepared to disengage.

Think ahead of time about what you might say to get away from someone you're not interested in, and practice your exit lines. You can use the same ones offered earlier in the chapter for disengaging from someone else who's not interested, or you can invent your own. The most important part is to *walk away* after you've spoken your exit line. Don't wait for the other person to leave because not everyone is tuned in or aware enough to know that you're asking them to go away.

How to Decline Gracefully

You may be genuinely interested in speaking with someone, at a party, for example, but have no wish to continue the dialogue with them. When you are suddenly asked for a phone number or date in this case, you will want to be prepared to respond appropriately. Here are some ways to say no gracefully:

- "I've enjoyed speaking with you also. However, I'm not available to go out. I do appreciate the offer—thank you for asking."
- "Thank you for your kind invitation—it's very sweet of you to ask. However, I'm already dating/married to someone else, so I don't think that would be the right thing for me to do."

If someone is persistent after you've politely said no, you can simply say no once again, then excuse yourself and walk away. Avoid the temptation to explain yourself or justify your answer. Remember that you don't owe this to anyone. It is enough for you to say no and for your answer to stand alone.

Now that you've gotten past Breaking the Ice, making the most of Conversational Opportunities, Continuing the Conversation, and Maintaining the Connection, you're ready for the next step.

Getting to the First Date

After the first encounter, much occurs for the two people involved, both in internal and external dialogue. You reflect back on the experience of meeting this person, remembering how you felt and the energy that took place between you. Was it full of sparks? Were you wildly attracted or only mildly interested, or something in between? Was he/she attracted to you? Could you tell how much interest was coming from the other person?

You might find yourself making an analysis or judgment about this encounter. Well, he was cute but he didn't have much of interest to say. She had a great personality, but she was a little overweight for your taste. Maybe he was too young, perhaps she was too old. Did he say he'd been married? And how many times? He might not be such a good risk for a long-term relationship. These and other thoughts fill your mind.

This internal dialogue about the first encounter is basically about weighing the question, Do I go out with this person or not? You may even supplement your internal dialogue with external dialogue with friends. Of course, then you'll get lots of other opinions, but only you can decide what's best for you. Before making the decision to go out on a date, there are a few things you might want to consider:

Be careful of projecting too much into the future, either positive or negative. First impressions are just that and nothing more. People are like onions, and the layers take many months and even years to be peeled away fully. In the first encounter you get only a mere sense of who and what this person is about, so it's important to remain open-minded at this point. This means keeping both the negative judgments *and* the starry-eyed fantasizing to a minimum.

Avoid drawing conclusions based on the first encounter. He spilled his drink, so he must be a clumsy person. She made a disparaging remark about someone else, so she must be a negative person. Maybe he was simply nervous about talking to someone whom he found very attractive. Perhaps she had a very bad day at work and some of her negative feelings about her boss spilled over into the conversation. Be careful of drawing conclusions about someone's character at this point. Just because he has good manners doesn't necessarily mean that he treats women well emotionally in a romantic relationship. Take whatever happens with a grain of salt, both the positive and the negative, and remain *open to discovery* about this person. In fact, this is a good policy to follow throughout a relationship, even though it gets more challenging as time goes on, as we'll discuss further in Chapter Four.

Ask yourself simply, Is this someone I am curious to discover more about? You don't need to know if this is the love of your life. It's not necessary to predict the future and see your whole life unfolding blissfully because you've met Mr./Ms. Right, in order to sign up for a first date! In fact, that's just the kind of attitude that will set your expectations so high that you won't go on that date, or, if you do, it will be a huge disappointment. Develop a realistic perspective and look for only two things: Is there a spark of interest, and do you have a desire to know the person better? If the answer is yes, then that's reason enough to ask for/accept a first date.

Asking for/Accepting/Declining the Date

Throughout this next section, I will separate my coaching for men and women, again, not because the roles can't be reversed—they can be—but because generally men and women handle dating differently at this point. Remember that these aren't rules that you have to follow, but rather, guidelines that you can tailor to suit your personality and lifestyle.

MEN

When you call a woman after the first encounter to ask for the first date, wait a couple of days, but don't wait too long. Two days is long enough to give her time to make sure she really wants to go out with you. If you wait two weeks or more she will probably have assumed that you're not interested or not very available.

This conversation will set the stage for a potential relationship, so what you say and don't say are important. Some general guidelines are:

Keep the conversation fairly short. Save getting to know her for a face-to-face encounter, since there is so much more information available when you can look into her eyes and see her facial expressions.

Also, marathon telephone conversations set you both up for disappointment, and sometimes are an escape from the reality of seeing each other in person, which can be very disappointing when you've built your fantasies up after hours invested on the telephone.

Keep the conversation light. Now is not the time to get into your problems with your ex-wife or your boss. Your purpose in calling is to set up the date, not to have a therapy session.

Begin the conversation with small talk. Don't launch immediately into your invitation. Take the time to establish a little rapport. Ask about her day. Talk about where and how you met, make comments about how you enjoyed meeting her and talking with her, and express an interest in getting to know each other better.

Be ready with a specific invitation. Have an event or place, day and date, in mind, once you get past the small talk. From *Be Your Own Dating Service*, you know to schedule a coffee or lunch date initially, so a first invitation might sound like this:

"I'd like to meet you for lunch one day next week, if that's possible. I have either Tuesday or Thursday open, around noon, and I thought Sam's Grill on Maple Street would be nice. I have about an hour and a half available for lunch. How does that sound?"

Or, like this:

"How about we meet at the Barnes & Noble on the south side in the coffee shop on Wednesday or Thursday next week at about six o'clock in the evening? I have about an hour either day in my schedule at that time. Does that work for you?"

Of course, once you issue the invitation, be ready to negotiate the time and even the location, depending on her schedule and availability. But what if she doesn't readily respond to the invitation? She says she's busy that week, or she's going out of town, or she has to wash her hair, or whatever. If she quickly offers an alternative, then you're still in the game.

Sometimes, though, a woman is uncertain about going out with a man, and so she hedges, unwilling to commit to a date. She may put you off (i.e., "I just don't know my schedule yet. Call me back in a few days.") or she may agree to the date but still seem uncertain. She may not want to go out and has a difficult time saying no. If you aren't sure if she's really interested, you might want to address your concern and offer reassurance:

"You know, Susan, as we're going through this, I'm not sure I'm reading this correctly. Are you interested in going out, and your life is just very busy and full right now? Or, are you not sure you want to go out and can't find a way to say no? Because I'd like to go out, if you want to, and if you don't, it's really okay. I certainly don't want to pressure you."

This way, she has permission to say no, without losing face. If you're not taking rejection personally, it's much easier to offer someone the latitude to decline. When you make a date with an uncertain person, and don't address it, you will often get those last-minute cancellations or even a no-show.

Always accept a decline gracefully. Never, ever try to persuade a woman to change her mind if she says no to your invitation. First of all, she may feel harassed. Secondly, if you succeed in persuading her to change her mind, usually you'll find yourself getting one of those last-minute cancellations on your answering machine, or a no-show. In the end, all you've done is put off the inevitable. Thirdly, if she really wants to go out but is playing a game with you, then you're stepping right into an unhealthy relationship dynamic. If you want an open, honest relationship, then always assume that the answer you hear is the truth. Honor her response, thank her for taking the time to respond, and say good-bye. If you think she's unavailable at this time, but might be free later, you might end with something like this:

"I appreciate your honesty, Karen. It's nice to know where I stand with you. It sounds like you're involved in things or other relationships at this time and therefore not available. If you change your mind or your circumstances change, and you think of me, I'd love to hear from you in the future, so I hope you'll keep my phone number."

You've planted the seed, and you both know that the future is an unknown. It is now understood that you'll naturally go on with your life and therefore may be unavailable yourself in the future.

If you call her repeatedly and she doesn't return your calls, take that as a decline. Sometimes a woman has difficulty telling a man that she's not interested in going out, even if she appeared to enjoy the first encounter. Afraid of rejecting him and hurting his feelings, she just doesn't return his calls and hopes he'll get the message. So, rather than spinning your wheels, you can pretty much assume that if you've called and left three messages, that's enough. She's saying no by not responding.

If you don't want to ask her out, don't call her. Sometimes phone numbers will be exchanged at the first encounter, and men assume that this means they are obligated to call, even if they don't wish to request a date. I've been told more than one story of a woman who received a phone call after a first encounter or even after one date, from a man, who proceeded to tell her, more or less, that she wasn't his cup of tea. Realize that a woman will know you're not interested if you simply don't make any attempt to follow up or to see her. Of course, if she calls you, be prepared to decline gracefully.

WOMEN

Because we're usually on the receiving end of the request for a date, our job is to be clear with ourselves (know what we want) and to communicate that in a straightforward way. Guidelines for responding to calls from men are as follows:

Be responsive, and be totally honest. If a guy goes to the trouble of calling you, the polite thing to do is to return his call, even if you're not interested in going out. Don't ignore his calls so that he has to leave messages repeatedly, hoping that maybe you didn't get the previous ones. If you don't want to go out with him, call him back and say something like the following:

"Thanks, Greg, for following up with me and for your invitation for a date. I enjoyed meeting you the other night; however, I'm not available for going out, so I'm going to decline. It's nothing personal about you, it's my situation. Thanks for your call, and I wish you the best."

Don't put him off by making excuses and being unavailable, thinking that he'll get the message and quit asking you out. Men tend to think logically and don't always get the subtlety of repeated turndowns. He assumes that if you're too busy to go out this week, maybe you'll have time next week, so he may keep asking you out for weeks! Be direct and tell him that you're not interested:

"Gary, I appreciate the invitations that you've extended to me, however, I've thought it over and this just isn't a love connection for me, so there's no point in asking me out again. I think you're a great guy and I wish you the best."

Eliminate now any illusions that you are sparing his feelings by not answering his calls or by pretending interest that you don't feel. He's much better off going forward and finding someone who is thrilled about going out with him, than being stuck with someone who's ambivalent or even uninterested. We all deserve to have the best in a relationship, and a *strongly interested person* is the very least that we can expect.

If you're interested, show it! Contrary to popular belief, it is not in the best interest of an open, honest relationship to be coy and manipulative by putting him off or not returning his calls for days at a time. If he calls, return his call. If he asks you out and you want to go out, accept the date.

Keep the conversation short. Long, drawn-out telephone conversations with someone you haven't gone out with can actually short-circuit a potentially good connection. You are at your best in person, connecting through your eyes and your facial expressions. Studies show that most men fall in love visually first, so he needs to see you in order for that to happen. Good verbal skills are important, but are no substitute for face-to-face interaction, where so much more information is available to both of you.

Sometimes a woman worries that her physical presentation isn't the best it could be ("I've put on some extra weight," or "I'm looking every bit of my age," etc.). So, she reasons that she'll spend lots of time on the telephone first, hoping that he'll fall in love with who she is and that her physical appearance won't matter. This is usually a mistake. First of all, if he does fall in love with your voice, he may feel horribly let down when he meets you and you don't fit the image he's created in his own mind, which is no reflection on your attractiveness, but rather on unrealistic expectations that he may have developed. Secondly, real attraction has little to do with the physical but is a meeting of the souls and hearts of two individuals, and can't be stopped by a few extra pounds. If he doesn't respond to your physical presentation positively it's a reflection of a lack of connection emotionally, and you're better off discovering that sooner rather than later.

Keep the conversation light. Again, this isn't the time for baring your soul, but rather for maintaining rapport and setting up a date. Respond to his attempts to talk, but if he doesn't get to the point fairly quickly, you might say something such as,

"You know, Kevin, I really enjoy talking with you, but I've got some other things to take care of right now. If you want to go out, maybe we could go ahead and schedule a time to get together."

Accept the date with good boundaries. Sometimes a man is under the false impression that first dates should be long and romantic. He will try to schedule an evening with dinner, dancing, drinks, etc., and to pick you up at your house, complete with long-stem roses and a bottle of wine. This is TOO MUCH TOO SOON, and almost always will spoil a potentially good relationship. The object of a first date is not to fall immediately in love but *to explore the possibility of getting to know someone better.* Therefore, aim for circumstances that are safe, that encourage conversation, and that are not too long and drawn-out. You can steer the conversation to a better scenario for a first date like this:

"You know, Joe, I'm really glad you called and I'm looking forward to meeting you again. I think maybe a good place to begin is with coffee or lunch so that we can get to know each other a little better. If things go well, then maybe we can go out to dinner another time. How about if we meet at Starbucks on Wednesday at one o'clock?"

Most men are relieved to know that they don't have to make the big romantic statement on the first date, nor do they have to spend a ton of money on someone who may not be at all right for them. Remember that if he's truly interested, there's plenty of time to be courted later, once you both know there's real potential.

If you need to take a rain check, be clear that you're truly interested. Sometimes a man who's asked a woman out and been turned down will begin to think that she's not interested. Fearing more rejection, he'll just stop calling, assuming that she's not available. If you are truly too busy to go out when he asks, but you know you'd like to go out with him, offer reassurance when you say no:

"Oh, Bill, I'm so disappointed that I'll be out of town on business the rest of this week plus the weekend, so I can't accept your invitation. However, I really want to get together with you. How about looking at our calendars and planning something for a couple of weeks from now?" Or end with:

"I don't know my schedule yet, but please call me week after next when I'm back in town and let's set something up then."

Part of accepting a first date with boundaries is not to accept invitations that are issued at the last minute. This also applies throughout a developing relationship. You don't want to be a man's backup dating partner, nor do you want to feel that you are so low on his list of priorities that he can't remember to call you earlier in the week. Setting boundaries is really about maintaining self-respect, and communicating that to a prospective partner.

Realize that a man may not know not to do this, so it's important not just to write him off. After turning down one last-minute invitation from Jerry, then receiving another, Sandi, a client of mine, handled it this way:

"Jerry, I'd like to explain something to you. I work out of my home, so I'm here morning, noon, and night all week long. It's very important for me to get out on the weekends and socialize so that I don't find myself staying in all the time. I find that my friends aren't always available if I wait too long, and so I make my plans early in the week. I would really love to get together with you, but if you wait until Friday to call, I'm usually not available, so maybe you could ask me out a little earlier in the week next time."

The next time Jerry called to ask Sandi out, it was five days in advance! He turned out to be a wonderful man who became a dear friend. Had she blown him off because of his last-minute invitations, and not had this conversation with him, she would never have gotten to know and appreciate him.

Meeting over the Internet

Sometimes the first encounter isn't in person but via the computer modem. Internet chat rooms, the conversational vehicle of the new era, have become a popular way for singles, and others, to meet. There are also now Web sites that cater to singles and function as introductory services. This is the good news about meeting over the Internet:

- It's a safe way to make contact, without ever leaving the comfort of your home.
- It has revived the lost art of letter-writing, as E-mail correspondence escalates in popularity.
- It allows you to "preview" a prospective dating partner without having to invest time and money in face-to-face encounters right away.
- It's inexpensive, and in most cases, free.
- It encourages an intellectual connection.

The downside:

- As with personal ads, it can be deceptive when people aren't who they appear to be.
- There's the potential to use it as a substitute for real-life social interaction.
- It doesn't relieve you of the responsibility of screening prospective partners carefully and in person.

The love stories about meeting over the Internet, both good and bad, are beginning to circulate. One man carried on a flirtation for weeks with a supposedly sexy young woman in Florida, only to discover eventually that "she" was a he, a male resident of a nursing home. News stories ran about one woman who sued her husband for divorce upon discovering that he had an on-line relationship with another woman.

On the positive side, the CEO of one of the nation's largest computer companies got to know the woman who is now his wife by exchanging E-mail for weeks before ever meeting her. A popular television talk-show host also met his current wife the same way, through meeting and discussions over the Internet.

As with any other way of meeting prospective partners in life, there are both plusses and minuses. If you do "surf the Net" for a prospective mate, there are guidelines to follow that can work to protect you, although they cannot guarantee any particular outcome:

As soon as you make a connection that has any real possibilities, request a photograph exchange and a telephone conversation. Sometimes people go to a particular chat room, talk at length, exchange E-mail, communicate for weeks, and build unrealistic expectations about each other, without ever bothering to talk on the telephone or see each other's faces. The sound of your voice conveys a lot of information that simply isn't accessible on the computer screen. Exchanging photos quickly can prevent the building up of illusions (i.e., "His letters are so wonderful, his voice so divine, he's just got to be the sexiest, cutest guy in the world!"), which can lead to tremendous letdowns when meetings finally do occur.

Switch mainly to telephone conversations rather than E-mail or chat rooms, once you've connected with a particular person. Take the relationship off of the Internet and into the real world as soon as possible. This will enable you to discover what kind of potential there is between you much sooner than can be done in cyberworld.

Find out which one of you would be willing to move, as soon as possible. Some Internet relationships drift on for months, only to make the discovery that neither party is willing to move to the other's city. Of course, this is always the problem with long-distance relationships, whether you meet in cyberspace or otherwise, and it's wise to have the moving conversation as soon as possible when things start getting serious. But how do you talk about it without sounding as though you're asking for a premature commitment? Here's one way:

"You know, Sally, we've been corresponding by E-mail and talking on the telephone for the past couple of weeks, and I'm really enjoying getting to know you. I have no idea where this is going, or if we're right for each other, but I certainly want to continue our relationship to find that out. I guess I'm wondering how we would handle living in the same city if things continue to go well between us. I just want it out on the table if neither of us is willing or able to move to another city at some point in the future. This isn't about making any kind of plans or commitments at this point. I would just like to discuss the issue for informational purposes for both of us. Is that okay with you?"

This dialogue may be a little tricky as you don't want to convey any false sense of commitment or desire for that at this point. Just continue to reiterate that you're only wanting to get a sense that there's not an already-closed door to a potential future. *Don't give out information about where you live until you've thoroughly checked out the other person.* Of course, this is a judgment call, and as with any person you meet who's essentially a stranger at first, you absorb a certain amount of risk. You can minimize the risk by doing your best to ask questions about background, family, friends, and lifestyle. The sooner you bring other members of your partner's social circle into the picture, the better. Go to his/her city, stay in a hotel (don't invite him/her to your room!), and ask to meet friends and family. Take your time getting to know this person, and listen to your own intuition about potential problems.

A lot of these guidelines also apply to meeting someone through personal ads and dating services, especially if you're being introduced to people who live in other cities. The bottom line is to use discretion, follow your own best judgment, and listen to input from friends if you're in doubt.

Now that you're prepared to follow up after the first encounter, it's time to pause and take a close look at *the heart and soul of romantic love: communication*, all that it means, all that it includes, all that it conveys, and the special power of love that can be unleashed in a relationship when it's used well.

4

The Heart of Love

♥ ♥ ♥

Recently, I sat and looked around the restaurant where I was dining, and I imagined that I could distinguish the couples who were in brand-new relationships from those who had been together for years. The well-established couples ate in silence for the most part. Some appeared to avoid each other, making little eye contact, not exhibiting any warmth, and having the general appearance of very little connection. Others seemed comfortable and warm toward each other, eating in companionable silence.

The new couples, however, presented an entirely different picture. They made lots of eye contact, leaned slightly toward one another, listened attentively when the other was speaking, reached out to touch a hand or an arm occasionally, smiled and laughed frequently, and generally seemed very connected. The sparks and warmth between them were practically visible.

I was struck by the difference, and I reflected on the changes that occur in a romantic relationship whereby that early, wonderful connection can diminish and sometimes even cease entirely. One obvious influence over a couple's interaction is the movement through the stages of love itself that happens in every relationship. In the beginning, the chemistry is high, and we experience those delicious, seemingly never-ending sensations that add up to "falling in love." Eventually, those intense sensations fade somewhat, and are replaced by loving feelings overall with occasional romantic highs. Later, there are other emotional changes that occur as we discover the things about each other that aren't so charming, which we'll explore in Chapter Eleven.

The ebb and flow of feelings in a romantic relationship seems to be largely beyond our control, so that getting disconnected from each other is something that we say "just happens." We're told by conventional wisdom that this is inevitable, even though in our hearts we feel that something's wrong; it just shouldn't be this way. Yet we don't know what to do to maintain the loving connection of today for a lifetime. In fact, there is something that we *can* do. We can begin early in a relationship taking steps to ensure that connection with our mate lasts, but it's never too late to intervene.

Getting to the Heart of Love

The secret to sustaining love over a lifetime can be found in those earliest interactions. Looking once again at the new couples, we observe

- Genuine interest in each other and what he/she has to say
- Attentive, compassionate listening
- Body language that increases the connection
- Speaking with respect and caring
- Lots of warm eye contact
- Waiting turns to speak

And that's only a partial list. These behaviors and good communication habits directly influence the connection between partners. More importantly, these activities are fueled by the desire to have a wonderful connection, and this is a large part of what makes a deep interaction work. So why don't we naturally maintain that desire and those behaviors over time in a relationship?

The Bartender and the Stylist

The old stereotype is of the guy who goes to the bar, has a couple of drinks, and pours out his heart to the bartender. Later, he goes home and has only a couple of words to say to his wife before falling asleep. The woman, of course, gets her hair done the next day and confides in her stylist, yet has little to say to her husband at the end of the day. Why this unburdening of the soul to relative strangers and silence within our closest relationships?

Talking to acquaintances is easy. After all, the bartender has no investment in a relationship with the guy who's confiding in him. He has no preconceived notions about this man, so he can listen with complete objectivity. He doesn't argue, criticize, or turn a deaf ear. In short, he's a great listener, just like the woman's hair stylist.

Long-term relationship partners, unfortunately, can be critical, talk over us, put us down, and invalidate our feelings. When we don't feel safe opening up to them, we find others with whom to talk. Maybe it's the bartender or the stylist, or perhaps it's a best friend, therapist, or Twelve-Step sponsor.

Yet, this is not how our relationship with our loved one began. Once upon a time, we felt utterly safe being ourselves and saying anything. Somewhere along the way, we stopped doing what best friends do: listening to each other in a way that nurtures the relationship and promotes greater understanding. We stopped speaking to each other in a way that is respectful and caring.

The Drift of Relationships

What happens in a relationship to erode our ability to communicate effectively? The answer is largely in the passage of time and the building up of history. Let's look at one couple's story to see how this happens.

In the beginning, Lisa and Greg had what seemed to be the perfect relationship. Their values were in sync, they enjoyed the same things, and each thought the other was simply wonderful. They opened their hearts to each other, sharing their life stories, including the most painful aspects of their childhoods. They were naturally loving and attentive to each other each and every day.

Then, one day, they had a date for dinner at six o'clock. Normally, they ate out at seven and Greg, not checking his calendar, showed up at the usual time. Lisa, alternately worrying and fuming for a whole hour, unable to reach him, was very upset by the time Greg breezed in the door. Immediately, she launched an attack. "Where were you? I've been waiting for an hour! I thought you had a wreck or something awful happened to you. How could you be so inconsiderate of me? I would never do this to you!"

Greg, caught totally off guard, began to defend himself. "What are you talking about? Are you crazy or something? I'm supposed to be here at seven o'clock and it's only five after seven!" A heated argument then ensued, as both Greg and Lisa sought to defend his/her own position. Their anger was fueled by the shock they both felt that this heretofore loving, attentive partner now appeared to be an insensitive, uncaring person. Lisa could hardly believe that her Prince Charming was not only late, but defending his actions! Greg, having believed that at last he had found a loving, understanding woman, was now confronted with this shrieking, out-of-control person who was nothing like the sweetheart he had been courting.

Eventually, the misunderstanding came out, but not before hurtful words had been exchanged on both sides. The couple called a truce and the relationship continued but something subtle had changed. Each now viewed the other in a slightly different light. Greg now unconsciously began to think of Lisa as overly emotional, unfair, and maybe even a little unstable. Lisa began to view Greg as forgetful, defensive, and, because she had studied a little psychology, passive-aggressive. At this point, they were both willing to forgive and move on, but these negative assessments of each other lingered in the background. A little bit of history had been established in this relationship.

Unknown to both Greg and Lisa, a certain amount of emotional guardedness began to set in for each of them. Had they stopped to look at it, they might have seen that a little bit of trust was lost between them. Not quite as sure of each other as before, they held back a little of their hearts, afraid of being hurt again the way they both had been in their first confrontation.

Of course, this wasn't the last misunderstanding they had. As can be expected in the usual course of relationships, other events occurred that added more history of disappointment, hurt, anger, and loss. They both lost their hopes of a perfect love, and each new incident added another layer of armor around their hearts.

Being a thoroughly modern couple, they escaped to the natural refuge of wounded lovers in today's pop psychology, talk-show, self-help age of information: their intellects. Lisa analyzed and dissected Greg and his behavior, pouring through women's magazines, looking for advice and insight into it, and having endless conversations with her girlfriends about everything he did. Greg chalked up Lisa's behavior to the craziness of women, and the fact that men could never hope to understand them, and sought refuge in work and nights out with his buddies, who naturally took his side and agreed with his assessment of Lisa. Both secretly wondered if they'd made a poor choice of partner.

Yet all wasn't bad with Lisa and Greg. They truly enjoyed being together, were very attracted to each other, and wanted the relationship to work. They loved each other, and overall found the relationship sufficiently rewarding to continue. Like so many other couples, they moved forward, marrying and starting a family. They believed that the erosion of intimacy in their relationship was the way it was supposed to be, that this was the most you could expect from a marriage. Ten years later, witness a typical "discussion" between Lisa and Greg:

SHE: Well, it's about time you showed up. I guess you "forgot" that dinner was at seven o'clock, not eight.

HE: No, I didn't forget. I left a message for you this afternoon, didn't you get it? Or maybe you just have to have something to yell at me about, so you ignored it.

SHE: That's a really mean thing to say. How can you accuse me of something like that? You'll say anything to dodge the real issue and let yourself off the hook.

HE: And you never listen to what I have to say. You've already got your mind made up. It's my fault no matter what I do.

SHE: Why is it always about you? What about me and the dinner I worked so hard preparing that's now cold? You're so self-absorbed. . . .

HE: And you're so critical. . . .

As you can imagine, this argument only led to more hurt feelings and negative history in the making. Without intervention, this couple seems surely destined for divorce court.

The deterioration of Lisa and Greg's relationship shows how the breakdown of communication leads to the demise of the romantic, intimate connection. Over time, bad communication habits gradually caused them to lose the two most important things that a healthy relationship needs, and without which, romance is sure to die:

- Trust
- Respect

In the beginning, we say "Tell me everything! I'm all ears." We share openly and we listen with compassion. Trust and respect are abundant. As we get to know each other, we begin to listen less compassionately and with more analysis. We silently say, "Now that I know you better, I know why you act that way. Yes, go ahead and talk, but I've got you figured out." We share less openly and we listen judgmentally.

Issues come up, difficult ones that are painful to deal with. We tend to

- Avoid them: If we ignore this, maybe it will go away.
- Fight about them.
- Silently or openly struggle over them.
- Build up a case for leaving. I'm adding this to my file on you. If you do enough things that I don't like, then I'll have good reason to leave.
- Attempt to control each other: my way or the highway.

History builds up. We say, "Now I *really* know you, and this is clearly your problem, not mine. If only you would _____, then we could be happy together. We have to find a way to fix you. Maybe a really good therapist could make you a better partner. . . ." Open sharing has all but ended, and compassion is something we've forgotten how to exercise. Our communication now revolves around one or all of the following:

- The no-talk rule: We simply avoid talking, staying away from "hot" topics, and thus we avoid each other.
- One dominates and controls while the other avoids domination.

- Power struggle as we both try to get our way, no one wins, we both lose.

Distance builds up. As the passion and romance wane, we lose the incentive to work on the relationship. We become silently resigned, or we look for ways to escape. We eat too much, watch too much television, work too much, have affairs, anything to avoid dealing with the mess that we've inadvertently created. Miserable, we stay together, or we eventually divorce.

This is the way many relationships drift, if we allow it to happen. Bad communication habits gradually lead to the erosion of love and passion, siphoning away the fuel from our connection. Eventually, we become resigned to the way it is and give up hope of ever seeing the warmth and love we once shared.

But it doesn't have to be this way. *Good relationships do not have to deteriorate; they can actually get better with time.* By practicing the basic principles of good communication, a couple can use an incident like Lisa and Greg's first confrontation to increase their intimacy, bring them closer together, increase their trust and respect, and deepen the connection between them. If this happens with difficult situations, positive, rather than negative, history accumulates. Love grows and thrives, and romance can live forever.

The Purpose of Communication

In a practical sense, communication helps us

- Solve problems
- Manage the tasks of daily living
- Create and implement projects

At the beginning of a relationship, communication helps us

- Get to know one another
- Connect on a day-to-day basis
- Create intimacy
- Build romance and passion

Once a romance has begun and connections are made, communication helps us sustain that which is most precious to us: our love, trust, respect, intimacy, and passion. How do we accomplish that? Through one essential vehicle: understanding.

The true purpose of communication is not to get my way, prove a point, get you to change, guard myself from hurt, make myself right, or to get what I want from you. These impulses, largely ego driven, are destructive to the relationship and work against the very reason that we are together.

In a relationship, the true purpose of communication is one thing and one thing only: understanding one another. From this all other things flow. What we do in the beginning that is so effective is simply

- Open, honest sharing
- Compassionate listening

By practicing these two skills, which we do quite naturally in the first stages of romance, we come to understand and therefore to love each other. Or we understand, like each other, and realize we're not right for each other without the limiting and damaging effects of making judgments. Or we become lifelong friends. Or we become business partners. Whatever the outcome, it isn't forced, but naturally happens out of our ability to communicate well and *understand one another.*

As the relationship progresses and we continue to practice open, honest sharing and compassionate listening, we discover our true possibilities together. If we fall in love, we have the tools to sustain that love, not just for a few weeks or months, but over a lifetime. We discover our differences, and rather than struggling to change each other, we naturally find acceptance. We may disagree, but we always, always make it our primary goal to understand each other.

Listening: A Powerful Beginning

The source of all good communication is not how we speak or what we say, although those things are certainly important. The beginning, middle, and end result of all great communication, is *how we listen*. When we do it well, true understanding occurs, allowing all other good things to happen.

Misunderstandings, not purposefully hurtful acts, are the source of most negative feelings in a relationship. They can give rise to anger, fear, hurt, and resentment. Once we perceive a particular event in ways that are contrary (I see it one way, you see it another), we no longer have an understanding, and thus are at cross purposes. We cannot meet each other's needs or nurture our connection when that happens, and it all begins with a *failure to listen well*. We misunderstand each other when we

- Communicate hurriedly and incompletely
  "Dinner tonight? Okay, see you later."
- Make assumptions
  "Since you were late, and you aren't injured or dead, then you must have chosen to ignore our agreement."
- Form negative interpretations
  "Since you ignored our agreement, you are therefore a selfish, insensitive, uncaring person."
- Personalize
  "You did this on purpose to hurt me."
- Psychologize each other
  "You do these kinds of things because you have a bad relationship with your mother and are therefore angry at all women."
- Have an agenda
  "I'm only bothering to discuss this with you because I hope to get my way."

When a misunderstanding is not corrected, it leads to faulty conclusions that we form about each other which then contribute to the negative history between us. The communication errors listed above interfere with your ability to do good listening, what I call *Listening Empty*. This means clearing your mind of your opinions, assessments, judgments, and analysis of your partner, and making it your goal simply to understand him/her. When I work with a couple, the first thing I teach them is how to do this.

Listening Empty

Listening Empty is something that we naturally do in the beginning of a relationship, but which becomes increasingly difficult with the passage of time and the buildup of history. Listening Empty is *not*

- Thinking about my own opinions and point of view
- Getting angry because I don't like what I'm hearing
- Interrupting
- Making internal negative assessments about you while you talk
- Silently preparing my rebuttal
- Forming judgments and drawing conclusions
- Analyzing you or what you have to say
- Waiting for you to stop talking so that I can have my say

Listening Empty *is*

- Consciously and deliberately setting aside my own thoughts, opinions, judgments, assessments, and emotions while you are speaking (not that my thoughts and feelings aren't valid, just that I set them aside temporarily)
- Having only one goal while you are speaking, and that is to *understand* you and your thoughts and feelings about the topic

Imagine that you and your partner are containers, such as water glasses, and that your partner comes to you with a full glass (his/her communication) and attempts to pour it into yours (your listening). Imagine that you are full of your own thoughts, opinions, assessments, and emotions (glass full) when your partner begins pouring. What happens? As you can picture in your mind's eye, the glass overflows, leaving your partner feeling unheard, frustrated, hurt, and angry. You also feel upset and frustrated. Communication has broken down because no true dialogue has occurred.

Now imagine that your partner comes to you with a full glass, and asks that you Listen Empty. You take a minute or two and, mentally, set aside your thoughts, opinions, feelings, and so on (emptying your glass). Your partner then speaks, and finds that there is a receptacle for his/her thoughts and feelings (your Empty Listening), which results in feelings of relief (at last, someone listened!). You witness the emotional pain diminish and the light come back into your partner's eyes. You have given your beloved a great gift: The Gift of Listening.

Psychologists and psychotherapists have long known the benefits of this kind of listening. For many patients, the healing from life's disappointments and hurts begins with having someone just to *listen and understand them.* When done with compassion, good listening can restore self-esteem and hope to a discouraged person. In a relationship, Listening Well restores trust and intimacy, and promotes healing where there has been emotional injury.

Listening Well means *Listening Empty,* with compassion, and Mirroring. Here's how it's done:

• Consciously and deliberately, I choose to mentally set aside my thoughts, feelings, opinions, and judgments while you speak. I visualize in my mind's eye emptying my cup, so that I am ready to do one thing only: *understand you and how things are for you.*

• If I find myself getting upset while you're talking (my cup is filling up), I stop you. I take a moment or two and, again, set aside my feelings, reminding myself that my sole purpose right now is to understand you. I then ask you to continue.

• Every so often, when you pause, or when I've heard all I can remember, I repeat back the essence of what I hear you saying, beginning with the words, "What I hear you saying is . . ." This is called Mirroring, and it's how you find out how well you're listening. It's also the way that you show your partner that you're really hearing him/her.

• During Mirroring, I refrain from embellishments and assessments. If you say you ran out the door, I repeat back that you ran out the door. I don't add that you were obviously afraid, and that's why you ran out the door, and that furthermore, you slammed it.

• I ask, "Did I hear you?" after Mirroring, and if you say "no," I ask you to repeat what you were saying, continuing to Listen Empty and

Mirror until you say, "Yes, you heard me." I never argue with you that I did get it right and that you're just unwilling to admit it.

• I believe and respect everything that you say, in the sense that it's your point of view and therefore valid for you, even if I don't agree with you.

• I continue Listening Empty and Mirroring until you've said all there is to say on the topic.

Sound like a lot of work? You're right. Good listening is a skill that is learned and developed, and in the beginning may be quite challenging. It may feel awkward and difficult at first, but eventually, as with all learned skills, it becomes easier and more natural. When a couple practices this on a regular basis, they naturally listen to each other this way most of the time without having to think consciously about it. These couples find that most arguments and power struggles are averted before they even begin, eliminating most of the conflict from the relationship, and leaving them free to enjoy each other more.

Getting to the Heart of Love

To say it again, because it bears repeating, the true purpose of communication is *understanding one another*, and out of this all other things are possible in a relationship. In fact, if the power of creating this understanding were fully understood and utilized by couples and families, most therapists and psychologists would be out of work. *True, honest, heart-to-heart communication is more than beneficial, it is actually transformational, meaning that it can alter how I see me, how I see you, how you see yourself and me, and therefore the relationship itself.*

Let's go back to Lisa and Greg's first confrontation once again. This time, we observe what happens with the practice of good communication skills. Lisa, though worried, begins by making the assumption that Greg probably has a good reason for being late. She makes a decision to suspend judgment until he is there to explain.

SHE: Where were you? I was worried that you'd had a car accident or something. I'm so glad you're okay.

Greg, though puzzled by her reaction, assumes that there's been a misunderstanding and seeks to clear it up rather than getting defensive.

HE: Sure, I'm okay. Did I miss something here? I thought I was supposed to be here at eight o'clock, our usual time.

SHE: Remember the other day when we talked about catching that new movie tonight? We decided that we should meet an hour earlier than usual so we could have plenty of time to eat and get tickets early.

HE: Oh, no. I can't believe I forgot that! I didn't even look at my schedule today, I just assumed it would be our usual time. I'm so sorry, sweetheart. You must have been frantic.

SHE: Yes, I was. But I'm so glad nothing happened to you and that it was just an oversight. You must be really busy at the office these days. It's not at all like you to forget to check your schedule.

HE: (Looking weary) You're right. I don't even think about how stressed I'm getting. I just keep pushing myself harder, hoping I'll get it all done. Maybe this is a sign that it's time for me to slow down a little.

SHE: You really do work hard, honey. Why don't we just order out for dinner and eat in tonight? We can rent a movie and just curl up on the sofa together and take it easy. That show will still be here next week.

HE: That sounds great. I'll go get the movie while you order dinner. Thanks for being so understanding. I really love you.

SHE: I love you, too.

Rather than ending up with emotional wounding and loss of respect and trust, Lisa and Greg came out of this confrontation with two important things:

1. Understanding. They both realize that he's pushing himself too hard at work.

2. Increased intimacy. They both feel validated and respected, and therefore loved.

How did they accomplish this? Reember that the stage is being set before you actually face one another by virtue of your attitudes and beliefs about one another.

Good listeners always begin with a premise: You, like me, are basically an honest person, have your heart in the right place and intend only the best for you, me, and for our relationship.

Starting with this premise is more difficult with history, but even then it is possible. How can you have this premise when you've witnessed your partner do hurtful things? *By realizing that, with few exceptions, most human behavior, flawed and hurtful as it is, is motivated by either fear or by love, and rarely by the actual desire to harm another person.* In a loving state, we are more attentive to each other's needs, yet even then we make mistakes. In a fearful state, we fumble, become awkward, and even hurtful in an effort to protect ourselves. Then, our mistakes are even bigger.

We may understand these things about ourselves and our own behavior, yet tend to make assumptions that others are hurtful to us because they're selfish, uncaring, not committed to us or the relationship, emotionally defective, and so on. *This belief that others have bad intentions or are defective blocks communication.* People get in the rut of believing: If you meant to hurt me, then whatever you have to say about your behavior will just be making excuses, and I can't believe you or accept what you have to say. Therefore, I can't trust you, and I must protect myself by guarding myself emotionally. Thus, communication breaks down with the loss of respect and trust.

Good communicators also practice emotional discipline. They *suspend judgment until they have the complete story*, thus sparing themselves the agony of assuming the worst. Once the other person is present, they *Listen Empty* until they fully understand what happened.

Good listeners allow others to save face when they make mistakes. They don't attempt to nail their partners for shortcomings or errors, forcing them into confessions of wrongdoing, even when the other person is clearly in the wrong. In Chapter Eleven we'll look at resolving conflict: knowing when and how to confront someone about hurtful behavior.

Good communicators don't have an agenda going into a conversation. They realize that until they truly understand the other person and where he's coming from, there's no point in attempting a particular resolution. They don't childishly cling to their own desires and attempt to railroad the other person, but instead, seek primarily to understand what's happening between them and why.

Speaking: The Second Most Important Communication Factor

Listening Well (Listening Empty and Mirroring) is the most important communication skill, followed closely by the ability to speak effectively. It isn't enough to articulate well and refrain from name-calling when speaking to your partner. These things are certainly steps in the right direction, but there's much, much more to Speaking Well in a relationship. Healthy communication includes

- Respect
- Emotional boundaries
- A recognition of other's limitations, and
- The use of adult language

Respect is something you choose to bring to the conversation, even if recent events have you upset and doubting your partner. Healthy communicators understand that good people do hurtful things. They are still able to view their partner in a positive light even when he or she makes mistakes.

Having boundaries means never allowing myself to indulge in a free-for-all, anything-goes kind of confrontation. Good communicators have emotional discipline and are therefore able to discuss upsetting topics without raising voices, calling names, making emotionally wounding comments, or becoming violent.

Recognizing limitations means not expecting your partner to be in the exact same emotional place that you occupy, or having the same point of view, or always being able to articulate things fully. In short, a good communicator doesn't expect others to handle themselves perfectly or to respond always in the way they'd desire.

Using adult language means not attempting to control another person, or to disclaim personal responsibility, through the use of parental language, such as "You should...," "You need to...," "I need to. . . ," or "Everybody knows you shouldn't . . ." A good communicator knows that, as an adult, he makes choices, and is therefore responsible for all of his behavior. Adult language would be, "I would like for you to . . . ," "I would prefer that you . . . ," "I am going to . . . ," "I want to . . . ," or "That doesn't work for me."

One of the most damaging mistakes that we make when speaking to our partners is to begin sentences with the word *you*. This is almost always an accusation of some sort:

"You did that on purpose."
"You didn't call when you said you would."

Combine that with sweeping generalizations in the use of the words *always* or *never* and the damage worsens:

"You never get anyplace on time."
"You always do this to me."
"You never listen to me."

Add to the above a psychological assessment and you have the makings of a fight and possibly a breakup or divorce:

"You're always late, and it's because you're so passive-aggressive."
"You never listen to me because you're so insensitive."
"You're so narcissistic that I can never expect you to treat me right."

Speaking Well means communicating in a way that others can easily hear, thus increasing understanding, and here's how it works:

I *stay on my side of the psychological fence*. Instead of beginning my sentences with the word *you*, I begin with the word *I*. The focus is on *my experience*, *my feelings*, *my intuitions*, and *my guesses* about what's going on. Furthermore, I phrase my statements in a way that leaves room for doubt, allowing for your input:

"I feel angry when you don't call when you say you will. Maybe I'm not understanding our agreement and you can help me with that."

"It seems as though you're late a lot. I'm wondering if you're under too much stress, or if it's something else."

"My feelings have been hurt ever since yesterday when you went out to dinner with friends and forgot to invite me. Please help me understand what that was about."

I express feelings without blame or accusation. Instead of saying, "You made me angry," I say, "When you walked out the door like that I felt very angry." Rather than, "You ruined the entire evening with your offensive jokes," I say, "Sometimes I don't think your jokes are funny. In fact, sometimes I feel offended by them, and I'd like to talk with you about that more."

I take responsibility for my own emotions. Instead of saying, "I cried all afternoon because of your insensitive treatment of me," I say, "After our discussion this morning, I felt wounded inside. I guess it reminded me of the fights I had with my father when I was little, and thinking about that, I was sad and cried."

I tell you about problematic behavior of yours without casting you as a bad person. Rather than saying, "You're a real jerk for doing that," I say, "Doing that doesn't work for me. I would prefer that you . . ."

I keep the discussion to the here and now. I don't bring up old issues from the past, unless it has a strong bearing on today's issue, such as a pattern that I wish to highlight.

I keep the discussion confined to you and me. I don't tell you what my friends, my relatives, my doctor, or my therapist have to say about you or our situation. I express only my own thoughts and feelings, in a respectful way.

I express feelings appropriately, rather than acting them out. If I'm sad, I say so. If I'm angry, I say so. I don't yell, throw a fit, call names, hang up the telephone, or shut the door in your face when I'm angry. I don't push you away when I'm sad and hide my tears. I include you in my immediate emotional experience as much as I'm able to do so, without hurting you.

I'm responsible for being able to express myself to you. If I don't know how I feel, I say so. I ask for time to sort out my thoughts and feelings, rather than just sitting mutely and saying, "I don't know." If I can't do it on my own, I seek the help of a professional, rather than stonewalling you endlessly.

I talk about the things that bother me as soon as I realize them. I don't store up resentments and anger for weeks and months, keeping a silent running tab on your faults so that I can justify leaving. I understand that being forthcoming with my dissatisfactions, with an intention to understand each other and resolve the problem, nurtures our connection.

I never bring up the issue of breaking up while emotions are running high. I don't threaten to leave when I'm angry, nor do I make statements such as, "I don't want to be with someone who . . ." or "If you're going to _____, then maybe we shouldn't stay together." I focus on the issue at hand, trusting that whether it's appropriate for us to stay together or not will naturally emerge as we continue to communicate more fully.

I refrain from insulting statements or put-downs, even if that's how I really feel. I don't speak to others in a way that leaves them feeling shamed or disempowered, justifying it in the name of "honesty." I realize that not all truths need to be spoken, especially when they serve no purpose and they're hurtful to others.

Speaking Well is about remembering that you are addressing another person, someone with feelings and sensitivities, someone with basically good intentions also. It's not about winning, proving a point, or gaining power, but about promoting understanding. Speaking Well makes for easier listening by the other person, thus building trust, respect, and emotional connection. Practicing these skills maintains a good relationship and reverses communication breakdown in a bad one. Passion and love always have fertile soil in which to take root, grow, and thrive, when partners communicate in this way.

Listening and Speaking: A Gift

Learning to speak and listen effectively is a journey and a process, in the same way that finding a right partner and maintaining a relationship are. Don't expect yourself to be skilled at the things discussed in this chapter overnight, or even in a few weeks or months. Becoming a truly skilled communicator takes years, maybe even a lifetime.

Engage yourself in the process, and view each relationship encounter as an opportunity to practice these skills and develop emotional muscle. Expect mistakes, even welcome them, for it's through these fumbling, painful experiences that your greatest learning often takes place.

When you really listen to your partner, and speak to him/her in a healthy way, you are giving a wondrous gift. Good communication is truly the heart and soul of a romantic relationship, and is something that is consciously chosen by each individual.

There is no obligation to give this gift, just as there is no obligation for kisses, hugs, romantic dinners, and other relationship offerings. If you're in a relationship now, focus heavily on giving the gift of good communication, and very little on receiving it in return. Realize that your partner is in a process also, and be tolerant of mistakes.

Whether you're in a love relationship or not, you have the opportunity to practice these skills with everyone in your life: friends, relatives, your boss, and coworkers. The constant repetition of these basic skills will make them a natural part of your behavior, so *practice, practice, practice.* By so doing, you are preparing yourself for your future romantic partner, thus building a strong foundation for a healthy relationship.

Conversations That Work

One of my Internet readers, whom I'll call Linda, recently sent E-mail with this story:

> I have a friend who's going through an exceptionally awful divorce. When we converse, I'm tempted to give pat answers and "analysis." So far, I've managed to resist the temptation. I realize I'm tempted to intellectualize with her because I feel so powerless when she tells me what's happening. I don't want power over her, I just don't want to feel so vulnerable myself. Mary's story could happen to any woman.

Linda went on to comment that Listening Empty and Mirroring taps into our own lack of control over the ups and downs of life and love. "If we accept our own vulnerability, then it's not so hard to listen," she continued. "If we have a hard time with [that], then we want to cover it up with pat answers and analysis."

Dale and Cindy's story shows how this kind of communication opens hearts and paves the way for a deep level of understanding. Returning home from a dance lesson one night, Cindy was upset, feeling that she hadn't done well. She wanted to talk about her feelings, but made the assumption that Dale wouldn't understand because he was a much more experienced, confident, and skilled dancer than she. Both had often experienced a sense of struggle in their attempts to learn to dance with each other.

CINDY: You'll never know how hard it was for me to start dancing six months ago, showing up at the studio and starting to take lessons. (Notice that she's begun her statement with a "you," thereby potentially shutting down the communication.)

DALE: (Recognizing what she's done, and, giving her a chance to both correct her mistake and to save face.) Could you rephrase that?

CINDY: Yes. It was very difficult for me to start dancing. I was very scared . . .

(Now that she's gotten back on her side of the psychological fence, she goes on to describe her experience.)

DALE: (Feeling that there's now room to speak, since she's opened up and not assumed that he doesn't understand.) Did I ever tell you how I got started? After my first few lessons, we went to a club one night and watched the experienced dancers. We were going clump, clump, clump, and they were going whoosh, whoosh, whoosh, and I wanted to dance like that. So, I went to the lessons at the club, but at first, I sat a long way back and just watched. Eventually, I moved closer and continued to just watch. This went on for three months." (Tears now appeared in his eyes.) One night, I was asked to dance by one of the social club directors, one of the best dancers. I told her, "I only know two patterns." She said, "Then, I guess we'll do two patterns." (Tears were now streaming down his face.) Afterward, I apologized for my dancing, and she said, "You're dancing much better than you think you are."

CINDY: (Deeply moved) That encouragement must have really meant a lot to you.

DALE: I'll never forget it.

CINDY: I'm so sorry I assumed that you wouldn't understand my fears. I look at you now and how good you are and it looks so easy for you. I realize now that you've been through a lot of what I'm going through. Thank you so much for sharing that with me, sweetheart. I love you so much.

DALE: I love you, too.

This conversation created a connection where one had almost not happened. By making a small shift in her speaking, Cindy became more vulnerable and opened up the conversation. By Listening Well, Cindy understood Dale much better than she had before, realizing that they shared the same fears and anxieties. Dale, listened to and understood, felt much more connected to her. In an area where they often struggled, they at last found common ground, freeing them both to experience much more joy in an important area of their relationship. *This is the transformational power of good communication*: She shifts, he shifts, and the relationship is forever altered in a positive way. Needless to say, Cindy and Dale's dance lessons went much more smoothly in the future, and their love continued to grow.

Now that we've established some of the basics of good communication, let's go back to the dating process and look at what it takes to make a connection on that all-important first date.

5

Igniting the Spark

♥   ♥   ♥

She sits at her dressing table. Carefully, she applies her makeup. She flings open her closet door. She tries on dresses, skirts, and blouses one after the other until she finds the perfect outfit. She does her hair, making sure every strand is in place, then chooses her nicest earrings. Last of all, she dabs on her best perfume, staring dreamily at her reflection in the mirror.

He goes to the gym, gets in a good workout, then takes his car to the car wash. Later, he showers and shaves for the second time that day, and pulls out a freshly laundered shirt and new pair of slacks. On the way to pick her up, he stops at the florist and selects a single, perfect long-stemmed rose. He wonders what color. Red? No, too romantic. Pink? No, too girlish. White? Yes, that's it. Beautiful, simple, with just a hint of romance. He flips on his favorite rock station and sings along as he pulls out of the parking lot, thinking of the evening ahead.

What are these people doing? By now you know, of course, they're getting ready for a date! Putting their best foot forward, they are each hoping to *ignite the spark of love*. There's only one thing they've overlooked, something vital to the success of their date: the preparation that goes beyond clothes, hair, perfume, and roses.

Getting Ready for the Date

No, this part of the book isn't about what to wear or getting a new hairstyle! Yes, your physical presentation is important, in that you want to make sure you are presentable and as attractive as possible. Good grooming and a well-put-together look can certainly create a much-wanted favorable impression. Even more important, though, is your mental and emotional preparation, which *sets the stage* for maintaining the rapport that was begun during the first encounter.

If romantic sparks are possible, you can help them ignite during the first date. If not, nothing you wear, do, or say will force this to happen. Contrary to popular belief, you can't make someone like you or fall in love with you. *A relationship is an energy that flows between two people.* You can *influence* that energy, but you can never entirely control it. Therefore, your first step in mentally preparing for the date is to xrealize this and to understand the true purpose of first dates.

The purpose of a first date is *not* to make a huge romantic statement or to capture someone's heart. It is *not* to make someone fall in love with you or to get their undying love. It is not to hook them, attract them, or get what *you* want from them, sex, love, companionship, friendship, someone to show off, or anything else.

The primary purpose of the initial date in a relationship is to *create a connection*. Secondarily, it is to *get to know someone, explore the possibility of a friendship or romance, and to practice relationship skills.* Oh, by the way, it's even better if you can have fun along the way!

When you succeed in creating a connection, all other things are possible, though nothing is guaranteed. The paradox of dating and relationships is that we endeavor to connect with others, realizing that *we never know where that will lead.* Perhaps we'll only go out once, realize there's no friendship or romantic potential, and move on. Maybe we'll go out a number of times and eventually come to the same realization. Maybe we'll date for a while, realize it's not a love connection and become friends, maybe even close friends for life. Perhaps we'll do something in business together.

One common misperception is that there should be a desired outcome for every encounter or date; otherwise, it's a waste of time and energy. If there's no obvious love connection immediately, why go out again? In today's busy, hurried world, we tend to take the attitude that only quick-igniting romantic sparks are worth pursuing, and that there's no point in exploring friendship possibilities with those of the opposite gender. We make rapid judgments and instantaneous assessments, then close the door on future possibilities.

This bottom-line, results-only orientation to dating causes us to step over life's most precious opportunity: to connect with others and to build a community of friendship and support. The real waste of this outlook is the loss of these chances to include new and wonderful people in our lives. Furthermore, having a results orientation makes us more uptight, analytical, and less emotionally available. If I'm concerned mainly with finding a mate, then I may be too busy putting you through my Ideal Mate filter ("Are you The One?) to actually make a connection with you.

If you're overly concerned with getting into a relationship then you're probably not relating very well. If you're not relating very well, then you're probably failing to make some valuable connections that could lead to the love of your life. This then becomes problematic: *By overanalyzing and thinking about whether someone's right for you or not, you may actually sabotage the very process by which you could find a right partner.*

The way out of this dilemma is to do your mental homework before the date:

• Realize the true purpose of first dates, and make it your goal mainly to *create a connection* through the practice of good conversational skills.
• Let go of expectations that this will be either the love of your life or a complete waste of time.
• Be open to all kinds of relationship possibilities.

Alison and Barry met through mutual friends. They went out together about four times before realizing that there wasn't going to be a romantic connection. Rather than write each other off, they continued to participate in each other's lives and social networks. Six months later, they worked on a freelance writing project together, which led to another business opportunity. Barry became a surrogate dad to Alison's children. Each made connections with friends of the other, leading to other friendships and dating opportunities. Both of their lives were enriched in countless ways through their continued association, all of which came about through their willingness to explore all possibilities.

Setting the Stage

In order to fulfill the purpose of your date, set the stage for connection to occur. Tickets to a show are fine, but make sure there's plenty of opportunity for conversation. From *Be Your Own Dating Service* you know that first dates can be wonderful or they can fall completely flat when you're going out with someone you don't know. Therefore, the best first dates are short lunches or coffee dates. Meet at the restaurant or coffee bar, and don't drink. It is important especially at this stage to keep your perceptions clear.

First-Date Conversations

Creating a connection on a first date involves not so much science as art, *the art of conversation and rapport.* You can read technique all day long, but it's worth little until you practice what you've learned. An artist develops her skill by first studying the technique of painting, and then, most importantly, by picking up the brush, mixing colors, and applying them to the canvas. She does this, not once or twice, expecting great results, but over and over again, hundreds of times. In fact, a true artist loves the process of creation more than the end result. Gradually, technique gives way to originality, creativity, and spirit. There's an evolution that takes place, one that continues for as long as the artist does what he does, whether it's sculpting, throwing pottery, painting, or writing poetry.

The art of conversation develops in the same way, through an infinite number of interactions over a lifetime. In dating, the goal is to create a connection through this practice. Understanding what to say and what not to say is the technique that gives you direction for the practice that is so essential.

What Not to Say

Some time ago, I was sitting at lunch with a friend of mine, whom I'll call Karen. She'd gone out with someone new just two nights before, and declared it one of those regrettably unpleasant experiences that sometimes occurs in dating. "Some people really need to learn how to have conversations on a date," she said. "In what way?" I asked, and then she told me the story of what had happened. Our talk that day was very eye-opening, and, in fact, was a large part of what inspired me to write this book.

The guy, whom I'll call Jerry, made just about every conversational mistake possible. "First of all," Karen said, "he seemed to have an agenda of showing me 'here's what it will be like to go out with me' rather than just being himself. He talked about all the high-profile people that he knew and made it clear that he received invitations to all the important events of the social season.

"He pulled out photos of himself at various black-tie events, as if to say, 'this is the kind of life you'll have with me.' He kept them in the breast pocket of his jacket and they were quite frayed, so it seems that these were his 'first-date photos,'" Karen told me.

Jerry then went on to talk about his first wife and the conception of their daughter, including his ex-wife's favorite sexual positions. He talked about his second wife ("the most beautiful woman I've ever seen"), who seemed capable only of taking bubble baths and smoking dope. He disclosed graphic details of his intimate life with the women in his past.

"He probably thought that he was being open and honest by revealing these things to me," Karen said, "but it came across as indiscreet and inappropriate. I imagined that if we dated and were ever intimate that the next woman he dated would be hearing these things about me! Also, he never stopped talking about himself. Not once did he pause or give me the opportunity to share information about myself. He seemed totally oblivious to the fact that there was a person here to get to know, and he expressed no interest in discovering anything about me. I couldn't get in a word edgewise. His sole purpose seemed to be selling himself to me."

As I was writing this book, I called Karen to refresh my memory about this story, and she talked about her first date with the man to whom she's now married. "It was so refreshing," she said. "He didn't even talk about his ex-wife. We talked about what's important in our lives, what we enjoy doing, what our friends are like and how we feel about them, our dreams and hopes for the future. We wanted to get to know each other, and we both talked and listened, just being ourselves. I guess, looking back on the date with Jerry and how I felt with my husband, the experiences were worlds apart. With Jerry, it was High Performance Dating. With my husband, it was Championship Companionship."

Karen's story shows how important it is to focus on creating a connection on the first date, rather than trying to make a certain impression. Developing the skills that it takes to have a great first-date conversation can make all the difference in whether you ignite love sparks or can't wait for the evening to end. What you say, how much you say, and how you say it is obviously vitally important in this endeavor.

To avoid the pitfalls of saying the wrong things, or of saying too much, begin by keeping your focus on *creating a connection* and getting to know the person you're with. Some guidelines to remember are the following:

Keep the conversation fairly light. First dates are not an opportunity to bare your soul or have a therapy session. Be honest, but stick with the Cliffs Notes version of your life for now.

Listen more than you speak. When you talk, share honestly and openly, then turn the conversation back to the other person and Listen Well.

Use questions sparingly. Avoid the Twenty Questions routine, as this can be very off-putting and can even break rapport.

As Karen's story shows, there are some things that you are better off not even bringing up on your dates. These subjects can dampen even the brightest sparks, leaving your (potential) partner with a negative impression of you and eliminating any future possibilities. In dating, it's wise to be aware of and endeavor to avoid these conversational taboos:

Don't speak negatively about your former lovers or spouses. When you put down a former partner, you are issuing a warning to the person in front of you: "If you screw up with me, or if we don't last forever, someday I'll be telling someone new about all your faults."

Avoid statements like these:

"My ex-boyfriend was a real tightwad. He never took me out to nice restaurants because he wanted all his money for his own interests, like traveling with his beer-drinking buddies."

"My ex-wife was the most controlling woman I've ever known. I couldn't make a move without her checking up on me."

Hostility toward an ex-spouse or lover rightfully frightens the person who is with you. Just because the gun is aimed at someone else right now doesn't mean it won't be pointed at him someday.

Don't make sweeping negative generalizations about the opposite gender. This is also a warning to the person sitting in front of you. After all, she is a member of the sex you're putting down and therefore is included in what you're saying.

Stay away from these kinds of statements:

"Men are such jerks. They only want one thing, sex. They're insensitive and emotionally stunted. All they care about is getting what they want and being in control."

"Women are so selfish and withholding. They want you to take them out and spend lots of money on them and buy them a big house, but they don't give anything back. All they care about is a fat wallet."

Don't cast your past partners as villains and yourself as a victim. This tells the person you're with that she will be the next person to victimize you. It also reveals the fact that you're carrying a lot of emotional baggage.

Be careful not to say things like the following:

"I gave her everything and she wouldn't even be there for me. She was always more interested in her friends and the children than she was in me. Then, when I asked for a divorce, she raked me over the coals. She tried to ruin my life. . . ."

"He neglected me and he neglected our relationship. He broke my heart into a million pieces, and then he had the nerve to tell me he wanted to move on! Do you know what he did? Well, let me tell you . . ."

Don't disclose intimate details of your sex life with past partners.
This sets your companion up for the inevitable comparisons, especially if you are praising a former lover's skills. It can also be offensive
and inappropriate.

Statements like these are real turn-offs:

"He was the best lover I've ever had, and pleased me in every way.
One of his favorite things to do was . . ."

"She was the sexiest, most desirable woman. She was very adven-
turous and was willing to try everything, even . . ."

"We had sex frequently, but I hated it. His idea of foreplay was
to . . ."

Don't gush about a former partner's good qualities. This gives the impression that you might prefer being back with your old lover instead
of with your date. It also implies that you're looking for someone like
that person, and that you might discount the wonderful but perhaps
very different qualities of the person in front of you.

Refrain from these kinds of comments:

"Sherry was wonderful. She loved me more than any woman has
ever loved me. She was sweet and generous, and she never, ever put
me down. She's a brilliant attorney, very successful . . ."

"Dan stands out in my memory as the most fun companion I ever
had. He was always taking me dancing or on impromptu weekend
trips to fun places. I still remember the time we . . ."

*Don't complain about your boss, your children, your health problems,
or your circumstances.* Negative, whining conversation is unpleasant to
the listener and conveys the impression that you are unhappy with
your life. Most people don't want to take on the job of making your
life okay or being a continual sounding board for your latest gripes.

Stay away from these kinds of remarks:

"I've had this problem with my back ever since the accident two
years ago. First, I went to physical therapy; boy, was that a waste of
time. Then, my doctor put me on steroids and that made me really
sick. Then . . ."

"My boss makes my life miserable. He's always changing the deadlines on our projects and then expecting me to make it happen. He
never listens to what I have to say, and everything has to be his way.
Just the other day, he . . ."

"I like my friend Bob, but he's really a pain. He . . ."

"My daughter is driving me crazy. She's at that age when everything that comes out of her mouth is a smart-aleck comment. This morning she told me to . . ."

Don't discuss intimate details of your therapy, your Twelve-Step program, or your religious experiences. When you're talking to a relative stranger who doesn't have an emotional bond with you, this information can be too intense and overwhelming. Remember, this is only a first date. There's plenty of time as a relationship develops to disclose more intimate information about your life. Later, when you have an emotional connection, there's more safety to open up this much without fear of being judged.

Avoid this level of disclosure:

"I've been in therapy for five years because I was sexually abused by my father from the time I was eight until I was twelve. It all started when my ex-husband and I were making love and I had a flashback to when my father . . ."

"The Twelve-Step program saved my life. I was a falling-down drunk for years. I was about to lose my job and my wife had filed for divorce when I . . ."

Don't emphasize your success, wealth, or connections with influential people. This reveals your insecurity, which is the fear that you are not inherently a worthy person; that your value and worth are determined by externals such as money and influence. A healthy person will not be impressed but actually turned off by this.

These comments will put anyone off:

"Last month I was invited to a party at the home of so-and-so, where I met such-and-such . . ."

"I was looking over my portfolio the other day and realized that I could retire today and still buy a new Mercedes every three years."

No matter how long you date someone, some of these conversational topics remain taboo. Negativity, complaining, gossiping, bragging, and name-dropping are not ever going to be well received. Disclosing intense information about your past does have a place and time in a relationship, but it is *not on the first date*.

Creating a connection with someone works best with appropriate levels of disclosure that gradually increase. This means that you provide basically a sketch of your life in the beginning, and you reveal more as time goes on and your bond is strengthened. Always tell the truth, but realize that you are not obligated to fill in all the blanks right away. Self-disclosure, like all areas of communication, is a process that unfolds over time as you build intimacy and trust.

What to Talk About

Now you know what to stay away from in your early conversations, but what does that leave? One of the questions that singles ask me most frequently is, "What do I talk about on the first date?" Remember that the goal is to create a connection, get to know each other, and practice your relationship skills. Therefore, the most important thing to remember is to *be yourself*. That brings us to the first thing on our list of topics to talk about:

Share the essence of who you are. Don't worry about making an impression, winning someone over, competing with others he may be dating, or making him like you. If there are sparks of interest possible, they will naturally happen. You don't have to force them. Just be yourself and talk about the things with which you're most comfortable. Trust that *who you are* is sufficient.

Comments like this say something about you:

"I love animals. I have two dogs and a cat, and they're like my family."

"Going to the beach makes me feel peaceful. Sometimes I have my greatest insights while I'm digging my toes into the sand and listening to the waves crash on the shore."

"I'm naturally kind of shy, but I've forced myself to become a public speaker so I could overcome my fear of being in front of people."

Talk about people and events that have given you inspiration. Revealing who your mentors are tells a lot about you and your values, and it is uplifting to the person listening. Inspiration shared is a contagiously positive experience.

Share things like this:

"When I was a high school sophomore, my English teacher told me that I should be a writer. I've never forgotten her words, and I've drawn on them to keep me going when I get discouraged in my work."

"I admire Oprah Winfrey. She is a person who's been through great hardship and experienced great success, yet she manages to be very real and genuine. Her heartfelt stories have helped countless numbers of people, including myself."

Share what you've learned from your past relationships without being negative about your partners. This demonstrates your emotional healing and respect for others. It also creates safety for the one listening, realizing that you are someone who takes responsibility for your past relationship failures.

These kinds of disclosures show your humanity and make you approachable:

"I realize I made a lot of mistakes in my marriage. I didn't listen very well because I was always trying to get my way. It's a character trait that I'm working hard to change."

"I never should have moved in with my boyfriend. I realize now that I wasn't really in love with him. I know I hurt him a lot by not being totally honest with myself and with him."

Talk about how you've benefited from knowing your past partners without gushing about them, even if you had a negative experience in the relationship. This shows that you have the maturity to see your past lovers in a positive light even though the relationships have ended. Again, it creates emotional safety for the one you're with, knowing that you're not going to cut him down later if things don't work out. Also, it signifies that you're mature enough to wish your ex-partners well, even if they're giving to someone else what they never gave to you.

Offer statements such as these:

"My ex-wife taught me a lot about love. I wish I had been a better student at the time, but I wasn't ready to make a commitment to work on a relationship at that time."

"It's true that Joe was an alcoholic and that he refused to go into recovery while we were together, but I'm glad I was with him for those five years. That relationship taught me how futile it is to hope that you can change someone else just by loving them. I'm glad he's in A.A. now, and his daughter tells me he's doing well with his new wife."

Be honest about how many times you've been married, give just an overview of why it didn't work, and talk a little about what you've done to understand your marital failures. This shows that you have nothing to hide and that you're endeavoring to learn from past mistakes.

Tell the truth, in ways like this:

"I've been married twice. The first time, I was nineteen and didn't have a clue about what marriage was about. The relationship was over before it even began, due to my ignorance about communication and love. The second time, I was thirty-two and I really wanted that one to work. We struggled for years and she finally told me she wanted out. I realize that I was always the one pushing for more. Now I'm looking for someone who will be just as committed to working on the relationship as I am."

Talk about your background. Where you grew up and went to school, give an outline of your family, your education, and your career. Keep it simple and light. Remember that if a connection is made, you'll have plenty of time to fill in the blanks.

Make statements like this:

"I grew up in West Texas, but I've lived in Houston most of my adult life. I have two brothers, no sisters, my mom died twelve years ago, and my dad lives nearby. As for school . . ."

Talk about your hobbies, interests, what you love to do when you're not working, and why you love to do those things. Talking about what you love and why reveals a lot about you. Also, this demonstrates that you are a well-rounded person with a balanced life. It reassures the other person that you're not looking for someone to *be your life*, but rather, for someone to *share your* already rewarding and fulfilling *life*.

Share in these kinds of ways:

"I love ice hockey and try to make all the games that I can. It's exhilarating to me to get caught up in the spirit of the game, the sense of team, the intensity, and the desire to win. I guess it's the way I want to be in life: going for it without fear."

"Reading is my favorite relaxing thing to do, and mysteries are the best. I love the psychological tension of trying to figure out what's going to happen and who did what. I think of life that way: It's so unpredictable, yet if you're really observant you begin to see certain patterns."

Talk about current positive events in your life and what excites you about them. This gives the other person a small view into the day-to-day goings-on of your life, which reveals much about you.

Say things like this:

"Next week I'm going scuba diving with some friends in Cozumel. This is my therapy for the stress of my life. When I'm down there, just breathing and looking at all the beautiful fish, all my worries slip away, and I'm truly at peace."

"My best friend from Chicago is coming to visit in a couple of weeks. I'm so excited. We haven't seen each other in five years, and even though we talk on the phone every week, it's just not the same. She's like my sister, the one I didn't have in my family."

Talk about your hopes and dreams for the future. This tells the other person that you have a vision for your life, and allows him to look at whether or not it's a life he might want to be a part of. It also reveals a lot about you: your values, what's important to you in life.

Make comments like these:

"I love the law, and I'll probably stay in practice for a few more years, but what I want to do later is write legal thrillers. I've already got a few story ideas going."

"I've always dreamed of living by the ocean and hope to be able to at least buy a condo someday in southern California or in Florida."

Talk about what kind of relationship you're looking for. This is the beginning of finding out if you're on the same page. For the first date, keep it simple and light, and be careful not to imply that you've already found "the one" in the person sitting across from you.

Share about what you're looking for in ways like these:

"I'm ready to settle down again. It's been eight years since my divorce, and I really long for someone to be a companion in life, someone to travel with and open my heart to."

"It's only been six months since my divorce and I don't think I'm ready yet for a commitment. Right now, I'm mainly trying to meet a lot of people and make some new friends."

The examples I've given are indications of what to say and not to say, but they're not meant to be absolute guidelines. As you practice more and more conversation, you begin to get a gut sense of what's appropriate and what's not. How much to disclose on the first date depends to some degree on factors that you cannot predict, and that you'll become aware of in the moment, such as:

- How quickly the connection begins to happen
- The maturity of the person you're with
- How well you're both listening
- The level of emotional development of each of you. For instance, when two people who have both been in therapy for years get together, the conversation will be quite different from one between two people who have spent little or no time on introspection and self-analysis.

Maintaining the Flow of Conversation

Now that you have lots of things to talk about from the list above, keep in mind the keys to good conversational flow:

Listen more than you talk. Share a little about yourself from a particular topic, then pause, smile, and give the other person the opportunity to share in return.

Once the other person begins talking, encourage him to continue. Nod, smile, and make little comments along the way, such as "Yeah, I know what you mean," "Uh huh," "I hear you," and so on.

Don't drill the other person, peppering her with endless questions. Allow the conversation to unfold, trusting that all the right information will emerge.

Don't worry about whether or not you'll get your chance to talk. If you're with a good listener, it will eventually happen, even if it's not until the next date. Sometimes Listening Well is so refreshing to people that they inadvertently get caught up in talking too much.

Be emotionally present: Avoid analyzing and judging as you listen. Remember to Listen Empty, and later, after the date, you can reflect on what happened. Making a connection is about staying in the moment, experiencing the flow of energy between you and the other person, and enjoying the opportunity to get to know someone and practice your relationship skills.

Maintaining Boundaries

With all these things to talk about, you could easily fill up hours on the first date! If the connection happens very quickly, and you're feeling an exchange of lots of positive energy and sparks, you may be tempted to share too much on the first date and to prolong the encounter. This is understandable, especially if you've had lots of mediocre dates in which you didn't click. Sometimes, this leads to what I call the Marathon Date: You get together on Friday for coffee after work, and that turns into dinner, which progresses to more conversation at one of your places, which results in spending the night together. Before you know it, you're getting up on Monday morning, having spent the entire weekend together!

The problem with Marathon Dates early in the relationship is that you're doing Too Much Too Soon, and that accelerates the romance. Overnight, you become deeply involved. Sooner or later, usually within two or three months, one of you wakes up and realizes that you've become a couple without ever stopping to think about it. Suddenly, fear sets in:

"What have I done? I'm already committed and I never stopped to ask myself if this was the right person for me! What if I've made a mistake? How can I back out now that I'm so involved?"

After fear comes backing away and asking for "space." This sets off the other person's fears:

"What is going on? Am I with a commitment-phobic? Maybe he/she doesn't really love me after all. I'm going to get really hurt in this thing!"

Chaos then ensues, with both of you trying desperately to keep from getting hurt. Sometimes this sets in motion an unhealthy relationship dynamic that can evolve into Love Addiction.

Not always does this kind of scenario happen as a result of Marathon Dates, but it happens most of the time, and you may not want to risk sabotaging what could be a perfectly good relationship. A good romance is something that can be savored as you experience each delicious moment to the fullest, but don't get "full," then take time apart, and look forward to and anticipate the next wonderful encounter. You thoroughly enjoy each interaction, and at the end of each you both are left wanting more. This way, you actually create and sustain desire in the relationship, while you also maintain your separate lives, which is an emotionally healthy thing to do. You appreciate each other and the relationship more if you delay gratification for periods of time. This is actually a mark of emotional maturity. Do the following to avoid the Marathon Date:

• Keep in mind the perspective of healthy relationships, which you're endeavoring to create.
• Be more committed to long-term satisfaction than you are to immediate gratification.
• Have short dates in the beginning, from one to three hours, with several days in between, gradually increasing your time together.
• Leave yourself and the other person wanting more conversation, sharing, connection, and intimacy at the end of each meeting.

Too Much Too Soon: How to Slow Down

The other night I was watching one of those television shows about real-life crime stories, and they were profiling a man who had swindled a number of women out of their life savings by pretending to fall in love with them. His method was to approach a woman, take her to lunch, and proceed to tell her his whole life story, interspersing too much disclosure with comments about how well she listened. Lunch turned into an afternoon walk, which then became dinner, and later to dancing the night away. All the while he would engage her in long, drawn-out intimate conversations. The next date began early the next morning, and he typically had the woman engaged to him by the end of the second day! It usually took him a mere five or six days to finish the sting and get her money, vanishing as quickly as he appeared.

While this is an extreme example, it illustrates the falsehood of too much disclosure, and too much romance, too soon. When psychological boundaries are lowered too quickly, a false sense of intimacy is created, leading to pie-in-the-sky fantasies about people we don't really know. For most people, what then happens is a Skyrocket Relationship that soars very high, but very quickly fizzles, leaving heartache and pain in its wake.

If you want a lasting relationship, built on a solid foundation of trust that is earned over time, then practice first-, second-, and third-date conversations that have an appropriate level of disclosure. When you find that the person you're with is attempting too much intimacy too quickly, you can interrupt that process by saying something like the following:

"You know, Eric, I really appreciate how much you're willing to share, but, honestly, it's just a little too intense for me for a first date. How about if we stop for now, maybe go get an ice cream, and just take our time with getting to know each other?"

"Susan, this is nice, sharing our stories and all that. But, I prefer taking my time when I get to know someone. I find that it's more fun if I feel like I want to know more about you. That way, I can look forward to our next date, which I hope we'll have."

Someone with good boundaries will take this as a cue to slow down the self-disclosure, but if not, beware! While you may not have a con artist on your hands, you might have someone who's looking for a hot-and-heavy romance with no intentions toward a lasting love.

Ending the First Date

A few years ago, I had a blind date with someone recommended to me by a friend. We met for coffee, and proceeded to attempt a connection. It didn't take long to realize that we had completely different philosophies about life. We were coming from totally different places, and thus could not get in sync. After about forty-five minutes of exhausting effort, we both threw in the towel. We said our good-byes, got in our cars and drove away. It was clear that there wouldn't be another date, but because we structured it well, no harm had been done.

Sometimes your efforts to create a connection are successful, and sometimes they aren't. This doesn't mean you've failed. Not always is there enough common ground to create a connection, and it's important not to allow this to discourage you.

Sometimes you aren't sure how successful you were, so you may have a lingering feeling of ambivalence. By the end of the first date, you will usually be in one of these places:

- Thrilled about your connection and sure you want to see the person again
- Disappointed about the lack of connection and certain that you don't want another date
- Ambivalent about what happened and not sure if you want to go out again

Unless you're both totally turned off, one of you is sure to bring up the question at the end of the date, "Do you want to do this again?" How you handle this question sets the stage for whether there will be a next date or not.

Some general guidelines are:

- If you're sure you want another date, and the other person seems sure, then go ahead and agree that you will see each other again. Schedule it then or talk later to coordinate calendars.
- If you're not sure about your own feelings, or if you're unsure about the other person's, don't make any kind of commitment at that point. This allows you to take your time after the date to reflect on your experience and reach a decision. It also helps prevent last-minute cancellations. What you can say:

"I'm not sure about my schedule at this point. Why don't you call me in a couple of days and we can discuss it."

"Thank you for the invitation, however I'd like to take a couple of days to think about it. Let's talk on Thursday and see where to go from there."

- Never say you'll call and then fail to do it. If you commit to a later phone call, do it even though you may have decided you don't want to go out again. What you can say:

"I just wanted to follow up after our date. I said I'd call and I am, however, I've thought it over and realize that this isn't a love connection for me. I enjoyed meeting you, I think you're a great person, and I wish you the best."

- Never ask someone to call, or agree to talk later, and then fail to respond just because you don't want to date her. If someone goes to the trouble to call you, the respectful thing to do is to return his call and be honest. What you can say:

"Thank you for following up; I enjoyed meeting with you the other day. I appreciate your invitation, however I've thought it over and this just isn't a love connection for me, so I'm going to decline. I think you're a great person and I wish you the best."

• Never accept another date when you know you don't want a romance, without telling him the truth. Sometimes there's a connection made, but no romantic sparks. You want this person in your life in some way, so the temptation is to accept or ask for another date in order to be around her and develop a friendship. When this happens, realize that you don't have the right to tie up someone else's energy, leading him to think there are romantic possibilities that don't exist, just so you can sit back and enjoy what this person has to give. Tell the truth. What you can say:

"I'm so glad I met you the other day. I think you're a wonderful person, and I'd like to get to know you better. However, I must tell you that it doesn't feel like a romantic connection to me at this time. I realize you may not have room in your life for one more friend, but if you do, I'd like it to be me."

"This doesn't feel like a dating relationship to me, but I really like you and I think we have some common interests. If you ever want a buddy to go to the show with, or go to the museum, I hope you'll think of me."

First-Date Goals

Yes, you want to ignite romantic sparks when you're attracted to someone, but that obviously isn't always possible. Just because you realize there's no romantic love connection doesn't have to mean that the date was a failure. Remember that you are painting a much larger picture than this, that you're going for quality of life and paving the way for a great relationship, however long that takes. Therefore, keep in mind the kind of goals that empower you to continue in the process.

You've accomplished your goals for the first date if you've

• Endeavored to create a connection
• Focused on getting to know someone new

- Explored the possibility of a friendship or romance
- Practiced your relationship/communication skills

Congratulations! *This is an unqualified success.* You've built some emotional muscle, you've practiced your conversational skills, and you're undoubtedly becoming a better partner for your future mate.

If you've made a potential love connection, then the next step is to practice the kind of skills that optimize your chances of keeping it alive. At the same time, you are continuing to set the stage for, not just any relationship, but a lasting, healthy romance with a right partner.

6

Keeping the Connection Alive

♥　♥　♥

It was our first date, a man I hadn't seen in six years. We had so much to catch up on, and since our earlier friendship had been brief, we were just getting to know each other almost as if for the first time.

What began as a one-hour dinner conversation stretched out for three hours, with no signs of running out of what to say. We took turns talking, listening attentively, and making lots of eye contact. The energy was great: connected, alive, sparkling. Reluctantly, we left the restaurant, saying good-bye with a warm hug.

Later, a telephone call established that we were going out again. I felt a mix of excitement and a touch of fear. It was a familiar feeling, one that I had experienced more than once, and one that I frequently witnessed in my clients and friends. It is the bewildering mix of emotions that occurs when we step out of our safe cocoons of singlehood and onto the unpredictable path of a budding relationship.

Where Will This Connection Go?

First dates can be wonderful. If a connection happens, sparks fly, and you agree to see each other again, then you've begun a relationship. Yes, at that point *you have a relationship*, even though you don't know yet what it is or where it will go. You don't even know if it will last beyond the next date, yet something is definitely happening between you; otherwise, you wouldn't bother to meet again.

The paradox of dating and romantic relationships is that when a connection happens, you're in the relationship from that moment forward, yet who knows where it will go or how long it will last? There's both a desire for the good to continue, and a fear of loss. There's the energy that draws you together, and there's a longing for autonomy at the same time. Emotions soar, they fall flat. It's the push/pull of human nature and of relationships. It's both exhilarating and scary.

This mix of emotions, and the unpredictability of the process, can create some confusion, to say the least. Sorting out our own experiences is a handful, and as if that weren't enough, we're called upon to share what's happening with the very person that it's happening about! What if he doesn't have the same feelings, wants, or desires as I do? How do we talk about these experiences and feelings that emanate from the very core of our being, that are stirred up when we enter the game of love, in a way that's open, honest and respectful, and yet has healthy boundaries?

There is a way to practice good communication skills in dating and romance, and it begins with remembering the purpose of this whole exercise: *to create and maintain connection through understanding one another.* From that, all else flows. Questions are answered, commitment either happens or it doesn't, the sparks of love are ignited or they aren't, and you are launched with the love of your life, or you are not.

A relationship is an energy that flows between you, and while you cannot control it, you can certainly influence it. The way you listen and speak to one another directly affects the quality of the connection that you're creating, and thus influences the direction you're going and how long you are together. Make no mistake about this: There are no guarantees when it comes to love. However, *the practice of good communication skills is powerful beyond measure in matters of the heart.*

As you move forward from the first date, your task is increasingly both deeply fulfilling and infinitely challenging: to practice good communication, while realizing that you can't be certain about where it will go. *Falling in love with the process itself* liberates you from the need for a particular outcome. Certainly it's human and healthy to want a particular relationship to work, and to want it to last. Yes, desire it very much, and intend that it last. But focus mainly on your own personal growth, what you're discovering about yourself, about men, women and relationships, and becoming a better person.

Second, Third, and Fourth Dates

After the first date, you will naturally be making a decision about whether or not to go forward and meet again. A common misperception is that at this point you should be falling madly in love and "know" that you've met "the one." This is reinforced by the stories that happily married couples tell of meeting each other. "I knew from the instant I first saw her that I was going to marry her!" he'll say. "I knew right away that I could be happy for the rest of my life with him," she'll say.

Remember that these stories are told in hindsight. For every wonderful beginning that leads to a great relationship, there are three other great starts that eventually fizzle. Lifelong, very happy relationships don't all begin in the same way. Many of them begin with mutual disinterest, some even begin with dislike. The majority of great romances start with *just a spark of interest.* Rather than "I've just met my future spouse!" the feeling is more like "What an interesting person. I think I'd like to get to know her better." Furthermore, one of you may have more interest in the relationship than the other in the beginning. All of these are valid feelings and not to be discounted.

Therefore, the first test of relationship potential is simply, Is there a spark of interest between us? Followed closely by, Is there any compelling reason that I should *not* go out with this person again?

If you've done your homework from *Be Your Own Dating Service,* then you have your list of Negotiables (things you want, but could live without) and Nonnegotiables (things you *must* have in a partner/relationship in order for it to be healthy for you). If you realize early in the process that someone doesn't fit one of your Nonnegotiables, then that's a compelling reason not to go forward. You must have a nonsmoker and she lights a cigarette at the table. You absolutely want to marry someone Jewish and he turns out to be Catholic. You want three children and he doesn't even want one. She tells you she's married.

Other compelling reasons not to continue (in a romantic direction) include the following:

Having absolutely no physical attraction to the person. My test for this was what I call "the Kiss Test." If I looked at him and thought, "I could never see myself kissing those lips," then I knew it would never go anywhere romantically. On the other hand, I didn't have to have a strong desire to kiss him at that time, only the sense that if the relationship developed, yes I could kiss those lips!

Any kind of abusive treatment or strong evidence of an active addiction. Remember that we tend to put our best foot forward on the first date. If she has five drinks the first time you go out, chances are you're dealing with a nonrecovering alcoholic. If he puts you down or belittles your feelings this early in the relationship, you're probably headed for much worse as time goes on.

If there are no compelling reasons not to go forward, then ask for/accept the next date, even if you're not falling in love yet. Why? *Because you never know where the connection will lead.* You're seeking an expansive mentality, meaning that you're open to all kinds of relationship possibilities, and you're only excluding those that you strongly do not want to be with in any way. Rather than attempting to pigeonhole a new person right away (i.e., this is either the love of my life or a complete waste of my time), you recognize the capriciousness of relationship energy and are open to discovering what may be possible with this particular person.

Structuring the Dates

In a budding relationship, the mistake is often made of shifting from the dating mode to the "hanging out" mode. Once the sparks are lit, it's tempting to want to forgo the formality of structured dates and begin connecting via impromptu phone calls and last-minute get-togethers. Instead of making dinner reservations and selecting a show to go see, you go to one of your homes, order pizza, and sit around watching TV or progressing the relationship sexually. Before you know it, you're acting like an old married couple, without the benefit of a commitment.

The problem with this laissez-faire approach to dating is that it leads to emotional laziness rather than emotional muscle-building.

You usually find you take someone for granted or you feel taken for granted. You lose the special feeling of romancing each other. Your relationship quickly becomes ho-hum, much too early in the journey.

Couples who stay together forever happily almost always report that they have structured time together, yes, dates, even after years of marriage. It takes time and effort to coordinate schedules, plan something fun and creative, get dressed up and go out together. The reward is that you sustain the romantic energy that is the lifeblood of your relationship, plus you have the experience of being with someone who thinks you're worth going to some trouble. By investing it with this time and energy, you signify that your relationship is a top priority and that your romantic connection is something that you greatly value.

This takes a certain amount of discipline, much like that which you exercise in your career. Most jobs don't allow you to say, "I'll be in when I get there, and I'll do whatever I feel like doing when I arrive, and I'll stay only as long as I want to," unless you are the boss. Companies require discipline in the work place, meaning that you arrive at a certain time, you have projects with deadlines, and you are expected to pretty much stay until the end of the work day. If you own your own business, I promise you'll be working long hours and practicing discipline if you want to achieve any success.

Successful relationships also require emotional discipline, and that means making a habit of structuring your time together from the beginning, as well as pacing the relationship by spacing your dates apart by several days. When you have dates that are preplanned, there's a comfort that comes from knowing ahead of time when you're getting together next. You delay gratification, rather than picking up the phone every time you have an itch to see each other. Thus, you appreciate each other more because you have a chance to miss each other. General guidelines for structuring the next few dates:

- Keep them fairly short, two to four hours.
- Lunch and dinner are preferred choices, with possibly a date for a show.
- Continue meeting each other until the woman feels comfortable having the man come to her home to pick her up.

• Add activities that allow you just to have fun, such as dancing and shows, but keep lots of your date time for conversation. Remember that the focus is still mainly on getting to know each other, and this means lots of interaction.

Continue to have structured dates throughout your relationship, although as time goes on you will naturally get together more frequently and for longer periods of time. When you've been together for weeks and months, you will of course have times that are just relaxing and hanging out together, but never stop dating. If you form the habit early of expecting that most of your time together will be structured and include fun and romantic activities, then it will be easy to maintain this.

How do you talk about structure? If you're the guy, you're probably doing more of the asking, so it's simple for you. You plan ahead and structure the date accordingly, then ask her out. If you're the woman, it's more complicated, as you're probably the recipient of someone else's requests, so this coaching is for you. If, after a couple of structured dates requested in advance, he suddenly shifts to a "hanging out" mode, you might address it like this:

"Bob, I want to clarify something about our dates. When you called last night, and you suggested that maybe we could get together on Saturday night sometime at my place, I found this difficult to respond to. I don't feel we know each other well enough yet to just hang out, and there was no mention of time or what we would be doing. If there's some problem with our dates, such as finances or whatever, I will be happy to discuss it with you. Otherwise, I would prefer that you decide what kind of activity you would like to invite me to participate in, and choose a specific time, and then call me back."

More Conversations

Beware of too much courtship, before you've gotten to know each other. Larry, when he met Celeste, was instantly mesmerized. He spent the first three dates gazing into her eyes and dreaming of becoming her boyfriend, and later, husband. He sent flowers after the second

date with a romantic note, and again, after the third date. He was
heavily into courtship when this conversation took place, on their fifth
date:

HE: (Gazing into her eyes) Do you have any idea how beautiful you
are?
SHE: (Blushing) No.
HE: (Noticing that she seemed uncomfortable) You know, Celeste,
I've noticed that when I compliment you, you get really quiet.
Hasn't anyone ever told you these things before?
SHE: (Bitterly) I guess it has to do with my last relationship. I was dating this guy for several months, and I was really crazy about him,
and he broke up with me for a twenty-one-year-old bimbo! I'm
only thirty-five, and I just couldn't understand why he left me for
someone younger. After something like that . . . I guess my ego
has taken a beating from this jerk.

After this interaction, Larry realized that perhaps Celeste wasn't
quite as ready for a relationship as he had hoped. He also realized that
there was much that he didn't yet know about her, and that he had
jumped the gun by moving so quickly into courtship. This conversation helped him realize that it was best for him to slow down, take the
time to get to know Celeste, and possibly be open to dating other
women for a while longer.

What are you talking about at this point? Getting to know each
other is primary, so keep your focus on conversations that explore
who you are and what's important to you in your life. As you did on
the first date, you'll be sharing about your past history, your dreams
and desires, your interests, and so on. With each date, if the connection continues and builds, you'll build more trust and intimacy, and
the conversation will move to deeper levels of sharing.

Talking about Past Relationships

Understanding what happened in your own and someone else's past
relationships is like having a window that looks directly into the inner
workings of your unconscious mind. We are more vulnerable in mat-

ters of the heart than in any other part of life. It is here that we live and breathe, connect and disconnect, and here that we discover autonomy, integrity, commitment, and our capacity to love and be loved. When we share our stories about past loves we reveal who we truly are, thus building a tremendous amount of intimacy.

Because of the emotional vulnerability that we generate in these kinds of conversations, it's important to have good boundaries. This means that we begin with the short version of our stories and we progress to the longer versions over time. A first-date relationship story might look something like this:

"I've never been married, although I've come close a couple of times. I've had two serious, long-term relationships, and of course I've dated a number of men casually. Jerry and I met in college and dated for six years, got engaged, and broke it off before we even set a wedding date. Carl and I met three years later, and dated for two years. We broke up a year and a half ago, and I've just started dating again."

After three or four dates, this conversation might shift to something like this:

"Remember my college sweetheart that I told you about? Well, the reason I broke our engagement was because I found out he had been seeing someone else. He said it was over and that he wanted to get married, but I just couldn't trust him again after that. I felt that it was better for us to move on."

And after dating for a couple of months, it might sound more like this:

"Ever since Jerry, I've had a difficult time really opening my heart up to men. For a while, I'd go out on two or three dates, and I'd find some excuse to break up, just so that there was no possibility of ever having to be intimate or trying to trust him. Now, though, I've had lots of time to deal with it, and I realize that it was a great learning experience. I had clues for a long time that there was someone else, which I chose to ignore. I've learned to trust my gut instinct more. I also had a great therapist who helped me deal with the grief and heal my heart. I think I'm really ready to love again."

With time, share more of your story, and at greater depth, but one area to stay away from is the details of your sexual intimacy with others. Unless it has a direct bearing on this relationship, there's no need for you to disclose the particulars of what you did with whom. The broad brush strokes, such as "We were lovers," or "I've never had intercourse, though I've done other things," are all that's important. Providing too much detail can be offensive, can trigger jealousy that creates comparisons to a former lover, and can be very uncomfortable for the listener ("Why did you tell me this? I'd really rather not have the images in my mind that this conversation has generated."). In Chapter Eight we'll cover more of the particulars of discussing sex.

When discussing past relationships, always follow the guidelines from Chapter Five. Be positive about ex-partners, and focus mainly on what you learned about *yourself* from those experiences.

Talking about Family

Sharing your family-of-origin history is much like sharing details about past relationships. Our first relationships in life are with our parents, and from those earliest interactions we form our basic assumptions about love, life, and even about ourselves. If we are nurtured, talked to, listened to, and treated with respect, we have one approach to the world. If our upbringing is lacking in one of these or other major areas, our developing personalities will be affected, as will all of our future relationships. Sharing our earliest life experiences reveals much about who we are and where we are headed, and again, creates intimacy.

How much do we share? As with conversations about past loves, these talks begin with the broad brush strokes and progress to more detail and disclosure. On a first date, your family history might sound like this:

"I have two sisters, both younger, and my parents still live in Baltimore, where I grew up. We're not very close, but we do get together at least once a year for the holidays."

Several dates later, it might sound more like this:

"My father is alcoholic and that made things very difficult for all of us. My parents don't have much of a marriage anymore, but they stay together. My sisters and I have our own lives and don't really enjoy being around my father, so we only go home once a year, usually at Christmas."

A couple of months later, the story is more in-depth:

"I have the tendency to believe that everything is my fault, and I guess that's because of what I went through with my father. He'd come home drunk and yell at my mother, and I would try to calm him down. I never really succeeded, but I guess I thought it was my job, so I have this overinflated sense of responsibility. It's something I work on all the time . . ."

A Powerful Connection

These shared stories, over time, build intimacy and trust, through compassionate listening. There is actually an emotional healing that takes place within a person with the repeated telling of personal history, going to deeper and deeper levels of disclosure. This is the basis of the Twelve-Step programs that have been so influential in the recovery of countless men and women. One person tells the group his story, honestly and openly, and the people present do all they can to listen without judgment. They don't offer sympathy or advice, they just listen. This experience is cathartic for both the speaker and the listener, and an unspoken connection is created as we are made aware of the commonality of our lives.

In a romantic relationship, we share our stories naturally in the beginning. It is powerful beyond measure if we can continue to listen to one another without judgment or advice-giving. With time, our stories go to deeper levels of disclosure and eventually we discover that underneath it all, we are the same. Your story and mine are different, the people and incidents are unique, but our humanity is alike. We may react today in a different manner and have very different personalities, but at the core level we are afraid of the same things: abandonment, rejection, and loss. As we come to realize that, we look at each other with a whole new level of compassion and tolerance.

A couple who begins and sustains this kind of listening builds a powerful connection that will usually stand the test of time. It takes months and even years to reach this level of disclosure in a relationship, and it's important not to attempt to accelerate the process. Pouring out too much too soon can actually short-circuit the connection by overwhelming the listener and frightening the speaker in retrospect.

Without the grounding effects of trust built over time, plus a stated intention to work on the relationship together, it's just too scary to open up this much or to be asked to hear a lot of emotionally charged material. When this happens a date becomes a therapy session, with no pay for the listener and no agreement about confidentiality for the speaker!

The Emotional Bank Account

Stephen Covey, author and coach to Fortune 500 companies, writes and speaks of the emotional bank account that every relationship possesses.* Each individual makes both withdrawals and deposits, of varying values, into this account on a daily basis. A large withdrawal might be forgetting an anniversary, while a small one might be neglecting to take out the trash. A large deposit might be surprising your lover with a weekend getaway trip, while a smaller one might be washing the dishes one night. Obviously, the more deposits you make, the more leeway you have to make a withdrawal. Highly evolved couples endeavor to make far more deposits to the emotional bank account than they will ever need to withdraw, making for a very wealthy and enriched relationship.

Listening Well to someone else's story is a deposit into the emotional bank account. This is a gift, which, like all deposits, is not required, and is more valuable when freely given. It cannot be demanded, although it can be requested.

Sharing your own story may be either a deposit or a withdrawal, depending on where the relationship stands. In the beginning, giving someone the broad brush strokes of your life is a deposit that helps him understand who you are and what you are about. This creates emotional safety and encourages the other person to open up as well.

Eventually, there will come a day when you wish to get into the deeper, more painful aspects of your story. You may wish to express fear, sorrow, and other intense emotions. Asking someone to listen at this point is a withdrawal, and Eddie's story shows what can happen if you do it too soon.

---

*Stephen R. Covey, *The Seven Habits of Highly Effective People: Powerful Lessons in Personal Change* (New York: Simon & Schuster, A Fireside Book, 1989).

After only two weeks of dating, Eddie opened up to Shelly. "I'm afraid that I'm going to mess up this relationship," he confided in her. Their connection was too tenuous at this point, so she naturally reacted unfavorably. "That makes me feel afraid to go forward with you," she told him. Suddenly, they were both on shaky ground and floundering. They almost broke up. After much discussion, Eddie declared that he intended to do everything in his power to have a great relationship, which reassured Shelly enough to stay. Both, however, felt the reverberations of this conversation for a long time to come. There was simply not enough in the emotional bank account for this level of disclosure. Eddie, in hindsight, realized that it might have been better for him to share his anxiety with a friend at that point.

Later in a relationship, if you've established a strong connection with lots of deposits already made, this much disclosure is usually not a problem. If your partner cares for you and possesses the listening skills and emotional maturity to do so, he/she is more than willing to give you this gift. The result is a deepening trust on both sides and a strengthening of the emotional bond between you, which turns out to be a bonus for both of you.

How Much Do I Ask?

Dating is a process of discovery, about you, about me, and about the potential of a relationship. The more we discover, and the sooner we do, the better, or so the reasoning goes. We don't want to "spin our wheels," after all, dating someone endlessly only to discover that there's incompatibility or emotional unavailability. It's tempting, therefore, to take the Twenty Questions approach, grilling our dates in an effort to insure that we won't take too much risk or get hurt.

In romantic relationships, as in all of life, there's no way to shield ourselves adequately from pain and loss. Paradoxically, our efforts to protect ourselves only lead us to greater hurt. By armoring our hearts we are unable to love freely and therefore can never discover the true potential of a relationship. It is only by being openhearted, free to love and be loved, that we are able to connect with another, and thereby take the true measure of our relationship.

Hiding behind lots of questions is certainly a safe place to be, and it's understandable that we might seek refuge there. But by doing so, we actually sabotage the very thing we are attempting to create: the possibility of love. Too much intrusive questioning can cause the other person to clam up, feel unsafe, and even be resentful.

Asking questions about someone else's past is a withdrawal from the emotional bank account, an account into which you've made little or no deposit in the beginning of the dating process. A far more effective approach is to

- Share first
- Then ask
- Question very little

Certainly you want the freedom to ask questions, but spend more time creating emotional safety by opening up first. Rather than asking, "How many times have you been married?" try this: "I've been married once, and it's been about two years since my divorce. I've had one significant relationship since then, and it lasted about six months. How about you?"

Instead of asking, "What kind of relationship do you have with your parents?" try "My father died six years ago and my mother and I are very close, but we weren't always. We've had a very stormy relationship but have finally declared a truce. And you?"

Many times the "How about you?" will not be necessary. The more you open up about your history the more others naturally open up about theirs. What you have is a dialogue, with both sharing, rather than an interrogation, with one person questioning and the other feeling grilled.

What if someone is attempting to interrogate you? One way to handle this is something like this:

"You know, Kevin, we've just met and I don't know you very well at this point. Rather than trying to answer all these questions at once, I think I'd rather just relax and go a little slower. Maybe you could tell me a little more about you and just let me share at my own pace."

If you've expressed a desire to slow down in the discovery process, and the other person is unwilling or unable to respect your boundary, you have the right to end the date. Subjecting yourself to the Twenty Questions routine with someone who's not opening up reciprocally is exhausting and you're not obligated to continue. Don't try to convince him that he's being intrusive unless he asks you why you seem uncomfortable. You might say something like:

"I think it's time for me to go. I've shared all that I feel comfortable with for now." Say your good-byes and leave.

Conversations for Discovery

These first dates early in a relationship are both revealing and pivotal. You are exploring your potential as a couple, and at any point you may decide to go forward or not. What you are looking for is *not* a guarantee that everything will be perfect and you'll live happily ever after. What you *are* looking for is:

- Are there romantic sparks? (Beginning with just a spark of interest.)
- Is there any compelling reason *not* to go forward? (i.e., Nonnegotiables not met, or emotional unavailability.)

Discussing Nonnegotiables is essential but presents conversational challenges. How do you discover each other's values without being too intrusive? Some guidelines to help with this process are:

- First and foremost, *trust the process itself*. Realize that when a connection is made, questions will naturally get answered.
- *Focus more on sharing*, trusting that your partner will reciprocate.
- *Pay attention to the truest evidence of values: behavior*. If he says he's ready for a relationship but rarely calls, this is telling you something. If she says she's over her marriage but can't seem to stop talking about her ex-husband, pay attention.
- Rather than judging people for what they reveal about themselves, be compassionate.
- Rather than looking for perfection, look for someone whose humanity (faults, quirks) you can live with.
- Talk about what's important to you in life and listen to what's important to her.

Examples of discussions about Nonnegotiables:

- HE: I've been a nonsmoker for fifteen years, and I really can't stand to be around it. I know myself well enough that I would never cease in my efforts to get someone to stop. I'd drive myself crazy and her nuts. It just wouldn't work.
- SHE: I don't feel quite that strongly about it, but I certainly enjoy kissing a nonsmoker better! I've never smoked because it just doesn't appeal to me.
- SHE: My spiritual growth is very important to me. I don't expect someone to convert for my sake, but I want to be able to share that part of my life, you know, talk about spiritual matters and maybe go to church together from time to time.
- HE: I haven't gone to church in fifteen years, but I admit that I sometimes long to get involved that way again. I'd really like to go with you sometime and see how I feel about it now.

The Shopping Conversation

When a connection is made, the possibility of love is created. You share stories, listen compassionately, look into each other's eyes, and like what you hear and see. Sparks fly and you begin to dream romantic dreams. *We're attracted to each other, we like each other, we share values, so of course this will lead to love!* Unfortunately, this is not necessarily the case. Many a budding relationship flounders later because of assumptions made at this point.

We date for a multitude of reasons, only one of which is to explore the possibility of a committed relationship and a lifetime partner. We date for social interaction, validation of our attractiveness, to salve our wounds after another relationship ends, and even as an insurance policy against loneliness, to name a few. Sometimes we date people who are very wonderful but just not the right emotional fit.

Rarely do we disclose our true motivations early in a relationship, even if we happen to be aware of them. It's unheard of for someone to say, after a few dates:

"I want to be honest with you, Sharon. I enjoy being with you and our dates are a lot of fun. I could even see us as lovers at some point.

But I don't have any intentions of ever getting married again, and even if I change my mind about that, I don't see what we have as lifetime potential. This won't last, but I'd rather be with you than be sitting home alone watching television, so what do you say? Would you like to continue?"

The dating world would be a lot safer and there would be far less emotional damage if everyone were, first of all, aware enough to be in touch with these feelings, and, second of all, honest enough to share them. We can hope for that someday, but the reality right now is that it's not wise to make assumptions about the potential of a relationship without checking them out.

Throughout a relationship, periodic You and Me Conversations help keep you aware of your own and your partner's thoughts, feelings, desires, and intentions. This is the kind of talk in which you put in the open those things about your connection that are scariest to reveal: *how I feel about you, what I want with you, where I see our relationship going, and where I want it to go.* What's so scary about this? It puts the entire relationship, or possibility of one, on the table. We may discover that we're not at all on the same page. You want one thing while I want something entirely different. As long as we don't talk about it, the reasoning goes, then we can just keep on seeing each other, and *that's better than being alone.*

The price for avoiding this risk is twofold. First, you may be putting off the inevitable. If it hurts now to discover that he's not interested in a lasting relationship with you, will it hurt any less in two years? In fact, it will probably hurt far more, and then you have the added baggage of resentment that you wasted that much of your life with someone who ultimately was not interested in the long term.

Secondly, You and Me Conversations build lots of emotional muscle, and avoiding them leaves you unpracticed in something that's vital to a lasting, healthy relationship: open, honest communication about where you stand with each other. Couples who begin talking about their relationship on their early dates build a foundation for every significant conversation they will ever have. They also create confidence within themselves that they can achieve this very high level of communication.

Where do you begin? The first You and Me Conversation is distinct from all the ones that follow, and I like to call it the Shopping

Conversation, because its object is to discover what you are both looking or shopping for in the dating world. When do you do this? Usually by the third or fourth date, if not sooner, when you realize:

- There's mutual attraction.
- There are no compelling reasons not to go forward.
- This has potential for a romantic relationship.

The following are examples of Shopping Conversations, each with a different outcome.

HE: Now that we've gone out a few times, Beth, I'd like to clarify where I'm coming from. It's been three years since my divorce and I would really like to get married again. I'm looking for someone who's interested in a relationship that can lead to that kind of commitment, and while *I don't know yet if that's you,* I think there's real potential here. I like you a lot, I'm very attracted to you, and I'd like to see where this can go. I guess I'd like to know if marriage is something you see in your future and if I'm any kind of a candidate at this point.

SHE: Wow, that's really honest of you. It's only been a year since my divorce, so I haven't thought much about marriage again. I guess I'm really afraid of making another mistake. I am attracted to you also, and I'd like to date and see where this goes. I guess if things went really well, I would certainly be open to thinking about marriage again someday, but not anytime soon. I don't know you well enough yet to have any idea if you're right for me, but so far, yes, you're a definite candidate!

HE: Thanks for that truthful response. Can we agree that we're exploring this thing, and that if either of us realizes there's a dead end, we'll let the other know?

SHE: Absolutely. It's a deal. Now, what movie are we going to go see?

SHE: I think it's time to talk about what's happening here, Jeff. I think it's safe to say that we're attracted to each other, and I want to let you know where I'm coming from. I'm not dating just for fun and games. I'm looking for someone who's ready for a lasting relationship, with the right partner. We're still getting to know each other, so who knows where this will go, but I think we have some real potential, and I'd like to know where you're coming from. Are you looking for a real relationship at this point or are you just looking for fun?

HE: Well, this is a heavy conversation. Honestly, I just broke off a five-year relationship a couple of months ago, so the last thing I'm looking for is any kind of commitment at this point. I can't say how I'll feel in six months, but right now I just want to date and have fun.

SHE: Are you saying there's no way this could lead to something, that I'm just not your type?

HE: Not at all. You're wonderful, and if I ever got comfortable with making a commitment again it would be with someone like you. I can't offer any guarantees, but I would like to keep seeing you and let this go where it will.

SHE: Well, I don't know if we're right for each other yet either, but it's important to me that you tell me if you decide that I could never be 'the one.' Can you agree to do that?

HE: Of course, that's completely fair. I won't lead you on if I ever realize that it's a dead end. I hope you'll do the same for me.

SHE: I will. Thanks for this talk, it really helped me know where we stand for now. I guess it's worth it to me to take my chances.

HE: Great!

HE: Karen, I want you to know that I've really enjoyed our last couple of dates. I really like you and see a lot of relationship potential here. I guess I wanted you to know where I'm coming from. I'm looking for someone to explore a relationship with that has the potential to lead to a commitment. I don't know yet if we're right for each other, but I'd like to date you and find out. What about you?

SHE: I'm glad you told me this, because I just don't feel the same way. I like going out with you, but I think of you as a friend. Maybe it's better if we don't go out anymore. I'm just not interested in getting romantic.

HE: Boy, am I disappointed. Thanks for telling me the truth. I'll have to let this soak in before I decide what to do next.

SHE: I'm sorry I can't return your feelings.

SHE: You know, Mark, now that we've gone out a few times I want to let you know how I'm feeling about this. I never expected to date you and I was surprised that you asked me out. As you know, my divorce isn't even final yet, and, the truth is that if my ex wanted to work things out I would try again with him. I am very attracted to you, and I want you to know that I'm not at all ready for any kind of commitment.

HE: I kind of thought that's where you were. I don't think I'm looking for anything lasting at this point, either. Maybe we could just go out and enjoy each other, and take it one day at a time. I wouldn't like it if you got back together with your ex, but I could certainly understand it.

SHE: Thanks for your understanding. Sounds good to me.

Keep in mind that the Shopping Conversation is *not*

- Asking for any kind of commitment
- Pressuring the other person to promise anything
- A way to make sure your heart is not broken

The Shopping Conversation *is*

- Your first You and Me Conversation, paving the way for countless others
- A way to explore what kind of potential you might have
- A brief talk without any agenda except understanding

With the Shopping Conversation, all things are possible and nothing is certain. The goal is to get out on the table your intentions at that time so that you can see what the possibilities are. Then you are empowered to make an informed decision about where you feel comfortable taking the relationship. If you discover that you're not on the same page, you may still want to continue. But, as you are advised by those warning labels on certain products, you do so *at your own risk*. Sometimes relationships that begin on differing footing progress to a course that is more mutually satisfying and sometimes they don't. But if you choose it consciously, you can learn from the experience, and though you may be disappointed with the outcome, you can be satisfied that it was your choice to follow this path with your eyes wide-open.

Be creative with the Shopping Conversation. There are countless ways to express where you're coming from, so tailor it to your personality. The Shopping Conversation sets the stage for the many You and Me talks that are sure to come up throughout your relationship. Each time you clarify where you stand with each other, you free yourselves for the real task of love: maintaining and enjoying the magic of your romantic connection.

7

The Dance of Intimacy

♥   ♥   ♥

Our second date was a week later, dinner at his house. We talked over candlelight and wine, and shared laughter and moments of sadness, as we chronicled our lives of the past six years. When he walked me to my car, we ended the date with another hug. A few days later, we had a picnic in the park. Then, there was the night we tried to go dancing but every place we went was closed. It didn't matter. The rapport from our first dinner date had led to the beginnings of a truly wonderful romance and we found ourselves enjoying the time we spent together no matter what happened.

Within weeks we were a couple, and then there was the fabulous, two-week cruise that we shared over the Christmas holidays. Our time together was almost magical, and I thought that, at last, I had found the perfect partner for me.

Then one week, something changed. He was more distant, I was bewildered. We tried to talk about it, but our communication broke down. One night, he told me it wasn't working for him, and we broke up, after only four months of dating. I was sad, but grateful for the relationship we had had. Still, though, I wondered, How could something this good end so quickly?

Months later, we met for dinner and talked about what happened, and the mystery was cleared up. We had a connection, but it wasn't as strong as it seemed. When stress came along, there just wasn't enough glue to hold us together. Even though we talked about getting back together, there wasn't enough passion on either of our parts to do so. We parted in a friendly way, at last settled on the fact that this was not meant to be.

As my story shows, romantic relationships are somewhat fragile in the beginning. We're still getting to know each other, and even though there are sparks, until there's a strong flame burning, they can be easily extinguished. We're making deposits to the emotional bank account, but at any turn we may inadvertently make a significant withdrawal and find that our budding romance has fizzled. This can happen within the first few weeks, or within the first months.

Like dancing, intimacy is an exchange of energy between partners. We're learning how to move together without stepping on someone else's toes. Through the test of time, we either become better partners, or we realize it's time for the dance to end.

New relationships don't have to flounder. Sometimes, through conversation, we may discover a new direction in which to go. Or, we may decide not to go forward, but have a real clarity about why. Along the way, there are many situations and communication opportunities through which we may deepen our connection, and strengthen our fledgling partnership, if we're looking for them and know what to say. *This is the dance of intimacy, and it all happens through communication and conversation.*

There are lots of dating situations that arise that call for special handling and for which we must rely solely on our conversational skills. Thinking about them in advance helps to prepare yourself for knowing what to say and how to say it, thus increasing the odds that you will stay in the dance. While we'll never be able to cover every contingency in this one chapter, we can look at some of the more common scenarios that occur early on in a relationship, and how to talk about them.

Their Feelings Seem to Have Shifted

Sometimes the first two or three dates are wonderful, and then it's as if the wind has changed directions. Warm feelings seem to grow cold, rapport seems to be broken, the connection is severed or weakened, and you're left puzzled and uncertain. Yvonne's story is an example.

"Our first date was great. We talked and laughed, and seemed to have lots in common. The second date was equally wonderful. We held hands a little when we walked, the rapport was very warm, and it felt appropriate when he kissed me good night. He was romantic but not pushy. I thought we were off to a great start.

"Then we had our third date, which was dinner and a movie. He seemed aloof and distant. Even though it was cold as we walked along, he never offered to put his arm around me. During the movie I made sure he could get to my hand, but he never made the effort to do so. There was very little rapport and no good-night kiss at the end. I was completely puzzled."

Yvonne expressed a desire to discover what happened, but she was uncertain about what to do. "I haven't heard from him in two weeks, and everyone says that whatever I do I shouldn't call him. What do you think?"

Being a believer in appropriate assertiveness, I coached Yvonne to do the following, something I recommend for women to do when he stops calling after a couple of dates and you don't know why. During the day, while he's at work, call his home phone number and leave a message, saying in an upbeat tone something along these lines: "Hi, Mark, it's Yvonne. We haven't talked in a couple of weeks, and I just wanted you to know that it's been fun going out with you. I would enjoy seeing you again, so if you're interested, give me a call sometime. If you don't feel the same way, it's really okay, and it's not necessary to call. If that's the case, I wish you well. Take care, and good-bye."

Yvonne actually followed this coaching with two different men with whom she had gone out and who had stopped calling. One of them never called back, so she got her answer. It was okay and was complete, so she invested no more thought or energy about him.

Mark, on the other hand, called back and wanted to talk. They met for lunch and he explained that he was no longer available, that an old girlfriend had come back into his life. They shifted to friendship and found that they had a lot to talk about. A couple of weeks later, Mark introduced Yvonne to his friend, Chris. Yvonne and Chris made a magical connection and are now very much in love.

Frank's story is very similar. After two wonderful dates with Lucy, they had two mediocre dates. Communication seemed to stop, and when he called her on the telephone she was too busy to talk. He wasn't sure if she wasn't interested or if something had happened to turn her off. Finally, he called and asked her for a few minutes of her time, and the conversation went something like this:

HE: Our first couple of dates were really great for me, and since then it just feels like we're not connecting. I'm really interested in dating you, and I'm wondering if something happened to throw us off course.

SHE: I had a good time with you also, Frank, but I realize that this just isn't a love connection for me. I like you a lot, and if you're interested in having a new friend, that's okay, but I'm not interested in dating.

He was very disappointed, but now he knew where he stood.

The lessons from these stories are:

• When the focus is on connection, and something interrupts that, you naturally want to understand what happened, even if there's no longer a possibility for a romance.

• Had Yvonne followed conventional wisdom, never contacting Mark, she wouldn't have met Chris, who may very well turn out to be the love of her life!

• Just because someone else breaks a connection doesn't mean you should automatically write him off. Taking the time to discover what happened gives you resolution, freeing you to move forward and meet someone new.

• Getting resolution about what happened also frees you to shift to a friendship connection, if that's appropriate for you both. And, remember, you never know where that connection will lead!

The Shopping Conversation Revisited

Sometimes a connection is made, you progress to the Shopping Conversation, that goes well, and you appear to be on the same page. Then, something happens. Instead of calling you two days later, he doesn't call for a week, and just doesn't seem as warm. You call her for your next date and she puts you off, claiming that she's very busy. What happened?

What you're probably experiencing is the aftermath of the Shopping Conversation. This first, highly significant, You and Me talk is somewhat scary, and there may be a delayed emotional reaction. Some of the possibilities are:

• Your partner said what she thought you wanted to hear, and not necessarily the full truth.

• Upon further reflection, your partner realizes that he is really not ready for a relationship, and is now embarrassed and reluctant to admit these feelings.

• Declaring where you stand puts you at greater emotional risk, and after doing so, fear sets in. The reaction is to withdraw somewhat.

• Another circumstance in the person's life is taking her energy and focus, and it may have nothing to do with your Shopping Conversation.

• The conversation itself was incomplete, so your understanding is inaccurate, causing you to be puzzled by the other person's behavior.

How do you know what's going on with the other person? The general rule is always, *When in doubt, check it out!*

Making assumptions is the basis of all poor communication, so nip that unwelcome habit in the bud by addressing your concerns as soon as possible. Remember, the goal is *understanding*, and once that takes place, you will naturally discover the next best step.

There are several ways to address this. You could wait until your next date to bring up the subject, you could call and attempt a telephone conversation, or you could just do nothing, waiting to see if his behavior shifts back to a more normal mode. Choosing which approach to take is a judgment call. Here are some things to consider as you try to decide:

• Sometimes doing nothing is the best solution, as relationships often have a tendency to self-correct when left alone. Obviously, doing nothing can be taken to the extreme, wherein you become a passenger in your relationship, always expecting the other person to take control. The other extreme is making an issue out of every incident or shift of the emotional wind in a relationship, which can be very exhausting and actually inhibit the flow of positive feelings in the future.

• Bringing up the issue on the next date has advantages, as you then have the benefit of being able to read your partner's body language.

• If you're having difficulty even setting another date, then a telephone call may be appropriate, rather than having to wait indefinitely to address the issue.

If you choose to address the shift in feelings that seems to be happening, keep these things in mind before you do:

• The other person may be feeling embarrassed, threatened, or just plain fearful.

• He/she may be feeling "cornered," whether or not you've done anything to cause that.

Therefore, make it your goal to *create emotional safety* for the other person so that understanding can occur. Some ways to do this:

• Begin with the obvious. Tell her you're confused, and ask for her help in understanding what happened.

• Replay the facts only, expressing a desire to understand.

• Give him a way to save face, even though you may have hurt feelings resulting from his behavior.

"Bill, I'm confused, and I'm hoping you can help me understand something. Up until lately, we've gone out at least once a week, sometimes twice, and I noticed that I didn't hear from you all last week. I wondered if I had done something that offended you, or if there was some other problem in your life that got in the way."

"Susan, I'm not sure what's happening, and I thought maybe you could help me clear up my confusion. The last two times I've called you've been too busy to go out, even though things seemed to be going great before that. Are you under a lot of stress, or is it something with me?"

• As the conversation progresses, don't stop just because she latches onto one of the offered excuses. Check out your hunches, with compassion, again offering ways to save face.

"I understand about the demands of your job, Bill, but I admit I'm still confused. I couldn't help but wonder if our conversation the last time we went out was a problem for you. I want you to know that if you've had a change of heart, or if you've realized you have different feelings since then, it's okay."

"Sounds like you do have a lot of stress, Susan, and I'm glad to hear that you're not upset with me. Still, though, I had this feeling that maybe something happened surrounding our conversation when we went out the last time, you know, when we discussed what we were looking for. I hope you know that if your feelings are different now, it's okay to tell me. I want what's best for you and for me, even if that means we shouldn't date."

• Don't stop until you've gotten to the bottom of what's happening. When you get that solid, sort of *thunk* in your gut, you know you've unearthed the truth.

• This particular guideline doesn't mean, however, that you hammer away at someone when she is obviously reluctant to open up. Anytime someone just won't express what's going on, take a break from talking, but let him know it's important to get back to the discussion at some point.

"We seem to be having difficulty talking about this. Why don't we just leave it alone for now. When you're ready to tell me what's going on with you, please know that I would love to listen."

Resistance to the Shopping Conversation

Sometimes bringing up the relationship and where you stand is so threatening to the other person that you just can't get through the conversation. Your partner clams up and won't say much. He tries to change the subject. You feel as if you're butting your head against a brick wall.

This could be because you're with someone who isn't emotionally available (a Westbound Train*) or it could be someone who's afraid of

---

*See *Be Your Own Dating Service*, Chapter Thirteen, for more about a Westbound Train.

being pinned down. Whatever the reason, you can make an effort to understand what's happening. Begin with something like this: "You don't seem to be comfortable with this conversation." Then go to one or more of the following:

- "I wonder if you're afraid that I'm trying to pin you down."
- "Maybe you're just not ready yet for a relationship."
- "You know, this isn't about making a commitment. It's about finding out if there's a built-in dead end."
- "I'm confused about why you won't talk about this. Maybe you can help me understand what's happening for you right now."

Pay attention to your hunches about what's happening and express them, with an openness to realizing that you're completely wrong. Usually if you make an inaccurate guess, the other person will correct you and tell you the real story, so wrong hunches are very valuable, as long as you don't cling to them.

If your partner still won't open up, you can let her know that you would love to hear from her when she gets her feelings sorted out. Let it go for now, but realize that until you can get through a Shopping Conversation, there's little chance that you'll be able to discuss with this person the other vitally important issues that are sure to come up later in a relationship.

Talking about Affection

One of the most awkward issues in a budding relationship is that of physical affection. Men wonder what to do and when, and women wonder how to handle it if he moves too quickly. Both find it very difficult to discuss. Because men are usually the initiators in this way, I'll again separate my coaching between the genders. You may want to read both sections though and realize that the shoe may easily be on the other foot.

MEN

One of the common misperceptions that men have about women is that if she's reluctant to be physically affectionate, she's a "cold fish," or she's uninterested in him romantically. Likewise, men may assume that if she's very touchy-feely (holding hands, hugging) in the beginning, that she's a "hot tamale," ready for sexual action with him. The truth is that almost any assumption you could make about a woman's affections, or lack thereof, is likely to be wrong. Here's why:

Women are very different, and how they express themselves through physical affection carries individual meanings, depending on personality, emotional state, circumstances, and desires for this particular relationship.

A woman may not feel safe being physically affectionate until she knows a man better. Even though she may love kissing, she doesn't want to do that with just anyone, only with someone special. This woman won't be receptive to a good-night kiss on the first date, but may be quite enthusiastic by the second or third.

A woman may be a very passionate lover, once she feels emotionally safe. She may not necessarily be very affectionate in the beginning, but once she sees that a man loves her, happily shifts to a physically expressive mode.

Sometimes a woman is attracted to a man and wants some, not all, of her physical needs met. She enjoys holding hands, kissing him, and being held by him, but has no desire to advance to sex until later in the relationship, or until marriage.

A woman may enjoy kissing a guy that she's attracted to, and it doesn't mean that this particular one is special, only that she finds him kissable.

As you can see, the possibilities are endless. How do you know when to hold a woman's hand or kiss her? Here are some general guidelines:

Get to know her as a person, first and foremost. Create a connection through conversation before you even consider being physically affectionate.

Pay attention to her body language. If she's maintaining lots of space between you physically, she's probably not ready to be touched.

Pay attention to the energy between you. If there's lots of warmth, if she's standing very close to you, brushing her arm against your arm, and so on, this is telling you that she's more open possibly to holding hands and maybe a kiss later.

Progress in stages, not all at once. If at any point you sense reluctance, back off.

If you still aren't sure, ask! Women love to be asked for a kiss, but be gracious and back off if she says no. If you're not sure what she's signaling, ask about that:"I'm confused, Gloria, and I don't want to overstep any boundaries. On our last date we kissed and it was great, but now you don't seem to want even to hold hands. Am I moving too fast?"

Never, ever try to persuade a woman to do more than she's comfortable doing, regardless of signals that you may interpret to the contrary.

WOMEN
Sometimes things flow easily in this department. You connect through conversation, you're attracted, the energy is good, and when he kisses you you're ready and thoroughly enjoy it. Sometimes, though, you're just not ready for his attempts to be affectionate. You can prepare yourself for those awkward times by realizing a few things and taking some steps.

Be aware of how you're feeling about a man. If you realize that he's someone you don't want to kiss, tell him you want to shift to friendship before he has a chance to go too far with his romantic expectations.

If there are romantic possibilities, but you're the type that likes to go slow, tell him, "Tom, I really like you and want to continue getting to know you. I am attracted to you and I don't want to confuse you. I am the type that likes to go very slowly in the physical affection department, so don't take it as rejection if I'm just not ready to kiss or hold hands right away."

If he moves too quickly, tell him, "I'm just not ready yet, Gary, for this. I'd like to continue going out and getting to know each other, and if that keeps going well, I'll be more comfortable kissing you later on."

Never continue to date a man who doesn't respect the boundaries you set. This is a warning signal for the possibility of emotional abuse, physical abuse, and even date rape.

Sticky Conversations

Some conversations, early in your relationship, seem easy on the surface, but underneath can actually be quite complicated, and if not handled well can become sticking points. Like flypaper, the misunderstandings you've inadvertently created on these important topics trap you over and over again. Three crucial areas that this tends to happen with are religion, children, and career, which we'll tackle separately.

Generally, some things to keep in mind about these sticky topics are:

• These conversations, like all your dating conversations, will unfold over time, going to deeper levels of disclosure. Don't expect every thought, feeling, and attitude to surface with the first talk, or even the second or third.

• Realize that not everyone is clear about how he feels on these topics. Your conversations may, in the beginning, serve merely to uncover how you or your partner are unclear on a particular subject.

• Make it your goal simply to get the topic out on the table and increase your mutual understanding.

• Do watch for compelling reasons not to go forward with the relationship, such as a radical difference in values that would be incompatible.

Religion

Discussing religious views is vitally important in a budding relationship, yet we tend to stay away from the topic for fear of stepping on someone else's toes or losing a potential partner. Like your list of Nonnegotiables, you may be tempted to avoid really looking at this area if you're going out with someone to whom you're strongly attracted. This is a mistake, as religion can be a make-it-or-break-it issue, depending on whether you have common ground or you're miles apart in your views.

Doing your homework in advance prepares you for the discussions that you will be having on this vitally important topic. Some questions to ask yourself are:

• What are my views about (1) God or a higher power, (2) Membership in an organized body (church, synagogue, etc.), (3) Public participation (going to services), (4) Private participation (prayer, meditation, study)?

• What do I want with my partner, with regard to his participation, both publicly and privately? (1) Attending services together, (2) Joint prayer/meditation, (3) Religious study together.

• What do I want with my future family and children with regard to religious participation? (1) Attending services, (2) Celebration of religious holidays, (3) Rites of passage into adulthood, such as confirmation, bar/bat mitzvah, (4) Other religious ceremony both in and outside of the home.

• How important is it that my partner share my religious beliefs?

• Are my wants Negotiable or Nonnegotiable? Am I unsure about that?

• How did my background influence the formation of my religious beliefs and wants for a future partner/family?

• Am I clear about my religious views or is there confusion that I'm attempting to sort out? How important is it that my partner be clear about his/her religious beliefs?

Once you've sorted out your own feelings, you are more easily able to talk with your partner; however, the conversation itself can bring new thoughts and feelings to light. Your basic beliefs will probably not alter, but your approach to spirituality can be influenced by your partner's viewpoints and by the energy of the relationship itself:

• Cathy, Jewish but nonpracticing, met David, who attended services every week without fail. As she listened to his spiritual views and began going to synagogue with him, she realized that she had been missing something very important, and thus reestablished the practice of her religion.

• Steve, raised in a very freethinking home, was open to all kinds of spiritual practices, and connected quickly with Jane, who wanted something more modern than the fundamentalist church she attended as a child. Together, they explored several religious groups, finally selecting one with which they both felt comfortable.

• Adrian belonged to a very select religious order, with specific guidelines for life and for spiritual growth, many of which Ellen could not embrace. They found that by praying and reading the Bible together, they were able to connect spiritually in a way that was very satisfying to both.

How do you discover where you and your dating partner stand on matters of religion? Through *conscious conversation*, in which you both practice the skills of speaking and listening. *The most important thing you can do in this, and in all discussions of sticky topics, is to be respectful of someone else's point of view, no matter how different from your own.* Even if you are agnostic, and your partner is a card-carrying believer, you can still converse about your views with respect.

Where do you begin? Once you know your own position (or as much as you are aware of for now), you have an idea of where to begin with the other person. Start by sharing your basic spiritual mind-set, opening the door for them to share theirs:

"I'm a practicing _____ since my upbringing as a child."

"I went to church when I was little, but haven't in many years. I'm not sure what I believe, except that I do believe in God."

"I'm a Christian and it's very important to me to find someone who will be a part of a church community with me."

"I believe in a higher power, and I get all the religion I need at my Twelve-Step meeting."

"I don't go to any particular church, but I would love to explore some and find a place where I would feel comfortable growing spiritually."

"I'm Jewish, but I don't practice as an adult, and it's really not very important to me to do so, nor is it important that my partner be Jewish."

"I believe in God but don't care much for organized religion. My spiritual practice is meditation and being in nature."

Listen respectfully to the other person's position. Again, share about yourself, and then Listen Well. Ask questions only for clarification, but avoid the temptation to grill her.

What you are looking for in these early conversations about religion is *not* for every thought, feeling, and belief to surface. It takes time and the build-up of trust for these conversations to go to any depth. Also, spiritual views, like other beliefs and attitudes, can actually shift and change with time, maturity, and life experience. So what you hear today may be very different from what you will hear in six months, two years, or ten years.

What you *are* looking for is fundamental approaches to religion that are incompatible (i.e., I'm a freethinker about spiritual matters, while you operate from a black-and-white viewpoint), or a violation of your own Nonnegotiables (i.e., I must have someone who shares my particular faith, and this person clearly does not). If you plan to have children, it's especially important to have compatible expectations about their religious training.

If you *absolutely must* have someone who practices your religion, and you know that this is a Nonnegotiable, then it's best to get that on the table as soon as possible. One way to say something like this is, "As you know, Carla, I'm very dedicated to my spiritual growth. It's so important to me that I can't imagine being married to someone who doesn't share my beliefs and practices. I'm looking for someone who is open to exploring that with me, or who already believes the way I do."

If you're doing a good job opening up and listening to your date, you'll probably not have to say this. It will be apparent that you either share religious beliefs or you don't.

What if you don't share faiths and you always told yourself that that's what you wanted? Do you immediately break up or do you go forward and risk compromising a Nonnegotiable? There isn't always an easy answer. Jason always thought he'd marry someone who was Jewish by birth, but then he met and fell in love with Sherrie, who was Christian although nonpracticing. Through the course of their early conversations, he came to realize that he had been trying to find a partner that matched his list of criteria but disregarding the lack of emotional connection. He decided that having a powerful love match was most important to him, and that as long as he could be with someone who was open to conversion that it was worth it to him to explore the relationship.

Religious Healing

Not everyone has positive experiences about religion from childhood. In fact, there are many who suffer from confusion at best, and the sense of great damage at worst, about their religious beliefs. These conversations may actually bring up pain and loss, and not automatically lead to clarity.

If that's you, it's important to seek help to deal with your feelings. Talk to a minister, talk to a therapist, get in a support group. Do what it takes to have peace of mind in your spiritual matters, and when you're dating, be honest about where you are, saying something like this:

"To tell you the truth, Carla, I'm not sure where I stand about my spirituality. I grew up in _____ religion, and it left me with more questions than answers. I'm still working on coming to terms with how I feel about my relationship with God."

Children

One of the most important issues to sort out for yourself and be able to discuss with dating partners is that of children:

- Do I want them?
- Am I unsure?
- If I already have them, do I want more?
- How important is it to have a partner who is willing to help raise the ones I already have?

And many other issues. Most puzzling of all is, *When do we discuss this?* Conventional wisdom says that this topic, like that of commitment, is death to a budding relationship, that it's too highly charged and threatening. The implication is that if we're discussing the possibility of children, then we've already targeted the other person for a relationship, that we're trying to force some kind of premature commitment. Yet time after time I've coached couples who didn't discuss this all-important topic early in the relationship and when it's time to consider marriage discover that they are totally out of sync. One desperately wants children while the other has no interest whatsoever in having them. Yet now they're in love and naturally quite reluctant to let go of the relationship.

Jennie's story illustrates the other typical scenario. When she and Cary started dating, both were still reeling from their divorces. Neither was in any kind of emotional shape to consider a commitment, so they proceeded with a relationship on the basis that they were just going out and "having fun." They made no attempt to discuss these difficult topics, including that of children. Of course, with time and intimacy, they got attached, and eventually, she wanted him to spend time with her and her children to get to know them better. He resisted, and finally, in a moment of honesty, confessed that he had no desire to help raise someone else's kids, and that their relationship had a built-in dead end. She managed to move on, but at great emotional cost for them both.

It's not unusual during premarital counseling to discover that the couple has never even broached this subject, or that they've only touched on it lightly in the past. Why would such an important topic be left undiscussed until practically on the doorstep of the church?

• Many times couples begin dating with the stated intention of "just having fun." Thus they don't bother to explore their attitudes, values, and beliefs, reasoning that it's not important since they're not planning on staying together. The heart, of course, has another agenda, and they eventually find themselves heavily involved and planning a future together, but without the awareness of where they stand on these important issues.

• Bringing up sticky conversations early in a relationship is scary. The belief is that "I'll scare them away if I bring that up!"

• Not knowing how to discuss these topics, we neglect them until it's finally imperative. By then, of course, we've built up so much anxiety about it that it's very difficult to discuss.

• We make assumptions about each other's beliefs, based on inferences from other conversations and based on behavior (i.e., assuming "He's so affectionate with his nieces and nephews; surely he wants children of his own!" when in fact, it isn't so).

The reality of failing to discuss children early in a relationship is that it leaves us unprepared to deal with our conflicting agendas later, when there's an established emotional bond that we don't want to break. This can have lifelong consequences.

• After marriage, many couples end up having children against the true desires of one partner. These children often grow up feeling unwanted and unloved, as rejection by even one parent can have a devastating effect.

• If one person gives up the need to be a parent and the marriage doesn't work out, there can be an enormous amount of bitterness later.

• Many couples conceive their children without conscious decision-making, rather than talking about the issues. The fear is that if we discuss it we'll find out we're not at all in sync, so unconsciously, we resolve any potential dilemma by just getting pregnant.

The biological and emotional drive to procreate is very powerful, particularly at certain ages, and it takes a great deal of personal and interpersonal consciousness to direct it in a way that is in the best interest of each partner and their future children. This means

• Getting clear with yourself about what you want, and then
• Choosing to bring it up early in a dating relationship

How can you address this sticky issue early in a dating relationship without scaring someone away? First of all, *set the stage for the conversation.*

Start out by expressing where you're coming from:
"I know we don't know each other very well yet, and this may seem like a strong topic to bring up so early. It's just that I've had the experience of dating someone for a long time and then discovering that our values and life desires were way off. It's very painful to have to break up with someone for those reasons, so I've learned to talk about these things up front."

Let the other person know that you're not targeting him for commitment with this conversation:

"I'm not at all sure that you and I are right for each other, or that we'll even have another date, so this isn't about getting some kind of commitment. My desire is simply to understand how we feel about the subject, so that if we're miles apart we'll know it. Then you can decide what's best for you and I can do likewise."

Express the gist of where you are currently with regard to children:

"I want to be a parent and I want someone who has an equally strong desire to have children."

"I already have two kids, and I'm not sure if I want more, but I want someone who would enjoy being part of a ready-made family."

"I don't have children and at this time I have no desire to become a parent."

"I don't have children but I would enjoy being a part of raising someone else's kids." And so on.

Listen to what you hear, particularly the emotional tone. You may hear uncertainty, and if so, ask if that's the case.

"I hear you saying that you want children, too, but you don't sound quite certain."

Respect her views, even if different from your own.

Believe what you hear! It's tempting to think that your partner will feel differently later when you fall in love, but you can never be certain of that. Yes, it could happen, because love often creates new possibilities, but it's important that you live today based on today's knowledge.

Remember that this is only the first of many conversations that you will have on this subject, and that with time and deeper trust, more will emerge. What you are seeking now is to determine if your desires are way off or in sync. If they're very different, you can now choose

To go forward, with your eyes wide-open. Realize that you can't count on your partner to shift a basic attitude such as the desire to have children. If you go forward, do so with an open heart and mind, and resolve that you'll be okay no matter how it turns out.

To break off the budding relationship. If you're certain of what you want and don't see the likelihood of getting it with this partner, now is a good time to end it, before a great deal of attachment has happened.

No matter how carefully you bring up the topic, you may still scare someone away. *If that happens, so be it!* Better to scare a few people away than to walk on eggshells and steer away from open, honest conversations that so profoundly affect your future and the lives of any children you may have. Having the courage to bring up difficult subjects such as this early in the relationship builds emotional muscle, which you will certainly need as time goes on and even more difficult conversations are necessary.

Career

This is a sticky subject that has gotten tremendously more so in the last few decades. With more women in the workplace than ever, with changing roles between men and women, and with today's financial imperatives, it's no wonder we're confused. Who works and who doesn't? Who stays home with the children and who works outside the home?

There are no easy answers. Many women today are torn between a sense of entitlement ("My mother didn't have to work outside the home."), the desire to be more available for little ones, and the reality of today's world, in which two incomes can make the difference between whether or not college funds are available for the children. Many men find that shouldering the entire financial burden is too much, and want a self-sufficient woman who will share the load. Others want the traditional arrangement: She works in the home while he works outside.

Even more confusing than the issues themselves is how and when to talk about them. How does a man tell a woman whom he barely knows that he has no desire to support someone entirely? How does a woman tell a man that she wishes to stay home with the children when she doesn't even know yet if there will be a next date? Yet the issue of career can have a great deal of impact on a relationship in the future, and is therefore one of those things that you want to know as much as possible about in the beginning.

Like the subjects of religion and children, what you are looking for are gross incompatibilities that will prevent you from ever being happy with this partner. If a man wants a self-sufficient woman and he dates someone who is looking for a financial provider for her and her future children, there's going to be a huge clash of needs later. If a woman loves her career and dates a man who expects her to give up her job when they get married, there are power struggles galore in the future. How do you discover whether or not you're in sync without waiting too long (i.e., after attachment has occurred)?

As with all these significant conversations, begin with the basics.

Set the stage by expressing where you're coming from, which is that you're not driving for commitment but rather for understanding.

Express the essence of what you want with regard to career, as it pertains to your relationship.

"As I've already shared with you, I do want children, and I think it's important that they have a mom with them while they're little. I'm looking for someone who would enjoy being the financial provider while I take care of the home and the children, at least for the first few years. Later, I'd expect to resume my career, unless we both agreed that that wasn't what we wanted."

"Regardless of whether I have children or not, I'm passionate about my work and couldn't imagine ever giving it up entirely. I want someone who will support my choice to work, even if that means that we pay for nannies and day care for the children."

Talk about what inspires you in your career (or not), about goals and objections, and visions for your future.

"I like the job I have now, but what I really want to do is be a full-time actor. I do it part time now, but as soon as I make enough money at it, I'm going to give up my regular job. What's most important to me is pursuing this goal, even if that means some years of financial sacrifice."

Talk especially about what might affect someone else's decision as to being with you (i.e., as part of the pursuit of career goals: plans to move away, putting off or not having children, making financial sacrifices, going back to school for advanced degrees, and so on).

Listen respectfully to the other person's views, even if different from your own.

Believe what you hear! Don't expect to change his/her mind later.

Treat this as one of many conversations that you'll have on this all-important subject. You're laying the groundwork, and if you make a connection, you'll undoubtedly revisit this topic many times.

Getting Ready for the Conversation

How do you prepare for these sticky topics? How do you know when to bring them up and when not to? On the issue of timing, keep in mind:

These conversations are earned through your deposits to the emotional bank account; they aren't a freebie. This means that you take the time to establish rapport and build trust before you attempt to discover someone else's thoughts and feelings about sensitive topics such as these.

Once you know there's attraction and a good possibility for a relationship, it's time to begin. Think of it as timing for the first round of these and other important conversations, and that's usually after a few dates or whenever you feel a connection beginning to happen.

Have a balance. Be on the lookout for good timing to bring up these topics, rather than forcing the conversation to happen. If you've done a good job with rapport and are paying attention, you will find the right opportunities and these conversations will naturally unfold in the course of getting to know each other.

Before you can have these kinds of conversations, you have lots of homework to do. Knowing yourself is vital to your preparation. I can't emphasize enough how important it is to do whatever you need to do to understand yourself and where you stand with regard to these and other make-it-or-break-it issues.

Do your self-development work now and as a relationship is developing. Keep a journal, go to therapy, meditate, go to Twelve-Step meetings, join a support group; in short, do whatever it takes to know yourself better.

Have compassion for those who aren't sure about how they feel. It takes years, a whole lifetime, in fact, to really know one's self, and everyone is in a different place in the process. Try to understand the essence of the person and where he's coming from, trusting that as that evolves so will the right direction for the relationship.

If you're afraid to talk about these issues now, realize that it will only get tougher as time goes on. Fear grows in proportion to the length of time that we procrastinate having difficult conversations. You can diminish your fear dramatically by plunging in and initiating these kinds of talks early in a relationship rather than later.

Have a far greater investment in a healthy relationship than you do in winning over a particular partner. In the face of wild attraction to a particular person, you may be tempted to hedge or cover up the truth, hoping that their feelings will change or that it won't matter. This hurts you, as you set yourself up for a great deal of pain when you can't get your needs met later. This hurts the other person, in that you're leaving someone else in the dark, having to make important choices based on inaccurate or incomplete information. Worst of all, this damages your relationship, setting a precedent of manipulation and deceit, rather than honest, open communication.

Having these open, honest conversations with your dates continues to build the kind of emotional muscle that you'll need as your relationship develops, and, additionally, it works! Knowing that you're in sync, wanting basically the same things, frees up your energy for connection, enjoyment, romance, and love. This, after all, is what you're here for!

Conversations That Worked

Use these guidelines as just that: indications of where to begin and continue the conversation. Be creative, and bring your own personality into the mix, like these individuals did.

Talking about Career. Joe, a wealthy middle-aged man who was looking for a self-sufficient woman, was talking with Beth, a woman he'd been dating for a few weeks. He asked her if she planned on working after marriage, to which she responded, "Well, I probably would, but I'd like the option not to have to if I don't want to." Mulling that over, and listening to what his gut was telling him, he then said, "It sounds like you won't be working after you're married." She paused, reflecting on this, and said, truthfully, "No, I suppose I won't. You're right." This cleared up the issue for Joe, allowing him to move on quickly, something new for him, as he typically dated women for lengthy periods of time before discovering that there were major value differences that rendered them incompatible.

The Shopping Conversation. Linda broke up with Mickey one night after dating for five weeks. She was frustrated because of his emotional unavailability and because of developing feelings for him that she wasn't sure were being returned. Looking at it later, she realized that she had acted impulsively without getting the whole story, thus leaving her hoping that they would get back together. She decided to go back and have a complete conversation with him.

SHE: I realize that I broke up with you without really talking about what was going on between us. It would help me have closure to talk about it some more. Looking back, I felt frustrated, not knowing where I stood with you. I do have feelings for you and was hoping that our relationship would go somewhere. I'm wondering how you felt about breaking up.

HE: I think you're wonderful, but the truth is that I felt relieved when you broke up with me. I knew something was happening but I didn't know how to stop it or to handle it. We started out just having fun, with nothing long-term in mind. I could tell that you were feeling more, and I felt bad that I just couldn't return that. I'm sorry I didn't speak up or take action myself.

They talked more, clearing the air and getting the reality of their brief relationship out on the table. After this conversation, Linda felt complete, her questions answered. She understood that her feelings had changed since their original Shopping Conversation, but his did not. No longer did she wonder if Mickey was a real possibility or not. She was free to move on.

Hot Topics

As you continue to build your connection, the two hottest issues in a relationship loom: sex and money. Not surprisingly, they are also the most difficult subjects to talk about. In fact, we are so uncomfortable about discussing sex and money that we actively avoid these discussions. The battles that married couples have over money and the continuing spread of sexually transmitted diseases, including AIDS, are testament to this.

You can spare your heart, and even your life, by being able to address these issues early in your relationship. In the next chapter, we'll look at the first of these two "hot topics" and how to have conversations with your date about it.

8

Sex Talks

♥   ♥   ♥

Nicole and Jason are on their fourth date. They dine by candlelight while sipping wine (three glasses for him, two for her). Eyes locked, they listen enraptured while the other shares the most intimate details of his/her life. After dinner, they stroll hand-in-hand down the street, entering a chic nightclub, where they dance the evening away. Afterward, they go back to Nicole's apartment, light candles and put on soft music. Holding each other close, they breathe the scent of each other, feel the texture of each other's skin, hands, and hair. They kiss, tentatively at first, then passionately.

Soon, they are taking off each other's clothes. Jason whispers in Nicole's ear, "Are you okay?" to which she responds huskily yes. They both stand and, stopping to kiss every couple of steps, go to her bedroom, where they make love.

Sound like a trashy novel? Actually, it's a portrait of the typical way that men and women today make the leap from just going out to being lovers. And what's the rest of the story? Depending on their individual circumstances, their future interactions with each other, and their emotional availability, it could be any of the following:

• After sex, Jason abruptly gets up and leaves, realizing that he does not want a relationship to develop with Nicole.

• The next morning, both look at each other in embarrassment, and quickly agree that it was a huge mistake that they don't wish to repeat.

• Two weeks later, Nicole gets back together with her old boy-friend and marries him a month later, leaving Jason heartbroken.

• Three months later, Jason gets back together with his wife and stops divorce proceedings, leaving Nicole heartbroken.

• Their first sexual encounter is the beginning of a wonderful rela-tionship. They fall in love and marry within two years.

• Six months later, Nicole gets a call from Jason that he's been diag-nosed with a sexually transmitted disease, to which he's exposed her.

• Six weeks later, Jason gets a call from Nicole that she's pregnant.

• And countless other scenarios, as you can imagine.

Sex Talk

Most people would rather have sex than talk about it. Sound like an outrageous statement to make? Our couple's story is testament to this unfortunate reality of human behavior.

Jason and Nicole did what most dating couples do: They followed their libidos first, rather than their minds or their hearts. The outcome could be good. Perhaps there won't be an unwanted pregnancy or ill-ness or heartbreak. Maybe they'll be lucky enough to fall in love and have a loving and healthy relationship. If it turns out well, though, it will mostly be by happenstance, not by creation. And, their luck will have to go against the odds, because they haven't done the ground-work that puts the odds in their favor.

Actually, what Nicole and Jason have done is much worse than sim-ply neglecting to be well prepared. *They've become sexually intimate, a huge step in a relationship, without the benefit of communication.* In today's world, that's tantamount to flying an airplane without check-ing how much fuel you have! Because not talking about sex can have consequences that are life-altering and even deadly.

Why We Don't Talk about Sex

With so much at stake, why don't we talk about sex before doing it? To put it simply, that's how we were trained. The first place we're taught not to talk about sex is in our families. Most parents don't know how to talk about sex with their children because no one talked about it with them.

Sex is such an intensely private part of life, and so many of us carry burdens of shame and guilt about sexual behavior, real or imagined, that we keep it all under wraps. Certainly that's the case within most families. Most of us don't know what Mom and Dad did alone in their room, nor do we want to know. They didn't talk and we didn't ask. Or if we asked we were told it was none of our business.

Our questions went largely unanswered because our parents were so uncomfortable dealing with the issue. So, we turned to our friends and peers, who were equally bewildered. Speculation and mythology abounded in our childish discussions, much of which lingered into adolescence and even adulthood.

Sex education at school seemed to be more of a plumbing lesson (this goes here and that's located there) or a nature lesson (the birds do this and the bees do that) than an actual discourse on something that is the basis of all life. At no point were we taught anything about the connection between love and sex. Ironically, the great debate about sex education in our schools today is, once again, do we talk about it or not?

The myth is that if we let children talk about sex, or if we educate them about sexuality, they'll be more inclined to do it. This is sheer lunacy and reveals how little insight we still have into what sexuality is all about. The reality is that plenty of un-sex-educated kids are sexual, while plenty of kids who know a lot about it aren't. Kids who have sex are mostly kids who are filling an emotional deficit, and they'll do it regardless of whether they're educated about sex or not.

In our own education, our instructions on what to do were simple: Boys were told not to get anyone pregnant, girls were told not to do it, and we all were told to wait until marriage.

Education or not, spoken or unspoken, we somehow managed to grow into sexual beings, but how healthy we were with it is another story. Many of us tried the path of promiscuity, eventually learning that there's a price for so much experimentation. Still others got married young in order to sanction our sexuality, and paid the price in unhappy marriages that later ended. Even if we made good relationship choices, chances are we carried our incomplete legacy with us, leaving us mixed emotions and uncertainty at best, pain and suffering at worst.

No wonder we have no idea how to talk about sex, even today as adults! It's mysterious, confusing, and strictly taboo conversationally. If we have a history of painful incidents about our sexuality (i.e., incest, rape, abortion) or shame and guilt about past behavior, then that's all the more reason we have not to talk about it. With all that emotional baggage, it's no wonder we'd rather just get on with it than discuss it!

Sexual Healing

To overcome this legacy of fear and silence requires a dedication to our own healing process. That means we have to learn to talk about sex, whether it's with a therapist or a minister, a trusted friend or a committed lover. *You can't heal what you can't talk about.*

When Helen began therapy, she was guilt-ridden about a time in her life, a number of years earlier, when she had been quite promiscuous. Reacting to a painful breakup, she began going out to bars, drinking heavily, and going home with men she didn't know. After a few months of this, she realized how self-destructive her behavior was and stopped, beginning with abstinence from alcohol. She got her life back together and eventually met Randy, whom she'd been dating for a couple of years when she first came to see me.

Deeply ashamed, she had been unable to tell Randy about her past. She knew that she couldn't marry him without telling him all about herself and knowing that he still loved her in spite of what she'd done all those years before. In group therapy, she finally shared her secret, and discovered, to her astonishment, that no one was shocked or thought any less of her. As she learned to forgive herself, she realized that she could take the risk of telling her boyfriend everything, and when she finally did, their relationship actually grew much closer. Soon after, she finished therapy, at peace with her past and ready to get on with life. A couple of years later, I saw Helen and Randy at one of my speeches, and her face glowed with happiness as she talked about their wedding and their life together.

Helen's story is testament to the power of getting sexual secrets, whether about your own behavior or about what others have done to you, out in the open through the powerfully healing medium of conversation. Start somewhere, anywhere. Get in a support group, read some good self-help books, talk to a therapist, confide in a trusted friend. Do a fearless inventory of your sexual history, or lack thereof, including attitudes, moral stance, fantasies, and feelings (guilt, shame, resentment, anger). Forgive yourself and others for wrongs and injustices, mistakes and errors in judgment.

When you've gotten yourself healed with regard to your past, then do a fearless inventory of your stance with regard to your sexuality. Get absolutely clear with yourself about where you stand regarding

- Whether or not to wait until marriage to have sex, and how much is okay before
- Emotional timing of sexuality in a relationship (before or after commitment)
- Health, pregnancy, and disease

Resolve never again to become sexual with someone without first talking to him about the full spectrum of what's involved (which we'll cover later). Think of this as a commitment to yourself, to your own emotional, physical, and spiritual well-being. After all, you can't be trustworthy to others if you're not first of all self-caring.

Does this mean that you can't have a relationship until you're totally healed sexually? Absolutely not! In fact, a great deal of sexual healing is possible through the power of love with a committed partner. Conversations with your lover about sexual hurts, fears, fantasies, and desires is potent medicine for the psyche. A great deal of trust must be present in order for this to happen, and that takes time to build. As with all of your conversations, you begin with the Cliffs Notes version about this part of life and you progress to deeper levels of sharing with time and increased intimacy. Let's start with the most basic Sex Talk.

Timing of Your First Sex Talk

Sometime *after* you've handled your Shopping Conversation, and you feel that you're in sync with your partner, and *before* you become sexually intimate, will be the time for your first sex talk. This could be a couple of weeks into the relationship or a couple of months, depending on how quickly the level of intimacy grows.

Once you see that there is a relationship, and that it's progressing toward sexual contact, or that it could, it's time to talk. This first Mini Sex Talk basically covers the following:

- Moral stance regarding sexuality
- Emotional timing of sexuality

If you don't wish to have premarital sex, now is the time to tell your partner. If premarital is okay for anything but intercourse, express that. If premarital is okay, but you want a commitment before you sleep with someone, express that. If you're still a virgin, tell him. If you want a no-strings sexual partner, by all means disclose it now.

- "Even though I've had sex outside of marriage before, I've decided that I want my next lover to be my wife. I want to wait until I'm married before having sex."
- "It's very important to me to feel an emotional bond with someone before sleeping with him. For me, that means taking the time to date for quite a while, possibly even several months, until I feel like I'm in love and the person I'm with loves me the same way, and we have a commitment to work on the relationship together."
- "I'm not ready for any kind of commitment at this time, and I'm really just wanting someone to be a friend and lover with no strings."
- "I'm a virgin and I intend to remain that way until I get married. However, when I date someone for a while and I feel close to him I enjoy expressing it physically, as long as it's understood that there won't be intercourse."

This first talk notifies your partner of your moral and emotional stance with regard to sex. This is setting a boundary for you, ensuring that you're getting started on a course for mutual fulfillment and well-being.

Some say, "That's so intense! I might scare someone off if I disclose where I'm coming from so quickly." An understandable fear, as so many of us are intimidated by open, honest discourse about this part of life.

What you *don't want* is yet another relationship with no depth of conversation, especially about a part of life that is so integral to your well-being and to the health of a romantic relationship. What you *do want* is a partner who's willing to take these bold conversational steps with you, even if you're both uncertain and a little scared. By bringing up difficult issues for discussion, you create the opportunity for that to happen.

So what if you stumble around and feel a little awkward? So you feel a little embarrassed, or you get tongue-tied, or your date's mouth drops open. Maybe he won't even ask you out again, but so what? This tells you that you're dealing with someone who's not ready for this level of communication, and that makes him a poor risk for a relationship. Wouldn't you rather find this out now, instead of after you're intimate and falling in love? I say, scare a few people off! Especially if that's what it takes for you to stop compromising your values, to stop risking your well-being and even your life for a less than fulfilling romantic relationship.

Time after time on our radio talk show, young girls call in who have gotten pregnant by guys who either don't love them or who are too young and immature to stand by them. Men and women call with broken hearts because they've slept with a "friend" and fallen in love, only to find out that the other person has no interest in pursuing a relationship. Sex often happens on the first, second, or third date, with no real communication. Misunderstandings are the rule rather than the exception, resulting in broken hearts and broken lives. *If these conversations are scary, remember that the consequences for not having them are far more so.*

When to Become Sexual

Even though celibacy before marriage might be the ideal, and a more desirable approach to sexuality, the reality of today's world is that most couples do not manage to uphold this standard. If you want it, and are committed to it, then by all means do it.

If your standard is somewhat less than that, then you might want to consider having this one: *No sex without a strong emotional bond.* At the very least, never settle for a sexual relationship without exclusivity, especially in light of the risk of AIDS.

Becoming sexual with someone is much more than a physical act. The nature of human beings is that emotional attachment *will happen*, given a continuation of sexual intimacy and romantic behavior. When the relationship begins with sex (within the first few dates), there's a great gamble going on: Will we manage to build an emotional bridge between us, or not? More often than not, these sex-first relationships lead to broken hearts, as one person falls in love and the other, while attached, just doesn't share the same level of feelings.

A few of these situations, and we all begin to be more emotionally guarded. Not wanting to be hurt, we may still sleep with someone, but we hold back our hearts. This doesn't work, as relationships are doomed to failure when there's emotional armoring. It's only by being open and vulnerable that we create the opportunity for love. Though we're right to seek some emotional boundaries, this is movement in the wrong direction.

The casual approach to sex that we adopted in the sixties, seventies, and early eighties created a lot of "walking wounded" individuals, as we became sexual too soon with partners and got our hearts broken repeatedly, not to mention spread sexually transmitted diseases. Erroneously thinking that there is a clear separation between sex and love left us misinformed and dangerous to ourselves and others.

Sex is a highly intimate act. Emotions are aroused by holding and caressing someone, even if those feelings aren't as deep as you might wish. It's tempting to fall into a Settle For relationship as a result of becoming sexually intimate with a wrong partner.

Also, by sleeping with someone too soon, you may skip over important groundwork in your emotional connection. Getting to know someone pre-sex is much less pressured, as it's generally easier to move on should you decide this person isn't right for you. Once you have sex, you inadvertently become a couple. Suddenly, you realize you're involved with someone you barely know!

At that point, someone may feel very afraid and begin backing off. The other person, misunderstanding why his lover is suddenly moving away, may become emotionally demanding or angry, all of which sets off a negative cycle of relating that can be very destructive to the couple's fragile ties.

Then there are the attempts to avoid emotional entanglements by agreeing to a no-strings sexual relationship. This almost never works, as invariably one person will fall in love while the other will not. This is a formula for hurt for both parties, and therefore not something that I recommend.

The approach that seems to work best, and which I strongly endorse, is that if you are not going to wait until marriage, then *put off sex for a while*. Go out, get to know each other, avoid circumstances in which you'll be tempted to take your intimacy to the next physical level, and allow a relationship to develop, first and foremost, if it's going to. Wait until you have a strong emotional bond, preferably until both of you are in love and you have a commitment to work on the relationship, before you sleep together.

Regardless of what you choose with regard to emotional timing, always, always practice Responsible Sex.

Responsible Sex

Responsible Sex, a concept that is much larger than mere Safe Sex, means *conversation before sex*, in which you clarify exactly where you stand with each other emotionally and with regard to your sexual history and moral stance

Responsible Sex means valuing yourself enough to wait until you understand where you and your partner are coming from. It means having enough discipline that you don't tumble into bed every time your libido soars; that you consciously choose your behavior and communicate fully with your partner. It means, in short, that *you care more about your well-being and that of others than you do about your imme-*

diate gratification. Responsible Sex means starting with your first Mini Sex Talk and progressing to your Second Sex Talk, before you become physically intimate.

Your Second Sex Talk

At some point in a developing relationship, whether sooner or later, you realize that you are headed for sexual intimacy. Rather than waiting until the heat of the moment, initiate your Second Sex Talk. *This crucial conversation prepares you to be lovers by attending to your physical and emotional well-being.* Its importance cannot be overstated.

This talk covers

Disclosure of sexual history

Some say that the past is the past, and is none of anyone's business. This is a viewpoint that has some merit. However, when it comes to sexual history, this just doesn't hold water. As the saying goes, *the person who sleeps with you sleeps with everyone you've ever slept with.* Your partner assumes a certain amount of risk by having sex with you, whether before or after marriage.

By discussing sexual history, you both "show your hand," so to speak, giving each other the entire picture from which to make a judgment call. Your partner has a right to be told critical information that might affect his decision to be with you. This is called *making an informed choice*, an essential component of Responsible Sex. What to disclose:

Approximate number of past sexual partners. Even though this information is potentially embarrassing and off-putting, it's something your partner has a right to know.

Any high-risk behavior you've engaged in that might put your partner at risk, such as IV drug use or sleeping with a drug user.

A past partner whom you now know engaged in behavior that puts you or your partner at risk. For example, knowing that your ex-spouse was highly promiscuous while you were together.

How do you talk about sensitive material such as this? The best way is just to be straightforward and matter-of-fact. If you've done your sexual healing (or a large part of it), then it shouldn't have a huge emotional charge for you. It's just information about you and your past, and you present it as such. If emotions do come up, such as shame or embarrassment, then be honest and express them:

"It's embarrassing for me to talk about this, but I want you to know that after my divorce, my ex-husband confessed to me that he was gay and that he had sex with lots of different men while we were together. I've tested free of HIV for the past three years, but I feel that I should still disclose that."

"I feel sad having to tell you this, but I went through a wild period after my marriage broke up. I slept with a lot of different men, and I didn't always use protection. It's been several years since then, and I'm free of disease."

Next, your talk covers

Sexually transmitted diseases (STDs), past or present

Herpes sufferers have to go through this talk every time they begin a new relationship, and can testify to the discomfort that goes with it. Again, just be straightforward and to the point. It also doesn't hurt to offer reassurance with this:

"I've had herpes for fifteen years. I take an antiviral drug every day, and I've never given it to a partner as far as I know. I'm very cautious and use every protection to make it as safe as possible for whomever I'm intimate with."

Protection that you will use against the spread of STDs

Until you have evidence that your partner has been tested negative for HIV since his last sexual partner, use protection. This is your responsibility to yourself, and something that you should never just trust the other person to be credible about, unless you know him very well and are certain of his integrity.

Bill, having the Sex Talk with Angie, discovered that she didn't want to use protection against STDs. He abruptly called their evening to a halt, unwilling to assume the risk to his health, no matter how much he desired to be with an attractive woman.

Testing for HIV

In today's world, it just doesn't make sense to take any risk with a disease that is life-threatening, indeed almost a death sentence. Responsible Sex means practicing Safe Sex, and that means making sure that both you and your partner are tested for HIV prior to being sexual. Never assume that because someone is nice and well groomed that they aren't risky! AIDS is no discriminator and can strike virtually anyone.

This is too important an issue to gloss over or to compromise. *Be willing to end the relationship if your partner won't get tested!*

Birth Control

Women: *You are always responsible* for making sure that you don't get pregnant! Men: *You are always responsible* for making sure that you don't cause a pregnancy!

A very wise doctor once told me that if a man and woman are absolutely sure that they don't want to make a baby, then they don't. However, if even one of them is ambivalent, then a pregnancy is likely to happen.

I would add that being uninformed about birth control can cause pregnancy, even if both sincerely don't want that to happen. Lots of babies are created because of inaccuracies and misconceptions about conception. It is always your responsibility to be fully informed about this before having sex with someone.

Talk about what form of birth control you wish to use, then make sure it happens. Men: Even if she seems like a responsible person, ask her if she ever misses taking a pill. If she says yes, use an additional form of birth control, unless you're willing to take the risk of which you've now been informed.

Exclusivity

If you're becoming sexual with someone, sexual exclusivity is the very least you should ask for in the way of commitment. Most people also want emotional exclusivity, and there is a difference.

Sexual exclusivity means that you don't have physical romantic contact outside your relationship. You don't touch, kiss, hold, or have sexual relations of any kind with anyone else.

158 • *Date Lines*

Emotional exclusivity means that, in addition to no sexual behavior, you also do not nurture any other kind of romantic or erotic relationship, even if it's only verbal. You don't go out with anyone else, you don't encourage someone else's romantic feelings for you, you don't have sexually charged conversations, and you don't express to another person feelings that you deliberately withhold from your partner. The typical example of this is what's known today as an "emotional affair." There's no sex with the other person, but it's clear that you've gone outside the boundaries of your primary relationship.

How do you talk about this? Be straight, and ask for what you want. Make it clear that this is your minimum standard, below which you will not go:

"I would not be comfortable going forward sexually with you until we are both ready to be exclusive, both sexually and emotionally. That means that we're not dating anyone else, and that we have no interest in doing so."

"Having sex with you is a big step for me. It means that I'm ready to focus only on this relationship and give up the option of others, for as long as we're together. I want us to be sure that we're both ready to be physically and emotionally exclusive before we do this."

What this means to each of us, and to our relationship

Having sex changes your relationship, whether you believe it will or not. It is a more intense level of intimacy. Becoming sexual also brings up expectations that may not have existed before and that should be discussed, such as:

- Now that we're lovers, I want you to call me every day.
- This is a step toward commitment and maybe even marriage.
- I think of myself as your boyfriend/girlfriend, now that we're sleeping together.
- I want us to be sexually and emotionally exclusive.
- I expect to see you more often.
- I want a higher level of commitment if we're going to be lovers.

Talk about what this step means to both of you. There may be hidden expectations, many of which you won't be aware of at this time, but do your best to flush as many of them out in the open as soon as possible.

Sex Talk: Not Just for Anyone!

This level of communication isn't just for any old relationship. Obviously, talking about sex, thoroughly and completely, isn't something you are likely to do with someone you don't know very well! If you have a habit of getting sexual too quickly in a relationship, one way to end that behavior is to make a commitment to yourself to have this kind of talk about sex before you act on your feelings of attraction. Right away, you'll be motivated to put off sex until there's enough emotional connection to feel safe having this level of conversation.

Having full and complete Sex Talks prepares you for a loving, healthy relationship with lifetime possibilities. Even though it can't protect you from emotional pain, or even act as insurance against disease (there's always some risk, however small), it puts the odds in your favor. Most importantly, it builds the emotional muscle that you'll need for other difficult conversations, which will occur throughout your relationship no matter how long or how short your time together.

When Not to Become Sexual and How to Handle It

As you can see, this will be a rather intense talk, requiring an emotional depth for which either you or your partner may not be ready. It isn't wise to proceed with sex if you find that you cannot get through this talk. You may be setting yourself up for heartbreak at the very least.

Stop and reconsider before going forward if your partner

- Balks at disclosing his sexual history
- Refuses to discuss exclusivity
- Wants only a no-strings relationship
- Attempts to seduce you rather than continue the talk
- Gets defensive or angry during the talk

- Makes judgmental comments about what you've disclosed
- Attempts to persuade you to trust her, rather than taking precautions
- Doesn't want the level of commitment that you want, or seems hesitant to give it
- Does anything with which you feel uncomfortable and you find that you can't resolve with him before having sex

Stop and reconsider before going forward if you

- Know that this is a nowhere relationship, i.e., your values are not in sync, etc.
- Know that you would never marry the person
- Don't want the level of commitment your partner is requesting at this time
- Can't imagine spending the night after having sex
- Don't feel emotionally close
- Aren't sure that you trust this person
- Have strong feelings that this isn't the right thing to do, for whatever reason

If you decide not to go forward, tell your partner what you've decided. If you feel that there's enough rapport, tell him why, but don't do so if there's not a lot of connection and empathy. Giving explanations opens the door for arguments and attempts at persuasion when boundaries are poor:

"I'm just not comfortable with the way this is going, Sue. Maybe we should table this discussion for now and each take our time thinking it over before we take this step. Why don't we talk later in the week, say over dinner Thursday night?"

"I don't like what's happening in this discussion, Leon. I think it's best if we just break this off now, because this relationship isn't going to work for me."

"Since you're not comfortable using protection, and I'm not comfortable doing without it, I think it's best that we not go forward with this right now."

"It doesn't sound like you're ready for the level of commitment that I want before sleeping with you. I'd like to continue dating and put off the sex for now."

"I need more time for my feelings to develop in this relationship before we sleep together. You want more commitment than I'm prepared to give, so maybe we can just not do this now. I do want to continue seeing you, if that's what you want."

Conversations about sex that are abrupt, incomplete, or rushed do not work. This often happens when you wait until the moment of passion to talk. Stopping in the middle of making out and attempting an in-depth Sex Talk is almost impossible. Being so intent on getting to the bedroom that you'll say almost anything just to get through the conversation also doesn't work. Withholding vital information from your partner is damaging to him and to the relationship. Practice Responsible Sex:

• Anticipate the direction of the relationship, so that you can see you are headed for sexual intimacy.

• Talk about this with your partner so that you can both assess whether or not you want to go in that direction.

• On the telephone, or over dinner, bring up your Sex Talk by establishing a context for the conversation: "I want you to know, Angie, that since we've been dating I've been developing a lot of special feelings for you, and it feels like you have for me, too. I can see us becoming lovers sometime soon, and I would like to discuss some things about that. I want both of us to feel safe taking that step, both from a health standpoint and from an emotional one. It's important to me to get everything out in the open, so that we understand each other. This is a significant step for me, and I hope it is for you as well."

Establishing a context lets your partner know that you care about the relationship and that this is a decision that you don't take lightly. It also gives you credibility as a responsible person while setting the stage for a loving and healthy sexual connection.

Contrary to popular belief, these conversations do not take away from the passion and intimacy. With your worries about disease and pregnancy aside, and with an emotional foundation (exclusivity, commitment) in place, there is actually a great deal more freedom to be loving and expressive. Most important, a couple who manages this level of conversation prior to sex creates a bond between them that puts them miles ahead of most couples at this point in a relationship. A significant amount of emotional muscle-building has taken place, which prepares you for even more difficult conversations in other areas of your romance.

Advanced Sex Talks

In every relationship there are differences between partners about sex. One wants more frequency than the other (and not always is this the man!), one has more experience than the other, each has wants and desires that don't necessarily correspond to the other person's preferences. Your ability to discuss these sensitive issues will enable you to find lasting satisfaction with one partner. Some general guidelines for these advanced Sex Talks are

• Talk about sex at the dinner table or sitting in your living room, but rarely in the bedroom, unless you keep it to positive affirmation. If your talk goes offtrack, if there are hurt feelings or anger, you don't want that connected emotionally to your bedroom. When you're in bed together, try to keep your interactions positive and loving at all times.

• Use lots and lots of positive affirmation. Tell your partner what you *like* about his behavior, first and foremost. Do this both in bed and at other times.

• Never discuss what you don't like in a critical, angry, or blaming tone. Remember that most of us are extremely sensitive about our sexuality. Even the slightest bit of criticism can trigger massive feelings of sexual rejection, which will inhibit the flow of intimacy between you.

• Keep 90 percent of your conversations focused on reinforcing what your partner does well and how much you love her.

• Rarely, and only when it's vitally important, inform your lover of something you'd like to be different, whether it's stopping something you don't like or whether it's adding something you'd like. Keep this conversation short and light. Don't dwell on it, just make it matter-of-fact, and then move on to other things. Your lover will appreciate you for not making this a difficult conversation by hammering away.

• Bring conversation and eye contact into your lovemaking. This adds a special dimension of intimacy to your romantic connection that's very fulfilling. Instead of just bodies in heat, you're connecting mentally and emotionally as well.

Conversations for Sexual Healing

When couples begin their Sex Talks early in a relationship, it opens the door for a much deeper level of connection and intimacy. Over time, these conversations contribute to the development of feelings of love, trust, and psychological safety. With that kind of connection, a wonderful opportunity opens up for sexual healing.

Almost everyone has some work to do in this area. We've all been hurt, either through love relationships that haven't worked, or through painful adolescent experiences around our sexuality. Many of us have been deeply wounded, whether through shame and embarrassment as children, or by being victimized then or later. At the very least, we are all wounded by the culture we live in which says, simultaneously, *sex is bad*, and *here, go indulge in this pornography*.

Conversations about past sexual experiences can be very powerful, when allowed to unfold naturally over time. Safe in a caring and committed lover's arms, we can share what has hurt us, and by so doing, we begin to heal. Gradually, we leave behind the pain of the past. What emerges is a new, more vibrant sexuality. We are unchained from the burden of what has gone before, and we are able to be much more fully expressed as the sexual beings that we are.

Sexual healing like this can only occur in conversations that are emotionally safe between two people who love each other and have a commitment. Some things to remember when you're sharing your past sexual experiences:

Focus on feelings, rather than on explicit details. It isn't necessary to describe your sexual acts in the past, only to mention them and then to talk about the effects on you.

Never ask intrusive questions. Let your lover be the judge of when, how much, and what to share.

Listen nonjudgmentally. If you don't think you can, alert your partner that you're having difficulty with the conversation, rather than letting him continue with your listening shut down.

Don't try to "fix" anything. Offer reassurance in a loving way, and trust that she will be okay. If you think there's been a tremendous amount of damage to your partner, encourage him to get some therapy. Offer to go with your partner, if it helps.

Sex Talks That Worked

• Stacie decided that she wanted to have a one-night stand with Will, one of the guys in her singles group that she'd known for several months. She asked him to dinner, and informed him of what she had in mind when they got back to his place. He wanted to kiss and make love, skipping the Sex Talk, so she got up to go, telling him, "I'm sorry, but this just won't work." Realizing that she meant it, Will sat back down and completed the conversation. They went on to have a rather passionate two-week connection, which they conducted and ended with respect and dignity.

• Doug initiated a Sex Talk with Wendy after dating for a couple of months, at which time she disclosed that she was still a virgin. Although she expressed the desire to sleep with Doug, he decided not to go forward. Their Sex Talk revealed that he was not intending a long-term relationship while her feelings for him were much stronger, thus creating a risk of emotional damage that he was not willing to take.

• Anna and Steve had their first Mini Sex Talk on their second date, wherein she expressed the desire to date for several months before having sex. When their relationship progressed to the point of both being emotionally ready, they had more than one conversation about sex, disclosing past history and discussing where their relationship was headed, as well as STDs, protection, and the HIV test. When they did become lovers, it was with their hearts fully connected and the security of knowing that there would be no health risk. They are very much in love and planning a future together.

9

You and Me and Money

♥　♥　♥

Richard and Stefanie are on their fifth date, sharing a wonderful dinner. They talk, smile, and laugh at each other's jokes. Her eyes shine as she watches him, thinking, "This could really be a great relationship." He gazes at her, thinking, "She's so beautiful. I hope she can be my girlfriend." Everything's great, almost perfect, until the check arrives.

The waiter puts the check on the table, smack dab in the middle, no closer to one than the other. Neither makes any moves to pick it up. They continue to talk, both studiously avoiding any acknowledgment of this item. Ten minutes later, the check has become an albatross around their necks.

He thinks, "I've paid for everything we've done in this relationship so far. Some rather expensive entertainment, in fact. I think it's time for a little reciprocity. Surely she knows it's her turn to pay."

She thinks, "Why isn't he picking up the check? He's never made an issue about this before, and all my friends say I should never offer to pay. Besides, some guys get offended by that. What should I do? I guess I'll wait and see. Maybe he just didn't notice it yet."

Finally, Richard picks up the check and pays, but the emotional energy has shifted. The warmth and delight that was present earlier has all but disappeared. He feels silently resentful. Stefanie is bewildered. Without a conversation about money soon, this couple is headed for a huge case of clashing expectations, if they even manage to stay together.

Money Talks

Next on the "hot topics" list is money, something most of us would really rather not talk about. In fact, in romance and dating, it's considered almost as taboo a conversational topic as sex. *Yet money impacts the very nature of our connection with a potential partner.* Talking about it sets the stage for great workability, while avoiding it can set a time bomb ticking that one day explodes. Considering its importance, why do we avoid this pivotal topic?

Many of us are simply not comfortable with money and the power it holds. Most of us came from families that did not talk about money. Dad worked and Mom paid the bills, or they fought about it, or both worked and no one talked. Maybe there wasn't enough to go around. Where it all came from (or didn't) was quite mysterious, as no one was saying much about it. We got allowances, or we didn't. We earned money for chores, or we were just given whatever we asked for.

Money is associated with power. Those who have the most money are generally considered to be the most powerful and successful members of society, and this has been so for thousands of years. Maybe Dad exerted power over Mom by withholding money. Perhaps she fought back by overspending, or by getting a job.

Most of us got our first exposure to the connection between money and living in today's world when we went to college. Someone had to pay for our living expenses. Either we got an allowance, or we got a job. But either way, the bills came to us, not to our parents. We had to decide how much to spend and how much to save, usually without anyone to talk to about it. Throughout childhood, adolescence, and young adulthood, one consistent thread was woven: *Talking about money is taboo.* As a result, we learned to associate secrecy and fear with this vital part of life.

All of this lack of communication about money is our legacy today. It's a topic considered highly private, both socially and within business organizations. In fact, many companies fire on the spot anyone who dares to discuss his/her salary with another employee. The last thing you would do at a dinner party is share your income and ask others to disclose theirs!

In a dating relationship, money is one of those highly sticky subjects. How you handle it in the beginning sets the stage for either your dysfunction or your well-being with regard to this topic later. The discomfort and secrecy about this topic makes it very challenging to bring it up and to discuss it, yet not to do so raises the potential for power struggles and unhappiness in a long-term relationship. In fact, a great number of divorces and unhappy marriages are the result of conflicting needs, and the inability of couples to talk, about money.

• Barry and his wife Jill had so much difficulty talking about money that they became more and more estranged, as she ran up his credit cards and he became increasingly resentful. Finally, in desperation, Barry canceled the credit cards and opened a new bank account, thus making the preemptive strike that would lead to a bitter divorce.

• Lisa and Clark agreed that they both would pursue careers until the children came, at which point she would stay home and be a mom. A year into the marriage, she quit her job and did not seek another one, even though his income was by no means large and it was eight more years before their son was born. By that time, they were so out of sync that Lisa and Clark soon divorced. He was resentful of having been the sole provider and she was resentful of having given up her career for a marriage that didn't last.

Having the courage to talk about money while dating, and then discussing it repeatedly and regularly throughout a relationship, minimizes the risk of these kinds of scenarios. Not only do you increase your connection with your partner through these difficult conversations, but you also build emotional muscle and assure yourselves that you are still sharing the same goals and concerns when it comes to your shared funds. Each time you bring up a difficult topic like this you diminish the fear that surrounds it, demystifying it and making it more accessible.

So, where do you begin? Begin by *understanding your own attitudes, wants, desires, and needs about money*. Know, or invest yourself in discovering, where you stand with regard to

- Who pays for the date, now and in the future
- Who pays for what after moving in together/marrying
- Financial integrity (paying bills, debt or not, filing taxes, savings, investments, and retirement plans), yours and his
- What you expect financially from a partner

I've found, through personal experience and from my clients' stories over many years, that, *generally, what you're entitled to expect from a partner financially, provided you have it yourself, is*

1. *Financial stability.* She has an income that adequately supports her plus any children she might already have, in the lifestyle they enjoy.

2. *Financial integrity.* He pays his bills, maintains good credit standing, files his taxes, keeps a savings account, and has a retirement plan.

Anything below this standard, and you'll find yourself in the position of rescuing someone and creating a dependency. Anything above this standard is icing on the cake, and has very little to do with what makes a good relationship. You're not entitled to wealth from a partner. If you want financial prosperity, create it for yourself. If you want a prosperous partner, *be a prosperous person.* Don't focus on getting a partner who will be completely financially responsible for you. This approach to romance almost always leaves people very unhappy. Look for a partner with whom you can connect intellectually, emotionally, sexually, and spiritually, and the rest will follow, if it's meant to be.

Men, Women, and Money: Who Pays?

Generally, the first couple of dates take care of themselves with regard to money, but the rule of thumb in the beginning is

Whoever asks for the date pays for the date!

Men have traditionally been the initiators of dates, and this remains largely true today. Most men just assume that they will pay, at least for the first couple of dates. Women are beginning to take over some of this role, but it's a little trickier for them to discern what to do and how. Let's look at paying for dates from both sides of the fence.

MEN

If you take the traditional approach, assuming that it's your responsibility to pay for everything, and you feel okay with that, then just continue your usual system. Realize, though, that by paying for everything you are communicating something: that you're the responsible party with regard to money. It's your job to pay now, and to pay later, for all the entertainment, and even, yes, the living expenses. You are creating a relationship wherein you are likely to be the sole or primary breadwinner.

If that's not what you want, you may want to rethink your approach to dating and money. If you want an equal partner, a self-sufficient woman who takes care of herself, then you will communicate that early in the relationship by the way you handle the payment for dates. This leads you to your first Money Talk.

Once you realize that there's relationship potential with a woman, let her know where you stand with regard to who pays:

"I really enjoy taking you out, Sarah. I like finding good restaurants and seeing how much you enjoy the food and atmosphere. I also like feeling that there's reciprocation, you know, that the person I'm dating really wants to be with me. I'm interested in being with a woman who takes care of herself and is willing to share some of the entertainment expenses, or to reciprocate by cooking dinner and buying show tickets. I guess I'm saying that I want an equal partner, and I'm wondering how you feel about that."

"Gina, I want you to know that I'm a thoroughly modern kind of guy. I like to be asked out and treated to a nice evening just as much as I like doing that for a woman. It makes me feel like I'm with someone who really wants me, not just a meal ticket. What are your thoughts on that?"

The idea is to stimulate conversation, get a dialogue going on the subject of money. You may find yourselves sharing your experience with money in past relationships/marriages and how you handled it with former partners. This can be a very revealing discussion, helping you both understand where you're coming from and what your potential is as a couple.

What if she reacts negatively? Many women feel that they're entitled to have a man pay for every date, and unfortunately, that attitude has been reinforced recently with dating books that emphasize manipulating men into constant pursuit. Here are some of your options:

Ask her to talk about why she feels that way, but don't judge her too harshly for her attitude. Women have been given so many confusing messages, and many of us are still trying to sort out where we stand. Focus on understanding her and helping her understand you, rather than getting defensive or just writing her off.

Tell her how it feels to you to be expected to do it all. Many women aren't aware of how men are affected by the belief that they should always pay. Don't whine about the injustice of it, but let her know that it's important for you to know that being with you is important to her also, even if that means she shares some of the financial responsibility.

WOMEN

We've been given almost as many mixed messages about money as we have been about sex! Our training, both positive and negative, was most likely incomplete in this area. Maybe Mom worked only in the home, maybe she had a job outside of the family. Maybe she even pursued a career. Whatever the case, chances are you didn't discuss her role in regard to finances much, leaving more questions than answers for you to figure out on your own. Many of us, therefore, are left grappling with the question: Should we rely only on ourselves, or should we look for a man to take care of us?

While there are no right and wrong answers, here are some things to consider as you sort out your own feelings on this issue:

Having an education and a career empowers a woman to feel that she has choices. There's probably nothing more devastating to a woman than to be trapped in an abusive marriage because she lacks the financial means or resources to leave. It is an unfortunate reality in today's world that a woman must have the ability to care for herself and her children's physical, emotional, and financial well-being should she one day be left alone with the task.

The issue of who works in the home and who works outside it is a negotiation in the relationship that takes place once there's sufficient commitment. Many women make the mistake of looking first for finances, secondly for a relationship connection. This makes men feel like they are simply a means to an end, her agenda of getting married and having children.

In a healthy relationship, it's assumed that you will both take care of yourselves. Once you are planning to marry and have a family, that's the time to renegotiate the financial responsibilities. Because you have demonstrated your self-sufficiency, you're both coming from an equally strong position, rather than from a position of dependency or entitlement.

Because money is so strongly associated with power, most women find that letting a man pay puts them, however unconsciously, in a weaker position. He makes the money, so he decides how to spend it. In dating, if he pays for everything, there's likely to be the unconscious feeling on her part that she owes him something, and, on his part, a sense that he's entitled to her love and loyalty.

When you're dating, you're looking primarily for a *right connection*, given that you uphold your basic standards as we've talked about, and given that you don't compromise your Nonnegotiables. Beyond that, the relationship is an exploration, one upon which you both embark, and one in which you are both equally at risk emotionally. It may lead to the love of your life, or it may lead to a dead end.

Expecting a man to foot all the entertainment bills from the beginning creates an assumption that one of you is exploring while the other is already sure. Hopefully, you are dating this man to discover whether or not there is lifetime potential, and you haven't already targeted him for "the commitment." Also, it is hoped, you are not expecting him to court you endlessly, as if you are someone to be "won over."

There is great power in adopting a stance of "wait and see" when it comes to commitment to a dating partner. You may find that it works better to wait until you've gotten to know each other really well before you move to that level. If you want an equal partnership, then you act like an equal, financially as well as in other ways. Thus, you are striking a balance of energy, with both of you making deposits to the emotional bank account. This means that you contribute your own part, whether it be in the form of pay for entertainment, or whether it be in the form of cooking dinner and renting videos to watch in your living room. That way the money issue does not hint at a premature commitment on the part of one person who is solely funding the relationship's development.

You know you're on track if you're able to discuss it with your partner. Although I've heard women say, "I expect the man to pay when we go out," I've found that they are usually not willing to tell him this philosophy. This creates a hidden agenda that will inevitably lead to resentment on his part when he does figure out where she stands.

Jane's belief was that the man should pay for all of the dates, no matter how long they dated, a belief that she did not share openly with Dan. After about six months of paying for everything, Dan finally voiced his resentment over money that had been building for some time and asked her to share some of the expenses. They ended up having their first Money Talk and once their true attitudes emerged, they found that they were fundamentally incompatible about this crucial area of life, and the relationship ended.

If you believe that men should pay for all of the entertainment expenses, say so:

"I'm an old-fashioned girl, Dan. I was raised to believe that men should pay for dates, so that's the way I approach it."

There are some men who will agree with this philosophy and you'll be fine together. If you find that you cannot bring yourself to say this straight out to a man, or if you don't want to rule out all the great men who believe in a more egalitarian relationship, then consider revising your philosophy about men and money.

If you are clear that you are looking for an equal partner, and that you wish to be an equal partner, communicate this up front:

"Thank you, Doug, for paying for our first three dates. I really appreciate your generosity. I would also like to be able to treat you once in a while. Maybe you could leave the check on the table and give me a chance to pay every now and then."

Women can also communicate their desire for an equal partnership through their actions. When the check arrives, pick it up and pay. Do this often enough, and he'll get the message.

If your attitude is that it's fine to share the dating expenses, but you're looking for someone to support you after marriage, communicate that! One sure formula for divorce is to have one standard of behavior during courtship and an entirely different one after marriage, without getting that out in the open and agreed upon by both parties early on in the relationship.

Some men refuse to let women pay, insisting on paying for the date regardless of her wishes. If you want an egalitarian relationship, this is a huge red flag that you're probably not going to get that with this person. One woman I know attempted to negotiate "Dutch treat" for the first date while on the telephone, only to have the guy strongly insist that he would pay. Even when she expressed a desire to pay for her half, that it was her policy to do so on first dates, he still refused. Finally, she told him, "Thank you for asking me out, but this just isn't going to work," realizing that if it was this difficult negotiating with him on the first date, things would only be worse later.

Hidden Expectations

Because talking about money is so difficult, it's easy to fall into a pattern of not talking while developing expectations that can eventually clash if they are not shared with your partner.

Often men will
- Pay for dates over and over, even though resenting that she's not at least occasionally asking or attempting to pay her share
- Let the check sit on the table for a long time, hoping that she'll get the hint and pick it up
- Pay for the dates because he thinks he's supposed to, but not feel good about carrying the entire financial burden of dating
- Give a woman several opportunities to pay, and when she doesn't, write her off as a dependent, clinging vine

Often women will
- Allow the man to pay over and over, fearing that he will be offended if she offers to pay

- Allow the man to pay because she's been told that it's a good dating strategy
- Let the check sit too long on the table because she doesn't realize that he would like her to pay, but is going to pick it up if she doesn't do so rather quickly
- Pay her share but secretly hope that someday when he's in love with her, she won't have to anymore
- Allow a man to pay, and judge him as cheap if he isn't willing to do so at all times

These hidden expectations can destroy a budding relationship, as both men and women build up resentment over time. Later, this can lead to an intense power struggle, as each one tries to blame the other for the misunderstanding that has grown up in silence over time. Hidden expectations can also allow a relationship between two mismatched people to drag on for far too long, as both live in silent hope that the other's attitude will change.

To avoid this trap, make it your policy to be familiar with and to bring all of your attitudes about money out in the open as soon as possible. Once you've done so, you're in a position to negotiate a crucial part of your relationship powerfully, allowing you to avert one of the most common sources of conflict between partners.

When to Talk About Money

Your first conversation about money should occur very early, usually around the fourth or fifth date, once you have a sense that there's good relationship potential with your dating partner. This conversation can be very brief, but honest and to the point. Basically what you are covering is

- Who pays for the dates
- Your general expectations about entertainment expenses

Maybe you feel that you and your partner share similar views about money, so you don't see the point of having this discussion. While that may be true, you also may be making an incorrect assumption. Often one or the other of you is feeling uncomfortable about the way money is being handled, but is afraid to bring up the subject. You might get into the conversation in a nonthreatening way by introducing it over dinner, at a time that feels comfortable. Begin with a statement of how you feel about the relationship, and a little bit about how important it is to you to be able to discuss difficult topics:

"We seem to get along so well and it's just so easy to be with you. I feel comfortable talking with you about almost any subject so far, and that's important to me."

From there, move into the conversation about money:

"Talking about money is kind of a difficult thing to do, but something that I'd like to get out in the open. So far, I like the way we're handling the issue of who pays for our dates. It seems to work well for you to pay most of the time, and I enjoy picking up the bill occasionally. But I'm wondering if you're comfortable with it, and I would welcome your thoughts and feelings."

At this point, your dialogue will most likely be well underway. Now is your opportunity to get some of your general attitudes about money across to your date. At this point, you will probably not take the conversation to much depth, but you will hopefully clear the air about who pays, for now. Also, you will have set the stage for comfortable talks about the subject later.

Understanding about Money

In this and many, many future money conversations, you are seeking an understanding of each other's ideas about this area of life. Like it or not, money is an integral part of functioning in our world, and our ability to converse about it is vital to a healthy relationship. In a way, you are beginning an ongoing negotiation with regard to money. Unless you are both lottery winners, or each possessors of vast independent wealth, you live in the real world wherein there is Your Money, My Money, and Our Money, and none of the categories are unlimited financially. As your relationship progresses, you must uncover which money goes into which of these categories, as well as how you will spend your money, what you will save, and how you will financially plan for your future together.

If you begin talking about money early in your relationship, you have a distinct advantage. You create a history of comfort between you when it comes to discussing a difficult topic, and you alleviate many of your fears: that you might be dating someone who is more interested in your money than in you; that you might be dating a deadbeat; that you might be getting involved with someone whose values about money are miles apart from yours.

I've had clients express to me that they wish they could simply demand a complete financial statement on the first date! While this seems like a good idea, in fact it is not. Even if someone looks good on paper financially, that doesn't mean that he shares your values. One client of mine dated her ex-husband for about six months and married him in a whirlwind of trips, cars, diamonds, and a dream home. She gave up her own very lucrative business, thinking she had it made. Ten years later, when his company began to go under, she discovered that he was, in fact, very dishonest about financial matters. She wound up with a massive IRS debt and barely enough child support to keep her children fed.

Don't let your assumptions get you into a similar position. You can never have a completely risk-free relationship in this regard, of course, but talking about finances early on will increase your chances of understanding what your date's ideas on money are and how they mesh with yours.

Far more important than someone's current financial status are her values with regard to the handling of money. More crucial than net worth is his integrity. These are things that cannot be found on a financial statement, but that can be found through the art of conversation, in the many, many honest, heart-to-heart dialogues about where you come from and how you handle this and other related areas of life.

These conversations are best approached, not through intrusive questioning (i.e., "How much do you earn? When did you last file your taxes?"), but through sharing your stories. It's much easier to miss how incompatible you are with someone through short answers to quick questions than it is through shared stories. Rapid question and answer doesn't reveal much other than the bare-bones facts, many of which may be false or misleading when given alone with no context. Sharing your story, however, begs for reciprocity. When your values are in sync with your date's, this naturally happens, and when they aren't, you'll get a blank stare or stonewalling, either of which are clear warning signals that you have some differing opinions to address.

So, *share and listen*, and do it regularly. Pay attention to how much your partner is opening up to you in return.

Talk about how your parents handled money. Share about your family-of-origin, beginning with broad brush strokes and going to deeper levels with time. This encourages the other person to disclose the clues to the origins of some of his own attitudes. Doing this you will each discover how you became the person you are today, and reveal where you are headed in your own personal growth.

Talk about how you handled money in a previous relationship or marriage. Focusing on what you learned from the past, you can reveal much to each other during these conversations. Share not only how you negotiated the issue of who pays, but how you felt about you and your past partner's financial connection. Are you seeking the same thing again, or something different?

Talk about past mistakes and what you learned from them. As you develop trust in the relationship, take the risk of sharing some of your darker moments with regard to money. We all have them, and, like our sex secrets, our hidden money stories have the power to taint a budding relationship if we withhold them.

Talk about hopes and dreams, and the value of money to you. Whether you dream of retiring in luxury, or whether you would just as soon go live in a cabin in the woods and forgo the need for money, share these personal views you have with your partner. Talking about future dreams with regard to money is where the rubber meets the road, so to speak. If you are tremendously far apart in your vision, you may be fundamentally incompatible, so you might want to discover that as soon as possible.

Negotiating the Money Balance

Like everything else in a relationship, there's a negotiation about money that begins with the first few dates and probably never ends as long as the relationship itself continues. A lot of the fighting that goes on during divorce is about money, and you can see in these heated conversations a reflection of how the couple interacted over money from the beginning of the relationship. Clearly, how you handle these negotiations can make or break your connection, as well as set the tone for your financial and emotional well-being.

In the beginning, there's Your Money and there's My Money, and the question is, Whose Money pays for our dates? This first negotiation may go quickly and smoothly. He pays, she pays, and both are comfortable with the arrangement. Or, he pays, and both like it the old-fashioned way.

Sometimes this negotiation is not always so smooth, due to factors that change the picture and clash with the values either one or both of you have. Maybe one of you is still a student with almost no income. Perhaps you've lost your job and not found a new one. Especially if the man in the relationship is in this situation, it presents a dating dilemma: How do I ask you out when I have very little in the way of financial resources? Imbalances in the money equation call for some creative money conversations. Some things to consider:

- One of you may make significantly more money than the other
- One or both of you may be currently very short of entertainment funds
- These conditions may be ongoing or they may be temporary

Talking about money gets these issues and how you feel about them out in the open so that you can choose the best course of action. Be honest about your thoughts, and don't pull any punches. Just say it straight out, and, though it may be difficult, your honesty will definitely benefit you both in the long run:

"The truth is that I'm still paying off my student loans for the next couple of years, and I don't have a huge entertainment budget."

Offer solutions along with your very honest disclosure:

"I would be happy to cook for you and rent videos to watch in order to cut our overall dating expenses. I also enjoy long walks in the park and maybe taking a picnic lunch along."

If one of you makes significantly more than the other, you may decide that you will balance who pays accordingly. Whatever you decide, the agreement is workable only if both agree that it is mutually satisfying.

What you decide today may not always apply. Later, you may find yourselves renegotiating who pays, depending on changing circumstances.

• Louis enjoyed the traditional role of breadwinner, paying for all the entertainment expenses for Lorry and him. Then, a job change caused a downshift in income for him, and they renegotiated. Even though both preferred it the old way, necessity dictated that she help out with the entertainment budget until he could get back on his feet financially.

• Naomi made a career change, starting her own business, after dating Jeremy for a year. Their renegotiation money conversation went something like this:

SHE: It's embarrassing to no longer have the financial means to share all of our entertainment expenses. We go out a lot, and I don't want to stop doing that, but I just can't afford right now to split everything fifty-fifty the way we have. I also realize that it's important for you to be with someone who is self-sufficient, and I can see how this might make you uncomfortable.

HE: Thanks for realizing that.

SHE: What I would like is for you to consider my contribution valid if I pay some of the time, and other times cook for us. Also, we can take my car a lot of the time, so that's another contribution.

HE: That sounds very reasonable to me.

SHE: When the check comes to the table, please just assume that if I'm able to, I'll pay. If I leave it there, I'm not, and I'd appreciate it if you didn't make an issue out of it by asking if I'm going to pay.

HE: That's fine with me. I know you're trying to build something very worthwhile with your business, and I admire you for taking that risk. I realize what's important is that you're going for it, and I support you in doing that.

SHE: Thank you, sweetheart. That means a lot to me.

HE: Of course. I love you.

SHE: I love you, too.

• When Marvin came out of his first marriage, he carried the emotional battle scars of someone who had not been successful negotiating money. He resolved that he would find an independent, self-sufficient woman to be with after that experience. He eventually met Karen, who was very successful in her career. From the very beginning, they split everything right down the middle. "Our friends used to look at us like we were crazy, coming up with our equal share of the tab down to the penny"—Karen laughed—"but it worked for us." They travel frequently and own a beautiful home in an expensive neighborhood. They thoroughly enjoy their lifestyle, earned by both of them equally. Now, though, they are considering a renegotiation. Karen is thinking of leaving her career and either retiring or taking time off before pursuing something else, a move which will call for changes in the way they handle money, and possibly a downgrade of their lifestyle. Having spent ten years with a system that worked wonderfully for both, and having practiced many Money Talks, they are both confident that this transition will not be difficult. They have built a great deal of trust between them by dealing with this touchy subject head-on from the beginning of their relationship.

• Ted and Carolyn made it their policy from the beginning to throw all the receipts into the fishbowl, then tally it up and split the total at the end of each month. Even though his income and assets were considerably higher, both considered it very important that she pull her own weight financially. Nine years later, they decided to move across the country to a city where the housing costs were considerably higher. They renegotiated their arrangement for the purpose of buying a new home, with Ted supplying almost all of the down payment, as well as the costs for home improvements. Their commitment had moved to a high enough level, and the trust between them was great enough, so that this worked for them both.

Negotiating money early lays the groundwork for all your future financial talks, from who pays for the date to who makes the mortgage payment. It can also give you clear indications about what to expect in the future. What you encounter today you will find tomorrow, except then it will be on a much larger scale. *Stop and reconsider the relationship if your partner*

Refuses to discuss money. This is a danger signal that you want to discover as early as possible. One man I know didn't bother to discuss money with his girlfriend until after they were married. She absolutely would not engage in the talks with him, and they finally wound up in divorce court, fighting over—you guessed it—money.

Refuses to negotiate. This is the equivalent of "my way or the highway," a very dangerous position for a relationship. This leads to unilateral decision-making, meaning that each person acts independently of the other, regardless of the effect on the other person.

Is secretive, evasive, or defensive when the subject comes up. This is also a clear warning signal, telling you that this person may be hiding something vital that will affect you later. One couple had only one Money Talk prior to marriage. His overall secrecy led to an explosive conversation after they'd been married two years in which he confessed that he'd lied about his true financial picture.

Money Talks, when initiated at the beginning of the dating curve, help form a trusting connection and a partnership in a relationship. The point isn't *what* you decide so much as it is that you *talk about it* and that you *decide together*, finding a point of mutual fulfillment. Use these talks, first of all, to understand one another and your individual values about this fundamental part of life. Secondly, aim for a respectful negotiation that takes into account each person's circumstances and needs. Try to find an agreement that works for both, but don't try to force that to happen. If your values aren't in sync, be willing to let the relationship go before you get too involved.

Assessment and Connection: Finding a Balance

Dating is a process of discovery, about yourself, about your partner(s), and about the possibilities of a lasting relationship. When you meet someone special and begin going out, there are many questions to be answered, some of which are:

- Are we looking for the same kind of relationship?
- Do we have a connection that's meaningful and positive?
- Are our values in sync?
- Do we share basic goals in life?

and, perhaps most importantly, as one famous comedienne puts it: *Can we talk?*

Introducing sticky and scary conversational topics (i.e., religion, children, career, sex, and money) serves a very important purpose in a budding relationship. It helps you understand each other, so that you can make an informed choice about moving forward into greater levels of commitment.

Underneath the conversations themselves, there is that all-important question of whether or not we can discuss and negotiate (*Can we talk?*), without the resolution of which every other question becomes moot. Some couples simply cannot navigate the waters of communication successfully. No matter how hard they try, they always end up arguing or failing to come to a resolution on their issues. While therapy can help, it can't cure all communication problems, especially if they stem from a fundamentally incompatible viewpoint.

After only two weeks, Lisa realized that she could not go forward in a relationship with Edward. Every time she attempted to tell him how she felt about something, he minimized her feelings and refused to listen, telling her things like, "That's not important. You're making a mountain out of a molehill." She knew that she would never be able to negotiate from equal ground with this man, so she broke off their budding romance.

By daring to venture into deep conversational waters, you test the very fabric of your relationship. If you start to do this while you are dating, you stand to learn a lot about your partner much earlier. You may save yourself a future divorce by seeing the warning signs before you reach a formal union.

Carol and Lon were stuck on the decision of whether or not to get married. Through their conversations about money and children, they discovered a communication breaking point. Despite extensive training to the contrary, neither of them could refrain from judging and blaming the other when their needs clashed. They were unable to negotiate successfully so that both could be fulfilled, and eventually chose to move on from each other. While this decision was very painful for both of them, it was less traumatic than a divorce.

Determining compatibility is the goal, and connection through conversation is the vehicle by which that is accomplished. This means that, to some degree, you are called upon to make assessments of your new partner in the beginning of a relationship. Not to do so would be to set yourself up for heartache. However, sometimes we carry this too far.

In our zeal to protect ourselves from heartbreak, we sit in judgment of each potential partner, continually evaluating the person in front of us. Is he smart enough, caring enough, handsome and rich enough? Are her values good enough, her morals high enough, her beauty sufficient? In our heads, we are separated from our emotions, our hearts. Thus, we fail at the primary objective, *to make a connection*. For without that, we can never take the true measure of a relationship's potential.

Some carry the risk-taking to the other extreme. Anxious to be in love, craving attention and intimacy, we quickly become enraptured, falling in love at the drop of a hat. Values? It's not that important. Life goals? We'll figure that out later. Totally in our feeling states, we are unable to make a rational, logically based discernment about the feasibility of a long-term relationship with this person.

What works is to create a balance between Assessment and Connection. Though they are fundamentally different positions from which to relate, both are needed in dating. Paradoxically, one is ineffective without the other when it comes to choosing a lifetime partner.

Also, you generally need more connecting than you do assessing. So, if we had to divide it into percentages, I'd say about 80 percent is connection and about 20 percent is assessment.

I coach my clients to create this balance by practicing these things:

When you're on the date and with your partner, do your best to connect. Make eye contact, practice your conversational skills. Share and Listen Well. Open up, dare to be vulnerable, tell him a lot about yourself.

Nurture the connection while you're together and even when you're not. Call her up, say romantic things, send cards, send flowers, express your appreciation. Be genuinely openhearted and willing to love.

Focus more on what's right about your partner than you do on what's not. Refrain from critical listening and judgment. Consciously look for the good qualities of the person you're with: After all, this is someone you chose!

Endeavor to understand this person, first and foremost. Secondly, endeavor to be understood by him, for it is only through this mutual knowing of one another that you are empowered to choose each other. *Occasionally, and rarely, stand back and make an assessment.* Ask yourself how you feel about

1. Your partner's values.
2. Your partner's goals in life.
3. Your ability to communicate with your partner.
4. Your partner's emotional availability.
5. Your partner! (Am I falling in love? Does the potential for that exist?)

So, it goes something like this: *Connect, connect, connect, enjoy good feelings, love, . . .* Assess. *Connect, love, enjoy feelings, connect, connect, . . .* Assess. *Connect some more.* The assessment part should gradually diminish so that by the time you move to the next level of commitment, you're pretty much out of that mode.

Regularly delving into sticky conversations enables you to rapidly determine your compatibility quotient with a potential partner. This frees you up to focus primarily on what your romance is about: loving and being loved, making discoveries about yourself and about your partner, and nurturing a passionate and loving connection that has the potential to last a lifetime.

10

The You and Me Conversation

♥　　♥　　♥

Cheri and Zack were not having a good day. Sitting in the therapist's office, the day of reckoning had finally arrived. Painful as it was, Zack told Cheri that he just didn't have the heart to work on their relationship. Cheri was both angry and sad, wondering how things had gotten to this point. Zack felt guilty, knowing that in some respects he had failed to be entirely forthcoming about his feelings for Cheri all along. Both eventually became aware that they had failed to talk about their relationship and their feelings for each other from the beginning. Both had hoped everything would turn out okay, but this was just wishful thinking.

You and Me: Staying Silent

You've been dating for weeks, maybe even months. You enjoy each other and you think there may be potential for something lasting. You want to know where you stand with each other. So, what do you do? If you're like most dating couples, you do absolutely nothing!

Most couples take the approach of just continuing to go out and hoping for the best. Why talk about the relationship? Let's just enjoy it. After all, if we talk about it, we might mess things up! If it's not broken, let's not try to fix it, we say to ourselves.

The reasoning behind avoiding a "relationship talk" usually falls into one of the following categories:

- If I bring that up, it'll scare him away
- I'm not ready to make a commitment yet, and those kinds of talks always mean you have to either commit or break up
- The last time I brought up a "relationship talk" with someone, he broke up with me shortly after
- I don't want to "show my hand" by revealing my true feelings
- My friends say that I should avoid those kinds of talks like the plague
- A popular book on how to capture someone's heart says that I should never talk about the relationship until he brings it up
- I'm not ready to let go of this relationship, and if we talk about it I'll have to reveal my true feelings, which may cause my partner to want to leave
- Maybe it will all turn out okay if I just do nothing

The You and Me Conversation

This thing that we are so studiously avoiding is what I call the You and Me Conversation. It is one of the most important conversations to have in a developing relationship, and, in a nutshell, it covers who we are to each other and where our relationship is headed.

When we discuss You and Me seriously we begin opening our hearts to each other, *sharing our thoughts and feelings about each other and about our connection*, in a way that allows honesty and paves the way for commitment. Its true purpose, like that of all heart-to-heart communication, is to *further our understanding of each other* and of the potential of our romance.

We fear this kind of talk because

It calls for us to be emotionally vulnerable. To have a successful You and Me Conversation means that we know ourselves and how we feel, and we express that to the other person. It means being openhearted, sharing what we really think and feel about each other and about our relationship. It means taking the risk that the other person will misunderstand, laugh, ridicule our feelings, or even reject us entirely.

It calls for us to examine our feelings. Let's face it: It's much easier to just drift along, dating someone endlessly, enjoying going out, the companionship, and the sex. It's much more challenging, and far less comfortable, to stop, do some introspection, and admit to ourselves how we're feeling about this person. This involves some soul-searching, and we don't always like what we come up with, which might be:

1. Maybe I'm ambivalent, and I realize that my partner is falling in love
2. Maybe I'm falling in love, with someone whom I fear does not return those feelings

It puts the relationship itself on the table. By having a You and Me Conversation, we take the risk of realizing that we're on two entirely different pages, and therefore we may decide to break up. Maybe I'm not yet ready to give up this relationship, even if I know in my heart that it's just not right for me. Or, maybe I'm falling in love with someone whom I know deep down isn't in love with me. Having this conversation puts me at risk of suffering a loss.

It can reveal the fact that we're in a "Settle For" relationship.** Okay, maybe one or both of us knows that this is not a forever kind of deal, but, let's face it, being in this relationship is better than being alone. If we have this conversation, and we're truthful, we will undoubtedly bring this information out in the open, possibly leading to a breakup. Again, having the You and Me Conversation raises the potential for loss.

It can reveal the fact that one of us is a Westbound Train.*† Maybe I'm still getting over my divorce, and just not willing even to consider a commitment. Perhaps you just broke off a five-year relationship and really want to date around, while I'm ready to be exclusive. If we get all of this out in the open, it might be a painful awareness for one or both of us that we're just not likely to get what we want from this relationship. That might lead to a breakup, so, once again, we're taking the risk of a loss.

It prevents us from clinging to fantasy. After discovering where we stand with each other, we may continue to date, but it's painful now

---

*See *Be Your Own Dating Service: A Step-by-Step Guide to Finding and Maintaining Healthy Relationships*, Chapter Twelve, by Nina Atwood, for more about the Settle For Relationship.
†See *Be Your Own Dating Service*, Chapter Thirteen, for more about the North and Westbound trains.

because we can no longer delude ourselves that everything will just magically work out. This is adult reality, which is very powerful, but to the vulnerable little person inside of us, it just plain hurts.

With that much fear, how can we possibly hope to bring ourselves to consciously choose the You and Me Conversation? First, let's consider the alternative: *Not to have regular You and Me Conversations means drifting along in the dark, unsure of where you stand with someone in a relationship, or making erroneous assumptions that lead you to much more heartache and pain later.*

Yes, having these talks now is uncomfortable, and can even be quite painful, but that is a legitimate pain. We hope for much and do not always get what we want, especially in romantic relationships. The truth is that to live and to love means risking loss, and taking that risk means letdown, sorrow, and pain. No relationship, no career, no accomplishment can ever live up to our expectations completely or satisfy our every desire and need. After all, according to the Declaration of Independence, we are guaranteed only the right to *pursue happiness,* not actually to have it. Thus, we know, as adults, that along with joy and pleasure there will always be a certain amount of pain. *This is an inevitable part of life and love.*

Suffering, on the other hand, is optional! We create suffering for ourselves and for others when we

- Stick our heads in the sand, refusing to see reality
- Avoid honest introspection, numbing ourselves with alcohol, food, sex, and too much work
- Put off making painful decisions, because it is uncomfortable, creating a vastly larger mess down the road
- Avoid honesty with our partners, telling ourselves that we're "sparing their feelings"
- Take a passive stance, indulging in the belief that our lives are not our own, and that we're controlled by invisible forces outside of ourselves, such as someone else's disapproval or judgment

In short, we create suffering when we do what feels comfortable today, knowing that we're creating more pain in the future.

Time and time again, as a therapist, I've sat with shocked and heart-broken people in my office who have drifted along for years with a partner, only to have that significant other suddenly leave. Almost always, this is the result of my client's making the assumption that his/her relationship was okay, and never bothering to put a finger to the pulse of it with the You and Me Conversation. The irony is that we often neglect this kind of communication, fearing that we will scare someone away with such serious discussion, only to find ourselves eventually left alone by that very person for lack of connection.

There are no shortcuts to an emotionally fulfilling relationship. There are no guarantees of happily-ever-after, and there's no way to avoid pain and loss in life. Paradoxically, the more arduously we try to prevent them, the more pain and loss we create.

The goodies that are available through a healthy romance are earned, they are not freebies. We bring them to ourselves through the regular practice of that which strengthens a relationship and our own emotional muscle: difficult, often uncomfortable conversations. We do this, not once every five years, but regularly and frequently, *beginning with the first few dates.*

Having the courage to bring up "the relationship," clearing the air about where we stand with each other, frees us up to enjoy being together and deepen our emotional bonding. The confidence and emotional freedom that You and Me Conversations give us is priceless. It paves the way to a deep and lasting love with a partner who is right for us. Regular practice of You and Me Conversations keeps the path of your love cleared of emotional obstacles.

You and Me Conversations do not guarantee a happily-ever-after outcome. Often they reveal emotional realities that are not resolvable, making it necessary for you to move on from the relationship. In the short run, this brings up sorrow, anger, and loss. In the long run, you are free to find someone who is much more right for you.

As we've already discussed, the first significant talk you'll have is the Shopping Conversation, in which you basically inform each other of the kind of relationship you're looking for, as well as the potential you have to be that for each other. At some point as you continue to date, you will have your first You and Me Conversation.

Where to Begin: The Emotional Portfolio

One day I was discussing the You and Me Conversation with a friend of mine who's a financial adviser. I asked him if he understood what I was saying, and he drew this analogy: "In the relationship, you are trying to get from Me to We, and form a connection. Each of you comes into the relationship with your own portfolio." He dubbed it the Emotional Portfolio, and we decided that it includes

- Family-of-origin
- Past romances
- Career history/education
- Children
- Social network (activities, friends, family, workplace)
- Spiritual (beliefs, participation)
- Physical programs (working out, etc.) and health
- Emotional programs (therapy, counseling, Twelve-Step)
- Finances
- Goals
- Marriage (past and attitudes about future)
- Things you're afraid to express (secrets, fears, past failures, thoughts, emotions, beliefs)

Each time you sit down to discuss the relationship, you are each speaking from your own individual Emotional Portfolios. Like it or not, whatever is in those portfolios influences the conversation at hand. If your conversations are allowed to flow to a deep enough level, these things will eventually emerge.

If you are unconscious of your own Emotional Portfolio, you are severely handicapped in the You and Me Conversation:

- You can't discuss You and Me if you don't know the Me part
- If your partner doesn't know his Me part, you won't be able to complete the conversation
- Until both of you are aware of your Me parts, you cannot successfully get to We, and commitment is thus blocked

Without commitment, a romantic relationship cannot flourish, and you can't reach a true commitment without some successful You and Me Conversations. In Chapter Twelve we'll examine commitment more closely and the conversations about it. What you can do now is take whatever steps are needed to become conscious of your own Emotional Portfolio:

- Get in counseling
- Talk to friends
- Get in a support group and talk to others
- Begin and write in a personal journal every day

In short, do an inventory of your life, and get whatever help you need to get in touch with yourself about each of these areas.

Even if you are not totally clear with yourself about these areas, you are strengthened in your ability to have a You and Me Conversation just by getting into the process of discovery. Get started on the journey of deeper self-knowing, anywhere and anyway you can, as a commitment to yourself, your well-being, and your relationships.

Timing for the You and Me Conversation

There's no rule about when to have your first "relationship talk." Generally, it will be sometime in the first three months, once you've realized that

- This is more than just a casual dating relationship, on one or both your parts
- You're beginning to fall in love with your partner
- You think your partner may be falling in love with you
- You're headed for a sexual relationship
- There's potential for a long-term relationship including the possibility of lifetime and marriage

The bottom line is that it's time for a You and Me Conversation when you feel the need to know where you stand with your dating partner. You don't have to wait until you're sure of your feelings to have this talk. *You don't have to be ready for a commitment or have a particular outcome in mind.* What's important is that you initiate the conversation and allow the interaction itself to reveal what you need to know. There's great power in simply beginning the discussion and trusting that the appropriate outcome will occur naturally.

Preparing Yourself for the Conversation

Relationship talks being somewhat scary, it's wise to do some mental preparation before you begin the conversation. Take some time alone, write in a journal or just focus inward, and have a little internal talk, reminding yourself

Whatever the outcome, I will be okay. Even if I discover tonight that my partner isn't on the same page with me, or doesn't share my feelings, I will take that information to empower myself, not put myself down. I will absorb the hurt or the loss, if that's what happens, and decide what's in my best interest now that I know the truth. I will be my own best friend, in this and whatever comes my way.

However special, this person is not my only chance for love. I will maintain a realistic perspective about my partner, such that no matter what happens I will not be devastated. I am confident that I am a worthy, lovable person, and that if this person doesn't love me or want what I want, that someone just as wonderful will come into my life who will.

Talk to a friend for reinforcement, if necessary. Whatever you do, always make sure that you take a mentally healthy attitude into a You and Me Conversation. *This means that your basic stance is one of self-caring first, and exploration of the relationship possibilities second.*

Set a Goal for the Conversation

Before you go into this conversation, get straight with yourself about your objective. Ask yourself *Am I doing this with a goal of getting something from this person?*

If your answer is yes, then you're headed for trouble! Having an agenda going into any significant relationship conversation is a setup for heartache for both of you. In relationships, as in no other area of life, even people who are normally very honest and straightforward will hedge about the truth in order to avoid hurt feelings, both for themselves and for others.

If your goal is to get the other person to make a commitment or declare feelings for you, then you won't be very open to hearing something different. This makes you vulnerable to self-deception, and the other person vulnerable to skirting the truth. You are likely to find yourself in a relationship with someone who's ambivalent about you, or the reverse scenario, so that there's no real foundation of commitment. Without that foundation, you are sure to flounder in the rough waters of a normal relationship.

If you want a powerful, loving, honest relationship, go into the conversation with only this one goal:

To understand where you are with each other.

From this understanding of each of your thoughts and feelings all other things will naturally flow. If your partner senses that you're open to whatever the truth is, she will be more likely to be forthcoming with thoughts, feelings, and desires. If your partner senses that there truly is emotional freedom to choose the direction of the relationship, then whatever is decided will be genuine and heartfelt, not a result of guilt or obligation.

If you are genuinely interested primarily in understanding how your partner really feels, then you are more likely to detect it if you're just not on the same page emotionally. You are more likely to choose what's best for you, even if that means saying good-bye to this person, or changing the direction of the relationship.

The First You and Me Conversation

This conversation will establish a precedent in your relationship, so it is very important. *Do not* have this talk when you're angry, tired, or feeling too emotionally vulnerable. *Do not* have this talk in the middle of an argument about something else, even if you think this is what your fight is really about. Choose your timing carefully. Have this discussion when you will not be interrupted, when you're both re-laxed, and there's no pressure to be hurried.

First, *set the stage for the rest of the talk.* This means doing a little self-disclosure about where you're coming from:

- "I really am enjoying going out with you, Susan. I haven't felt this good about a new relationship in a long time."
- "You're becoming very special to me, David. I'm so glad we met at Jerry's party a couple of months ago."

Then, *introduce the subject of your talk* with the next step:

- "I think it's time for us to talk a little bit about what's happening between us."
- "I'd like to discuss how we're doing so far in the relationship."
- "It's important for me to let you know how I feel about what's happening between us, and I'd like to hear how you're feeling."

Then, *set the stage for emotional safety.* Let your partner know that whatever happens, you will be okay with it, and that you truly want him to tell you how he really feels:

- "I want you to know that you can tell me whatever you're think-ing and feeling about this, and it's okay. I'll be fine, so please don't hold back because you're afraid of hurting my feelings or making me angry."

Lastly, *set the stage for freedom for your own emotions:*

- "Even though I want you to tell me whatever you're really think-ing and feeling, that doesn't mean I won't have a reaction of some kind. I might not like what I hear, but I promise to treat you with re-spect when I respond."

Now you're into the conversation. Share first, then listen. Make it your goal to understand where the other person is coming from, first and foremost, even if you don't like what you're discovering. I might even say, *especially if you don't like what you're hearing*, because it's at these times that we're most prone to deceive ourselves.

What to cover:

Our feelings for each other. At this stage, you may not feel undying passionate love, but sense that that's possible. A statement such as

"I feel very warm about you, and I could see this turning into love." Or

"My feelings about you are getting stronger every day." Or

"My heart is really opening up to you, more so each time I see you."

I personally don't like the use of the old cliché, "I think I love you." This is sort of a cowardly way of dealing with the issue. If you love someone, say so. Real love isn't about making sure that the other person feels the same before you express it, but rather, about what's true in your heart. If you aren't sure yet that you love this person, say something else or don't say it.

If you know you love someone but you're afraid to declare it, tell him you're not ready to talk about that yet, and why. For some, saying "I love you" signifies commitment at a higher level, rather than simply an expression from the heart. Rather than just stonewalling her, let her know that this is scary territory for you.

The relationship potential. Again, you're not making a permanent commitment at this point, but rather you're expressing what the potential is. If someone is just not a right partner for you long-term, this is the time to be honest and tell him so:

"I really like you and enjoy going out with you, but this just doesn't seem to be a love connection for me at this time."

If you see the possibility of something long-term, you can say so, even though you're not yet making any promises:

"I don't know where this is headed, but I see the definite possibility of something long-term with you. I feel a connection with you on a lot of levels, and I want to continue exploring our potential together, for as long as that feels right to both of us."

Agreement to inform each other if your feelings change significantly. This is a promise, in effect, that if my feelings about you or the relationship shift, I will tell you as soon as I'm aware of that.

"I promise to tell you if I ever decide that you're not 'the one' for me, and I'd like you to promise me the same."

Emotions in a relationship, especially in the beginning, can shift quite a bit. We can feel warm one day, cool the next, and something else the following day. These little emotional changes don't all have to be catalogued and reported, as they are a part of the ups and downs of intimacy and love.

It's perfectly natural to have questions in your mind about the suitability of a partner as you get to know each other on a deeper level. You're weighing your feelings for the person versus your dawning awareness that you haven't yet found that perfect person. One day you may feel you're with your ideal partner, a few days later, as you discover something about this person that you don't particularly like, you may wonder. It's not necessary, or even desirable, to inform your partner of each moment of doubt that you experience.

What is important to discuss is a significant change of heart that has an impact on the relationship. If you realize that, overall, you would never want to marry this person, tell him. As soon as you know that you're with someone who is not a candidate for a lifetime partner, she deserves to know so that she won't be spinning her wheels, hoping for an outcome that will never happen.

Exclusivity. If you haven't already covered it, this is the time to discuss your feelings about being exclusive with each other.

If you've been dating for several weeks or a couple of months when you have this talk, chances are you've already crossed the line into some emotional and possibly sexual intimacy. This means that you're going to have difficulty developing this relationship if you're still trying to date others, so now is the time to choose where you want your energy directed.

If you just don't want to give up your options to date others at this point, say so. Getting this out in the open is important for each of you to proceed in the way that is best for you both.

If you want an exclusive relationship at this point, say so, but don't try to force the issue. Persuasion in these conversations leads to insincere promises and agreements that usually break down over time.

Not an Easy Conversation

If you're beginning to think that this sounds like a lot to talk about for a new relationship, you're right! Remember that what you're striving for is not an ordinary, here-today-gone-tomorrow kind of love, but something deep and lasting. You're practicing the kind of communication skills now that build emotional muscle for whatever comes your way later.

What if your partner doesn't want to have this conversation? Maybe he or she is avoiding this talk, consciously or unconsciously afraid of the level of disclosure that is called for:

"I don't want to talk about this now. Let's just go out and have fun."

"This is too serious for where we are. I'm just not ready for this."

"I'm too tired to talk right now."

Don't try to force the issue. It's okay to agree to drop it for now, as long as you can get an agreement that you will talk later. Some things you can say:

"I realize you're uncomfortable with this, and I don't want to force this on you. However, it's very important to me to get my feelings out in the open and to get some idea of where I stand with you. How about if we make a date to have this talk in a few days?"

"If you don't want to talk right now, that's okay. When would be a good time to talk?"

Try to stay in the conversation long enough to get clarification about why she doesn't want to talk. Then ask for another time to continue:

"Are you telling me you don't want to have this discussion, or just that now is not the time? Is there something else wrong, or can we decide on another time to do this that's better for you?"

Listen with respect to your partner's fears and concerns, making sure that you maintain an atmosphere of emotional safety. This means that you refrain from the temptation to get angry and lash out because he won't talk.

You and Me: Not for Everyone

This level of communication is not for everyone. Not all people wish to have a relationship that calls for lots and lots of openness, honesty, and disclosure. Not everyone is emotionally developed enough for this kind of talk. Lack of insight into the Emotional Portfolio, or fear about being that vulnerable to a partner are only a couple of reasons why someone may not be ready for a You and Me Conversation. Sometimes an individual is simply not emotionally available for a relationship (a Westbound Train), so this conversation is not for him.

This conversation is for those who wish to challenge themselves to be the best they can possibly be in a relationship, to go beyond where their parents and grandparents may have stopped. It is for those who would rather work for a great relationship than to settle for a mediocre one. Chances are, since you're reading this book, I'm talking about you. And, if your partner doesn't want the same kind of relationship that you want, the You and Me Conversation will bring that out.

Sometimes just bringing up this discussion reveals where you stand, in your partner's unwillingness to have the conversation. If she simply will not engage in this discussion, after repeated attempts on your part to make it safe enough for her to do so, take this as a huge red flag. *If you cannot get through your first You and Me Conversation, you have little on which to build a lasting relationship*, the kind that you desire.

Listening: The You and Me Conversation

Remember that the goal of this dialogue is to *understand where you both are in your relationship*, so it's important that you practice good listening skills. Listen Well (Listen Empty) and ask questions for clarification only if needed. Avoid the temptation to grill your partner, peppering him with too many questions and backing him into a corner. Be careful that you don't take too many preconceived notions into the conversation; be open to the possibility that you may hear something you had no idea was in your partner's mind and heart.

Don't hesitate to say, "What does that mean?" in a gentle way from time to time. So often we assume that we know what is meant by the words people use, when in fact, their interpretation of them may mean something entirely different. This is especially true in relationships, which are populated by language that is so conceptual in nature. Words such as *love*, *commitment*, and so on, are subject to interpretation, and thus can be the source of great misunderstandings. Take the time to discuss what these things mean to each of you.

Listen to what's not being said, as well as to what is. This means being tuned in to the emotions behind the words, to the attitude underneath what's being said. This is another kind of emotional skill that's important to have in a relationship: the ability to detect the subtle nuances of communication that go beyond mere words. Body language, tone of voice, eye contact, and so on, are all vehicles of communication, sometimes conveying what's really going on in a far more powerful way than the words themselves.

If you sense that something's happening beyond what your partner is actually saying, it's okay to point it out, but it's not okay to use the information to manipulate the other person. Thus, you would *not* say,

"I can tell you're feeling scared, and even though you say you don't want to be exclusive at this time, I think you really want to be with me. Let's just call it what it is and make a commitment to this relationship."

But rather,

"Sounds like you're not sure of your feelings for me, so you don't want to commit to an exclusive relationship at this time. If you ever want to talk about what seems scary about that, I'm open to listening."

Different Pages: What to Say

What if you realize through this conversation that you're on an entirely different page than your partner? You've got a choice of

- Continuing forward, giving your partner the opportunity to "catch up" emotionally with you at a later time
- Changing the relationship to a platonic friendship
- Taking a break, then being friends later, if that's appropriate
- Ending the relationship now

If you're not sure, and you want some time to think it over, say so.

"It sounds like we're not at all in the same place, Brad. I'm ready just to date you and see what develops, while you're still playing the field. I'm not sure how comfortable I am with that, and I want some time to think it over."

Sometimes the conversation reveals you're in a different place, and by getting it out in the open, someone will have a change of heart. Don't be too quick to write off a person just because his heart doesn't have the same emotional timetable as yours.

If you're going forward unclear, make a promise to yourself and to your partner to stay in communication. Check back in from time to time and talk about how it's going and whether or not it's working for you both to take this approach.

The really big danger sign is if he tells you that you're just not the right kind of person for him. This is something that's not likely to change with time, so take that into account in your decision-making.

Ending the Relationship

Perhaps you've discovered that there's just no basis for you to continue, and you decide to end the relationship now. While there are many ways to say "it's over," the best thing to do is to just say it. Taking these steps will help you go forward from a breakup with the least chance of emotional baggage.

Thank your partner for investing the time in the relationship so far:
"I have truly enjoyed your company these past few weeks, Harvey. Thank you for the lovely dinners and that play you treated me to last week. I especially appreciate your honesty with me."

State your decision:
"In light of our conversation, however, I realize that we're looking for two different things and this just won't work for me, so I'm choosing to move on."

Answer questions, but don't get into an argument:
"There's nothing wrong with you, Mary. I just realize I can't get my needs met in this relationship, so it's best for me to move on."

Address the question of "friendship":
"I'm open to being platonic friends, if that works for you." Or
"I'm not sure I can be friends right now because my feelings for you are still so strong. I'll let you know if and when that changes."

Say good-bye:

"Good luck, and good-bye." Or
"I wish you the best in everything."

This kind of breakup conversation is suitable for a short-term relationship, but will be very different for a romance that has gone on for months or years. In Chapter Twelve we'll address breaking up again, when the relationship is at a more advanced level.

You and Me Conversations That Worked

Regardless of the outcome, the You and Me Conversation is a success if you reach an understanding of where you are with each other. You don't have to follow the format I've presented here rigidly in order to do that. What's important is that you speak from your heart, that you Listen Well to the other person, and that you persist until you have an understanding. If that's what you do, then the conversation may take many forms and you may address it in many ways, as the following stories illustrate.

• On their fourth date, one couple had a conversation that went something like this:

SHE: It's been such a short time since my divorce, and I'm just beginning to enjoy being single. I don't think I'm ready for a relationship at this time. I just want to enjoy my children before they leave for college, and my girlfriends. I also realize that I'm way past the point of wanting any more children, now that mine are almost grown.

HE: I guess I'm in a different place in life. I'm really ready to find someone and fall in love. I've come to realize that I want my own children, or I want to help someone raise her little ones, and I don't want to miss out on that part of life.

After this conversation, they downgraded their relationship to a clearly platonic friendship, and occasionally participated in each other's lives more as buddies.

• Liz and Charlie dated for about two months, while her divorce was pending. The day it finalized, she had an emotional about-face and began pulling away from Charlie. After two frustrating weeks of trying to talk with her, and her avoiding it, he finally got her on the telephone and insisted that she tell him where he stood with her.

SHE: I don't want to talk right now, I have friends coming over.

HE: I've heard this for two weeks, and I'm not going away until you give me some answers. I deserve to know what's going on.

SHE: All right. I guess I just don't want to date right now. Maybe later, or maybe we'll just be friends.

HE: Thanks for telling me the truth. What do you want me to do?

SHE: Just let me call you. Leave the ball in my court; I don't want any pressure from you or anyone else.

HE: Okay.

Charlie didn't like the outcome, but now he knew where he stood and was able to begin preparing to go on with his life. Three weeks later, after not hearing from Liz, he called her and got a recording that her number had been disconnected with no forwarding information. He was disappointed, but not totally shocked, in light of their most recent conversation. He had his final answer, and then moved on.

• Two couples sitting at dinner together one night decided to play a game: Describe your ideal day, from start to finish. Louise and Sam, who had been dating about six months, went first:

HE: My ideal day would be a day at the beach with Carol [his four-year-old daughter]. We'd play all day, building sand castles and just enjoying the sun. That would be perfect, everything that I could want.

SHE: (looking slightly put off by Sam's answer) My ideal day would begin with taking care of myself. I'd get my hair done, get a manicure, and maybe a massage and facial, early in the day. Then, I'd go to lunch with my girlfriends, and maybe see a good movie. That night, I would have my sweetheart over, make a roaring fire, and just snuggle with him in front of it, talking about whatever comes to mind.

• The second couple, Kay and Russ, who had been dating a couple of years, then took their turns.

SHE: Mine would be a day in Manhattan in December with my honey. First, we would go down to Rockefeller Center and see the tree, and maybe go ice skating. Then, we'd walk down Madison Avenue and window-shop, ending up somewhere really nice for lunch, where we could talk. After that, we'd go back to our hotel room and make love all afternoon. That night, we'd go dancing.

HE: My day would start with two hours of counseling with my sweet-heart. We'd both get all our stuff out, maybe cry a little, and then go to a really great restaurant for lunch. After that, we'd go home for a little dance practice, and then, after that, we see what happens (with a mischievous smile, meaning they make love).

Without even realizing it, these couples were having indirect You and Me Conversations. The first couple's disclosures revealed how out of sync they were, with nothing in common about their day. His ideal day didn't even include her. The second couple was clearly much more in tandem in the relationship, with their ideal days having several things in common. This You and Me Conversation was highly prophetic, as the first couple broke up a short time later due to incompatible goals in the relationship.

• In their first You and Me Conversation, Melissa disclosed to Kevin that she didn't see him as a lifetime partner, but that she cared for him and wanted to be with him. Even though he didn't like what he was hearing, Kevin knew where he stood and decided to go forward, taking his chances that her feelings might not ever change.

You and Me Conversations can also come up in the context of other topics, allowing you to get there through the back door.

• After dating for six months nonexclusively, Gail announced to Perry over dinner one night that she had been invited on a cruise with a man whom she considered to be a friend, although she had dated him at one time. This caused Perry quite a bit of discomfort, which led to a discussion about where their relationship was headed. This was a turning point for them, as they arrived at the mutual decision to date only each other. They continued forward, and today, ten years later, are still blissfully happy with each other.

You and Me: Conversations for a Lifetime

Periodically through your relationship, you will have You and Me talks. This allows you to

- Continue to clarify where you stand with each other
- Consciously declare deeper levels of emotional involvement and commitment
- Disclose a significant change of heart
- Strengthen your emotional muscle of open and honest communication

You and Me Conversations never end, and, in fact, are needed throughout a relationship, even for a lifetime. This is a checkpoint for love in which you pause to see where you stand and if there's maintenance needed, much as you take your car in for evaluation every so often to keep it running well. As time goes on, these conversations will be more and more revealing. As your connection deepens and your history goes on, you may uncover

- Fear, of commitment, of intimacy, of being vulnerable in a relationship
- Pain from the past
- Upset in the present
- Hidden resentments
- Differing emotional timetables
- Infidelity
- Differing emotions: one's "in love," while the other merely loves

to name a few. Getting through these conversations tests the strength of your bond and prepares you for a lifetime love through the building of emotional muscle.

A word of caution: Sometimes the You and Me Conversation can be overdone, when it's covering the same ground over and over with no new outcome. Be careful that you aren't doing this with too much frequency or hammering away at someone. One therapist put it this way:

> *If you're always having to talk about the relationship, you're not really doing it.*

The purpose of these talks is to clear the way for intimacy and joy, and shouldn't become the primary focus of your conversations. Although there are times when you're having these talks more frequently, such as when you're deciding about living together or getting married, most of the time your energy is better spent just enjoying your connection.

So, have You and Me Conversations from time to time, and be creative in the way you approach them; there's really no right or wrong way to go about that. Keep your finger on the pulse of the relationship, and you'll have the emotional freedom to enjoy your romance more fully. With this kind of honesty, you are empowered to live, love, dance, and play together, secure in the knowledge of where you stand with each other.

11

Handling Hot Topics

♥   ♥   ♥

You've been dating for weeks or months. So far, everything has been great. You're on the same emotional page and clear about your intentions toward each other as well as the possibility of a future together. You're in love and believe that, at last, you've found the perfect partner.

Then, something happens. A tiny little shift occurs in the relationship; a dawning sense of discontent about . . . something. You don't like his best friend. You have problems with her child. Sex isn't as good as it once was. Those little habits that, in the beginning, were so endearing now drive you right up the wall.

You have your first argument, and this brings you into point-blank contact with reality. Your so-called perfect relationship is . . . (shudder) flawed! Your ideal partner, your Princess/Prince Charming is also . . . (shock) not perfect! Even worse, this person with whom you've never had any difficulty talking about anything, suddenly is becoming difficult. She's angry. He's withdrawn. She wants to talk it out and you don't. You begin to struggle for power, either silently or openly. Deep in your heart, you fear that this just isn't the way it's supposed to be.

When we first realize that we don't have a perfect partner, nor a perfect relationship, our initial reaction is usually shock, followed by anger, disappointment, and then sadness. We are surprised that, once again, we've chosen someone who is unable or unwilling to meet all of our needs. We are angry that he/she just won't give us what we so desperately want, be it love, validation, or simply our way in a particular matter. We are disappointed that the future won't be a rose-strewn path of never-ending bliss as we were so sure it would be this time around. And, we are sad that we have to give up some of our false expectations and maybe even some of the things we want so much from our lover.

This is the beginning of what will either be the breakdown of our romance, or of our path to a deeper connection. We will either escalate the power struggle, which will most likely lead to a blowup and possibly a breakup, or we will begin to seek new ways of handling conflict. We will either move through the emotional disappointment, or we will become convinced that we've chosen the wrong person and begin to disengage. We will either move in the direction of healing and greater intimacy, or in the direction of breakdown and separation. *Which direction we go will largely depend on one critical factor, how we communicate.* The way we speak and, primarily, listen to one another will have everything to do with where the relationship goes from here.

Speaking and Listening: Making New Choices

In most relationships that reach this point, the attitudes that we hold about each other and about communication can make or break the ties we have. Your attitudes are positive or negative and are defined basically by *where you come from* when you deal with your partner. Negative attitudes that get in the way of good communication include beliefs such as

I *must win in any confrontation, even if that means you lose.* This attitude leads to anger, arguments, and attempts to put the other person down, all of which inhibit understanding and resolution. It also contributes to the buildup of toxic resentment and overall negative feelings in the relationship.

I *must prove that I'm right in any conflict.* The need to be right has caused more human suffering than perhaps any other attitude. It is in the nature of human beings to seek to be right about their feelings, thoughts, and beliefs, but it is also in their nature to have tremendous diversity of thinking and feeling, between various cultures, religious and ethnic groups, and between different generations. Men and women, especially, tend to think and emote in different ways, leading to even more divergence, especially in romantic love.

Thus, it's almost impossible for one or the other to be right all the time. Someone once said, "Do you want to be right, or do you want to be happy?" It seems that when it comes to love, we cannot have both.

I must make sure that you don't dominate or control me. This attitude comes from the belief that it's possible for one person literally to control the other, as if pulling the strings of a puppet. It leads to other false beliefs, such as: "You made me feel that way!" and "You made me do what I did!" With this frame of mind we relinquish our own personal power, and then blame the other person as if it's his fault that we gave away our power.

If you can't give me what I want, then you're obviously the wrong partner for me. This attitude is a result of the erroneous belief that in successful relationships there is no conflict or clashing of needs, but only perfect harmony. It inhibits the flow of love, as we continually step back and evaluate our partner negatively, clinging to the childish belief that there is someone out there who will be better able to love us.

If you want a powerfully loving relationship, take a look at your own negative attitudes that are inhibiting your ability to communicate with your partner. Choose new ones that open up the lines of communication and that restore a loving connection.

Develop a win-win attitude. Decide now that when you have conflict with your partner, you will endeavor to find a solution that is a win for you both. Be willing to give up some of your wants in favor of the higher good of the relationship. Let go of your stubborn desire to get your way at the expense of your partner and your connection. Focus on understanding, with a strong intention that there is a way for both of you to have what you want.

You become a winner by growing, and that comes from understanding your own and your partner's Emotional Portfolios, and then learning how to bring them together.

Give up the need to be right. Relinquish the desire to prove that you're right. Or, find ways to prove that you're *both* right, because, in essence, you usually are. If you both have good hearts and loving intentions, chances are there's some validity to both your positions.

Discover the power of genuine self-expression. Rather than trying to control the other person, or avoid his domination, put your attention on knowing and expressing yourself fully. Claim your personal power by taking responsibility for your own life, your own thoughts and feelings, and your own behavior. Rather than having an agenda in the conversation (i.e., to get what I want, or to keep you from getting what you want), make it your goal simply to understand your partner, and then to speak your own mind and heart to the best of your ability.

Claim your choice of partner. You have chosen this person as your romantic partner, and it's time to take responsibility for that. If you've spent a significant amount of time with him/her, and you've invested a relationship with your energy and heart, then you've done so for a purpose. *Relationships are a mirror of who we are, even though we don't always like what we see.* The temptation is to use our view of our partner's flaws as an excuse to avoid our own issues. This is like trying to stay focused on the rearview mirror as you're driving down the road!

The real opportunity of discovering your partner's flaws is to develop compassion, first for yourself and, by extension, for another. This promotes growth and healing, and paves the way to a deeper connection. Open your heart to the person you've chosen, to the possibility of this being a completely right person and a great mirror for you.

How Not to Have a Loving Relationship: Communication Habits That Don't Work

Because of negative attitudes held in the past, and for other reasons, it's easy to develop communication habits that don't work. Before you can correct these habits, it's necessary to identify them and understand them. The following is a list of unworkable communication habits, along with examples to illustrate some of them.

Putting words in your partner's mouth, aka mind reading. Assuming that you know what the other person is thinking and feeling, and then telling him, leaving no room for him to dispute what you assert. "You say you love me, but you really don't. You're just going through the motions, hoping someone better will come along."

This one can be done out loud with your partner, or silently in your own mind, or with another person, such as when you tell your friend what you believe your partner is thinking as if it's the indisputable truth.

Accusing, blaming. Almost any statement that begins with the word *you* is an accusation or a blame, and, again, leaves no room for the other person to assert the truth of his feelings.

Disguised "you" statements, with no room for argument. This is a clever way to sneak in a "you" statement, as in saying, "I feel that you . . . ," and then being closed to any dispute as to the reality of your assertion.

Interpreting, analyzing. This is playing the role of psychologist by assessing or labeling your partner's state of mind or behavior. Even if you're correct in your analysis, this kind of activity is damaging to the relationship, as it places distance between the two of you, and it puts you in a one-up position such that you no longer view or treat your partner as an equal.

"She's codependent." "He does that because he secretly hates women." "She's insecure and neurotic." "He's a control freak."

Expecting mind reading. This is the erroneous belief that it is someone else's responsibility to know what you're thinking and how you're feeling and what your needs are.

"If you really loved me, you'd know that I wanted you to rub my back. I even gave you hints, telling you how tired I was after my day. You should have known!"

Passive-aggressive. Instead of being direct and telling your partner that you're angry about something, you neglect or "forget" something important, like an anniversary or an agreement to do something for him.

Unilateral decision-making. This is the assumption that you know what's best for the two of you, having arrived at this conclusion in your own mind and implemented it without consulting your partner. This is one of the most damaging actions that you can take in a relationship, as it leaves the other person out of the decision-making process regarding issues that directly impact him.

Clamming up. Instead of telling your partner what's on your mind, you stonewall her, refusing to speak and forcing her to pull information out of you. Meanwhile, you clearly exhibit the signs of someone who's upset, causing her concern and worry. This is a highly manipulative thing to do in a relationship, as it puts all the cards in your hands, and leaves the other person in a powerless position.

Name-calling, labeling. This one is self-explanatory. It can be done out loud to the person, or it can be done silently, and either way it is very damaging.

"You're so stupid." "You never do anything right." "You're such a ****!"

Not allowing differing beliefs, opinions, preferences. This occurs when you attack or put down the other person's ideas. It shows a lack of respect and boundaries and its message is, "If you're not just like me, there's something wrong with you."

Sarcasm, teasing, ridicule. Even when done with so-called humor, if you are making fun at the expense of the other person it's hurtful. The recipient of this can't win, as there's a one-two punch: Not only is there a put-down in the teasing, but your unspoken message is that there's something wrong with him if he doesn't just take it and, yes, laugh about it, too.

Judgment. This is damaging even if it's not done out loud, as it puts a wall up between partners, and creates a situation in which someone always has an upper hand in the relationship. There's no psychological safety for your partner to open up and be herself if she's being judged, so communication will shut down completely if you employ this one: "You're wrong, sick, or bad because you [fill in the blank]." The other unspoken part of judgment is, "I, on the other hand, am much more strong, healthy, wise, and good because I don't do what you're doing."

The odd thing about judgment is that deep down, we don't believe the second part. It's all just a smoke screen for our own insecurities. We're really passing judgment on ourselves.

Pretending to listen when absorbed in something else. The obvious example is when you are watching television or reading the paper while your partner attempts to communicate. Even if you do possess the ability to concentrate on more than one thing at a time, it's still off-putting to the speaker not to have your full attention. It is a signal that you are not interested enough in what he has to say to give him your undivided focus.

Criticizing partner to others. With this habit you can find yourself quickly building a negative case against your partner, thereby tearing down the relationship. Also, it works to weaken your emotional muscle in being able to take your complaints directly to the person who can do something about them. Moreover, it can result in disapproval of your partner by friends and family, and thus erode the support you receive to deal with the relationship when times are rough. Lastly, it's usually not even accurate, as it is so one-sided.

Discussing your relationship with others in a way that you don't with your partner. When you confide in someone outside the relationship about things that you should be taking to your lover you cross your loyalties and weaken the connection you have with your partner. In the extreme, this can lead to affairs (i.e., the married man confiding in another woman about how awful his wife is). There are times when this is appropriate, such as in a therapy session, with a Twelve-Step sponsor, or with a trusted friend, as long as you use the conversation as a springboard and go back to your partner with what you discussed.

Speaking for partner. You tell others how your partner is thinking and feeling, without consulting her or making sure that your perceptions are correct. The assumption that you know what another person is thinking without asking him is the root of bad communication and should be avoided at all costs. By taking this one step further and representing another's unconfirmed thoughts to a third party, you could be creating false impressions about your partner that are potentially damaging if you've gotten it wrong.

Telling one on your partner without consent. Telling a story about your partner that casts her in a negative light without making sure she is okay with that is potentially embarrassing and hurtful. Likewise, repeating secrets that your partner has shared with you without consent is very damaging to trust as well.

Trying to "fix" partner. This is when you see your partner as deficient in some way and in need of help, then focus your energy on getting her to change. This is damaging because it works to diminish your partner in your eyes and in the eyes of others as well.

Lying, covering up, and withholding the truth. These things directly erode the trust that is so important in a relationship. Additionally, they interfere with you and your partner's ability to take the true measure of your connection.

Lying and withholding important truths casts a smoke screen over the relationship, preventing you from knowing what you really have together. Withholding the truth is a way of trying to cling too tightly to the relationship. This always leads to suffering, as staying together for false reasons means that we live a lie, and there are few things that are more destructive to the human spirit, and thus to the very fabric of our lives. On the other hand, in love, as in all of life, honesty keeps the energy and information flowing for the good of both people. Telling the truth reveals what we really have or don't have together, thereby propelling us to greater levels of trust and commitment or bringing about a breakup.

It's no coincidence that when couples are breaking up, they have nothing left to lose and often feel free enough to disclose their withheld thoughts and feelings, thus actually creating the intimacy they so wanted. They often then want to get back together, as their honesty has reconnected them and opened up new possibilities. The challenge in a healthy relationship is to keep the honest communication flowing *while you are together.*

Yelling, screaming, shouting. Any physical aggression, including property damage. Any threats, emotional, physical or otherwise. These are all acts of aggression, and destroy psychological safety in a relationship. If you or a partner ever does any of these things, seek help immediately. Violence, even when it begins as verbal abuse, tends to escalate, and can result in injury and even death.

Changing Old Habits

The first step in changing negative behavior is to acknowledge what you've been doing that hasn't worked. However, it's important that you *do not use this list to mentally beat up yourself or your partner.* In fact, putting yourself down can actually inhibit your desire to change, just as putting down your partner does nothing to promote her growth.

Spend some time with this list, thinking over old relationships and how you've handled the communication. Yes, you'll realize that your partners have made lots of these errors, but focus more on your own mistakes than you do on theirs. After all, you can't change another person, you can only work on yourself. Realize that they, like you, are flawed and are in a process of growth, no matter how hard it is to see that.

Reflect on your family and how communication was handled. How did your parents speak and listen to each other, to you and your siblings? This reflection will reveal the origins of many of your negative habits, either because you adopted your parents' attitudes and behaviors, or because you've bent over backward to try and avoid theirs.

Sometimes trying not to be like your parents only leads you into other negative habits. For example, maybe one of your parents held nothing back, constantly criticizing, nagging, yelling, and screaming. You, trying to be anything but that, withhold everything. You are not outwardly critical, but inwardly you are judging your partners as harshly as you yourself felt judged in your family growing up. Rather than disclosing your dissatisfactions to your partner and asking for change, you build a negative case until it is so overwhelming that you feel there's nothing else for you to do but leave. Thus, while you're technically doing things differently than your parents did, their legacy continues to influence your life.

Dealing with Anger

Before you can resolve your differences, it's necessary to understand and deal productively with the emotion that is inevitable when you clash. Anger is one of the most misunderstood emotions. Some say it's bad and you should never feel it. Others say it's good and that you should be free to express it whenever you feel it. The truth is

Anger is one of the natural emotions that all human beings experience at one time or another, and is no more unacceptable than your eye color. Anger simply *is*, and is part of the human condition. As such, you don't get a choice about whether or not to feel it, and it's impossible to judge it worthy or not worthy, any more than you would say that it is bad that your eyes are blue, or good that your eyes are brown.

Anger may appear to be about one thing, but in reality be about something else. Anger is often a smoke screen for emotions and situations other than the one it seems to follow or be attached to at first glance. The old cliché is the one that describes the guy whose boss yells at him; he then goes home and yells at his wife and kids. He's not truly angry at his family, but feeling powerless at work and taking it out on them.

Anger covers up fear. It hides the fear that I'll be hurt, that you won't love me, that I won't get what I want from you, that you'll leave me and I'll be abandoned and alone.

Anger covers up vulnerability and powerlessness. I feel out of control, small, and weak. I can't let that show or I'll be hurt even more, so I'll be angry and no one will see my true feelings of weakness.

Anger covers up hurt. I'm sad, disappointed, wounded, and feel small and helpless. I can't let you see my hurt or you'll twist the knife even deeper. I'll strike out with anger at you so I can put you on the defensive and then you won't have a chance to hurt me.

Without a full understanding of anger and where it comes from, we resort to knee-jerk responses when we feel it welling up inside. These fall into two basic categories that you will probably recognize:

1. Fight: We argue, try to win a current discussion, launch a power struggle, lash out, and look to get even.

2. Flight: We create distance in the relationship and can even leave or break up. If that doesn't work, we often do something nasty enough so that the other person will leave.

The fight or flight syndrome is the basis of all unhealthy expressions of anger:

Passive/aggressive. Rather than being up front with anger, we become "forgetful" of important promises, dates, or agreements. Also, *not doing* that which we know to be the loving thing; for example, I know that my lover longs to be greeted with a kiss at the end of the day, and, because I'm generally angry with him, I simply "forget" my usual affectionate greeting. This is a fighting stance, even though it is subtle. It is an underground way of getting even.

Attack/blame/criticism. Rather than owning your anger, you lash out at your partner, blaming her for your own painful feelings.

Toxic: Put-downs, name-calling, property damage, physical abuse. This is fighting that's crossed the line into violence and abuse and is unacceptable no matter how angry you get.

Leaving while angry. Rather than tell your partner that you're upset, you leave the conversation, either by emotionally disconnecting, clamming up, hanging up the phone, or physically leaving. In the extreme, you are working to build up a caseload of anger and then simply leave the relationship. Or, you drive your partner away with your behavior.

While you may have little choice about feeling angry, you always have a choice about how you act when you're angry. It's simply not true that people are totally out of control when angry. They may *feel* out of control, because the emotions are so overwhelming, but behavior and feelings are two different things, and it's important to distinguish between them now.

When violent individuals go into treatment, they discover that at some point in the anger cycle they have *relinquished responsibility for their actions*, in effect deciding that it's okay to lose control. This is the basis of the behavior that follows, not some invisible outside force making them do what they did. With cognitive and emotional retraining, people who find themselves in this situation are able to redecide to be responsible for their actions, and to choose new behaviors for dealing with anger that are nonviolent.

Healthy Anger

Sometimes, anger is empowering. When we've been truly unjustly affronted, getting appropriately indignant can provide the energy that is needed to stand up for ourselves.

Anger does not have to lead to toxic reactions, but can be very healthy. When handled appropriately, there's

Awareness. I am in touch with my own emotions. I endeavor to understand them and where they come from.

Responsibility. I realize that I am the originator of my own emotions, that no one truly has the power to make me feel a certain way, even if he does know my emotional buttons to push. I am capable of restructuring my own thought process when necessary so that I don't react in the same old ways.

When I realize that I'm too angry to deal with you in a productive way, I will find healthy ways to manage my emotions, such as taking a walk or doing other exercise, meditating, or taking an agreed-upon break,* before I speak with you.

Healthy expression. I take full responsibility for my own actions, and I choose to always follow the *three rules of healthy expression of anger*:

1. Do no harm to myself.
2. Do no harm to others.
3. Do no property damage.

Some ways to discharge anger appropriately include the following:

• Write a letter (not for sending) and say everything you'd like to say to your partner. Sleep on it, and the next day consider how much of it you actually wish to express. John Gray's Love Letter technique is a particularly powerful process for discharging anger and getting back in touch with love.†

• Use a foam bat, a tennis racket, or your fists to hit pillows or the mattress on your bed. Always verbalize (yell, scream, cry) when you do this, as the body has difficulty releasing these emotions otherwise. Do this when others aren't around, including children and animals, as it can be frightening to them. If you have problems with this technique and you suspect that you are carrying pent-up rage, find a good

---

*This means that rather than abruptly disconnecting or leaving, you inform your partner that you are too angry to talk right now and that you would like a break. Agree on a time to get back together and talk about what happened.

†John Gray, *Men Are from Mars, Women Are from Venus* (New York: HarperCollins, 1992).

therapist that does body work, such as Bioenergetics, to help you learn how to discharge anger.

• Take ownership of the anger with a statement to your mate. When you are angry, express your feelings to your partner in a way that implies these are your feelings, from you, and not caused by him, even if he did something to provoke your anger.

Use the basic formula "When you ———, I felt ———."

"When you came home without doing the errands I asked you to do, I felt very angry. I counted on you to keep that agreement and I felt let down by you."

As you practice healthy anger management, you will find that your fights are of shorter duration and less intensity, and that you both have more energy for the resolution of your issues. You also can prevent the buildup of toxic resentment and fights that break out between you both by following these guidelines.

In this next section, we'll outline the steps for a powerful communication process that will bring you back together during those times when you're angry and upset with each other, or when you're struggling for power. If you follow it step-by-step, you can resolve almost any difference that arises between you, and you can restore the flow of love and intimacy to your relationship.

How to Have a Loving Relationship: Communication Habits That Work

There will always be areas of life in which you and your partner will clash. Few of us have been trained in conflict resolution, especially when it has to do with the person to whom we're closest. This next section covers a step-by-step process by which most couples are able to resolve, on their own, the issues that arise in an intimate relationship.

The first step is to

Manage your anger in a healthy way. This helps you reduce the intensity of emotion before you attempt to deal with your partner. It's very difficult to resolve an issue when you're flooded with emotion, and if you're both feeling overwhelmed with anger, it's virtually impossible. Be self-caring first, then sit down with your partner. *Do not attempt these exercises if you are in a fearful, shut down, or angry mood.* Take time to nurture yourself, and each other (if possible), back into a loving state.

Choose a time when you can take as much time as you need for this conversation and can be sure there won't be any interruptions. I know one couple who hires a baby-sitter for the evening so that they can be alone and have these talks. *Both* of you must agree that you are ready to talk. It never works for one person to insist on his own timing for a talk when the other's not emotionally prepared. At the same time, not being ready is not justification for putting someone else off indefinitely.

Since the number one goal of communication in a love relationship is to *promote understanding*, the next step in conflict resolution is to

Listen Well. This means beginning your conversation in an emotional state that is open and compassionate, and then endeavoring to Listen Empty. You can declare to yourself internally and then to your partner:

"I am here to listen to you, to do my best to understand you as fully and completely as I possibly can, and to validate your perceptions and feelings. I promise to Listen Empty, setting aside my own thoughts, feelings, and perceptions about the topic, making it my goal simply to *understand you* and how things are for you."

As your partner speaks, maintain this frame of mind, and if you feel it slipping, stop her, get back into Listening Empty, and then ask her to continue.

Mirror your partner's expressions. From time to time as your partner shares with you, repeat back the essence of what's being said, paying attention to the underlying feelings, but being careful not to embellish the retelling with your own interpretation or analysis. Also, be careful that you're not simply parroting what was said but truly understand it and bounce it back in your own words.

The attitude behind Mirroring is more important than the actual words themselves. If you're *coming from a genuine commitment to understand your partner*, then however you say it will be okay, even if you fumble a bit. Your conveyance of compassion and caring about their feelings will more than make up for any awkwardness or fumbling.

"What I hear you saying, Valerie, is that when I forget to call to tell you I'm going to be late, you worry about me, and then you get angry that I was so inconsiderate."

"What I hear you saying, Steve, is that you don't like it when I remind you about the things you've agreed to do. You'd like it better if I just trusted you to get them done, even if that means you forget something."

Validate your partner's thoughts, feelings, perceptions, and beliefs, even if you don't agree with them. Show respect for your differences by honoring your partner's individuality, and by communicating your understanding.

A common misperception is that I have to agree with you in order to validate what you're saying. This is not true. *Understanding is not agreement.* Separate those once and for all, and you'll become a much better listener.

"I can understand how you would worry about me when I'm late and don't call, Val. I can also see how that might leave you angry, especially when I show up and act like nothing happened."

"I can see how my reminding you about your To Do list feels like I'm mothering you, Steve, and how much you hate that. I can understand that it feels like I'm trusting you more if I don't nag you about those things."

Check in to see if you're hearing your partner. The measure of how well you're listening is strictly in your partner's sense of being heard. Even if you think you're doing a great job, and he says he doesn't feel understood, then probably you haven't quite heard him. This is because it's so easy to *seem* to be Listening Well, when, in fact, your own agenda ("I'm right, you're wrong," "You're so screwed up," etc.) is getting in the way of really understanding your partner.

Ask "Am I hearing you so far?" and if the answer is no, then ask him to repeat what was said and start over with Listening Empty and Mirroring, until your partner acknowledges that, "Yes, you heard me."

Continue Listening Empty and Mirroring until your partner is done with the topic. (This exercise is much easier if you agree up front that you will cover one topic at a time.) Ask, "Is there anything else?" until the answer you hear is "no, that's all there is about that."

When it's time for you to speak, request that your partner Listen Empty. This is a vital step in communication that is often overlooked. It's tempting just to launch in with your side of the story, assuming that you'll be listened to as well as you listened to your partner, but this is not always the case. Requesting Empty Listening supports your partner in being there for you, and it also notifies you that there's psychological safety to open up. *Do not share sensitive material if your partner refuses to listen in this way.*

"I have some things I want to share with you, sweetheart. I'm a little anxious about it, and I would like you to promise me that you won't judge me or analyze me, or argue with me. I want you just to listen to me and try your best to understand me as I'm talking."

Speak Well throughout your communication. This means using "I" statements, expressing feelings without blame or accusation, and taking responsibility for your own emotions.

"I understand about not calling you when I'm late, Valerie, and I'm going to change that in the future. But, I'm still angry and hurt about the way you attacked me last week when I was late. When you raised your voice to me, and called me those names, I felt like a bad little kid being punished, so that it was very hard for me to feel sorry about your feelings. I want us to work together on these things, not be each other's enemies."

"I'm truly sorry about nagging you, Steve, and it's something I'm working on changing. But I'm hurt about all the broken promises you make to me. I want to be able to trust you, too, and it's hard to do that when you don't follow through on the things you say you'll do."

Share a little at a time, pausing to allow time for Mirroring. Be careful that you don't flood your partner with too much material at one time. Stop every so often and ask him/her to mirror what's been said so far.

"So, what do you hear me saying so far?"

Give feedback about how well your partner is listening. If you don't feel understood, gently express this and take more time to clarify.

"No, that's not exactly it, but that's close. What I really meant was . . ."

Keep going with these steps until you've completed what you have to say on the topic.

Maintain emotional safety after the exercise. Never use what your partner reveals in these sessions against him later. This is vitally important to remember and key to keeping the lines of communication open.

As you can see, this is a rather painstaking process, requiring a good bit of time, emotional energy, and patience. You will probably use conflict resolution in this form when you have major issues that are "stuck" for you, but not usually for the little everyday things that come up.

The interesting thing is that when couples use this process and train themselves to become very good at it, eventually it becomes part of their emotional repertoire, such that they no longer have to follow the steps formally. They just naturally Listen Empty most of the time and mirror each other. Thus, both feel listened to and understood most of the time, minimizing conflict and increasing love and connection. There's just not much to fight about when you and your partner truly understand each other and exhibit compassion.

Sometimes, though, listening and understanding each other is only the first step. Maybe there have been a lot of negative feelings in your relationship and that has led to resentment. When left unchecked, resentment can become toxic, building up in the relationship like poison in your system, until it becomes lethal to your connection. *It is vital to the continuation of love in a healthy relationship that you find some way to deal with resentment*, and this next process is designed just for that.

Renewing Your Love: Putting the Past in the Past

Randy and Denise had a problem. He had promised to take her shopping for some new furniture and help her with the purchase. When they went, he ended up chasing after his five-year-old son, and Denise was left to handle the salesperson on her own, the very thing for which she had expressly wanted Randy's help. This wasn't the first time he had failed to follow through on something he had promised, so she was very angry when it happened once again.

When Denise tried to talk to Randy about how she felt, he made the classic communication error that people so often do in these circumstances. Before she could adequately express her feelings, he interrupted her, acknowledged failure to keep his agreement with her, and apologized. When Denise tried to continue, he cut her off, saying, "Why are you going on and on about this? I said I'm sorry, what more do you want?" The conversation broke down, and both Denise and Randy went away angry. Over the next few weeks, they made several attempts to discuss this issue, each time building more resentment as Denise tried to express her anger and Randy continued to argue that they had already covered that ground. "Let's put the past in the past," he said, leaving Denise more and more frustrated and angry.

One day, Randy sat down to do some self-reflection, and realized that he had been asking himself a question that had no good answer: "Why is she such a b****?" Thinking it over, he had to acknowledge that this wasn't helping their problem, but only making it worse, as it led to only one conclusion: His partner was awful and the one to blame.

That day, he asked himself a new question: "How can we move out of this state of anger and blame and resolve the issue?" This shift in his attitude now opened new possibilities of partnership and resolution. He went to Denise and asked her, "What can I do to help us resolve this issue?" to which she responded, "How about just letting me talk about it, all the way through, no interruptions, no defenses, just expressing everything that happened and how I felt?" He agreed, and that's what they did.

As Denise talked, Randy did nothing but nod his head, say "uh-huh" and "I understand how that must have felt" and "tell me more about that" and "what else?" until she was finally through. When "what else?" elicited "nothing, there's no more," she asked him to say something that would convey to her that he understood how she felt and what the real issue was to her (Mirroring). So, he did just that. When all was said and done, it turned out that what had really been troubling her wasn't the events of that day but the fact that she had never gotten to express to him how upset she was and have her feelings validated. When he gave her that, she was finally released from the energy of the incident. They went on to have a truly wonderful weekend of intimacy and connection together.

Randy and Denise both wanted to put the past in the past and enjoy the present, and it took this one vital step to make it possible:

Full Expression of Feelings and Listening Well

Over and over again, I see couples who have become stalled in their relationship because of painful feelings that have never been fully expressed and listened to. Eventually, the anger and resentment is more about not being heard than it is about the incident itself. *The healing power of these exercises cannot be understated: Until we've been fully listened to, and our feelings validated, forgiveness and moving on are severely hampered if not completely impossible.*

Once our feelings have been heard, forgiveness often happens naturally. Emotional healing flows from compassionate listening and validation, both of which are gifts. Like any other loving behavior, we may withhold these gifts out of anger and resentment, thus unwittingly keeping the problem alive. Withholding compassionate listening causes the buildup of toxic resentment which, over time, erodes the very foundation of the relationship, your love and trust.

Thus, it becomes a vicious cycle. You hurt me, and you won't listen to me about how I feel about it. Therefore, I won't listen to you. We both walk around resentful, angry, and withholding compassionate listening. Do this for a long enough period of time, and you will certainly break up or divorce.

This cycle can be broken, and it only takes one person to break the deadlock. Like Randy, you can shift your attitude, open up the lines of communication by sitting down with your partner and giving the gift of listening, and begin the healing.

Shifting the Attitude

Ongoing resentment is highly toxic to a love relationship. It can lead to rage, health problems, abusive treatment, breakup, and divorce. *Most resentment is caused by a negative interpretation of your partner and of his behavior.*

What he did was bad enough, but what you think of him because he did it is even worse. "Not only did you forget about our plans for today and go do your own thing without me, but you are a selfish, self-centered jerk for doing that! Furthermore, I know you did it on purpose to hurt me, and that's unforgivable." Stewing in this kind of angry inner dialogue, you leave no room to hear anything new, so whatever he says later will fall on your deaf ears.

Typical negative interpretations that lead to resentment include:

- You did it *on purpose*, intentionally, to hurt me (belief in evil intentions)
- You knew better, and yet you chose to do it anyway
- You don't care about me or our relationship
- You're trying to drive me crazy
- You're trying to make me break up with you

It is possible, by the way, that you are right. Sometimes, people will deliberately do that which they know will yank your chain, or they will become careless of your needs out of their own resentment. This is to be expected, and is an unfortunate part of the human condition, not that that makes it okay.

If you believe that your partner is deliberately and maliciously setting out to hurt you *most of the time*, then either you're paranoid or you're in a relationship with an abusive person. Either way, you can address the situation by seeking professional help immediately.

Otherwise, *give up your belief in evil intentions.* Constantly thinking that your partner is setting out to harm you creates chaos in the relationship and shuts down communication. Shift your attitude back to a basic belief in the good will of your lover. Assume the best, and be surprised when you discover otherwise. Then, use this next process to clear out any old, lingering resentments.

Apology and Forgiveness

After you've listened to each other fully about the incident or issue, if you still find that you have resentment, you now have some important questions to ask yourself:

Am I willing to forgive my partner and move on? Or, is it more important for me to hold on to this resentment and keep my heart closed to my partner? Am I willing to pay the price for that? Do I want to be right, or do I want to be happy?

If you decide that you'd rather be happy, then this next process is for you. First, some basics on Apology:

Apologizing is different than saying "I'm sorry," which actually is a statement of feelings. "I'm sorry it rained today. I'm sorry I yelled at you." This reports on my internal feelings of regret about circumstances or about my behavior, and is certainly relevant at times.

Saying "I apologize for hanging up the telephone while you were talking to me last night. I know that I really hurt you," extends something new out into the relationship than saying "I'm sorry" does. More than a mere statement of feelings, it lets you know that I take responsibility for my actions that affect you. It also gives you the opportunity to address what I did to you.

Apology is appropriate for those things that we deliberately do to hurt each other. Difficult as it sometimes is to admit, we all do things from time to time to "dig" our partners, usually in retaliation for something we perceive that they did to us. Rather than expend tons of energy trying to cover up our misdeeds, it is far more powerful to admit our perpetrations, own up to the fact that we hurt our partner on purpose, and apologize.

Apologizing is also appropriate for those things we do unconsciously that hurt others. These are the apologies that often don't happen. The myth is that since "I didn't mean to do it," I therefore owe no apology to you. In fact, even accidentally hurtful things are still painful and can cause resentment that affects your relationship. It goes a long way toward healing in the relationship when we can admit our unconscious failures, as well as our conscious ones. Also, apologizing for the things we didn't mean to do makes us more mindful of the sensitive emotional buttons our partner has, and thus less likely to press them in the future.

Now, some basics on forgiveness:

Forgiveness comes from the heart and cannot be faked. Saying "I forgive you" is a gift that you give to your partner in the relationship. It says, "I hear your apology, and I appreciate you for making it, and I release my anger toward you. I recognize your humanity and the fact that you are not perfect. I willingly return to a state of love with you." In essence, forgiveness means "giving (love) as you gave before."

Forgiveness doesn't mean forgetting. Memory erasure doesn't come along with forgiveness, although by forgiving, you promise to hold the incident against your partner no longer. You consciously choose to let go of the energy around it, and to let it recede in your mind and emotions. You agree not to bring it up in the future as a weapon against your partner.

Forgiveness is not condoning the behavior. The myth is that if I forgive you, I'm sending a message that what you did was okay and that you have my permission to do it again. In fact, it's possible both to forgive *and* absolutely condemn the behavior. Forgiveness is in no way carte blanche for you or your partner to repeat hurtful behavior.

Forgiveness doesn't preclude an alteration in the relationship. In some cases there may be forgiveness but not an automatic return to the same old same old. Just because you forgive your ex-fiancé for his latest drunken episode doesn't mean the engagement is automatically back on. Sometimes forgiveness paves the way to new choices, and that may include a separation or breakup.

Forgiveness is not conditional upon the future. In other words, "I'll only forgive you if you promise never to do it again" doesn't count. This isn't true forgiveness, which is strictly about the past, but manipulation. In setting this condition, you are trying to get your partner to change, not really forgiving her.

Forgiveness doesn't have to be justified. Often we think, "I'll forgive you if I can find a way to believe that you deserve it." The truth is that no one deserves it, and everyone deserves it. As human beings, we all do bad things from time to time. We get up in the morning, eat breakfast, go to work, interact with people, come home and interact with our significant others, and we do things that hurt ourselves and others in the course of those activities. We are all flawed and therefore in constant need of forgiveness. None of us deserves it, yet we all crave it for emotional healing, both within ourselves and within our relationships. Forgiveness frees up the negative energy within ourselves and allows us, when we are the forgiver, to move ahead in a positive direction.

Forgiveness isn't necessarily permanent. As emotional beings, we may forgive one day, and get "hooked" into anger the next day about the same thing once again. This doesn't mean that the forgiveness of yesterday was a mistake, but rather, that what's called for today is to forgive again.

Forgiveness isn't a debt to be paid. We don't "owe" forgiveness to anyone. It is a gift in a relationship, freely given, from the heart, no strings attached.

Forgiveness is as important for self as it is for others. Experiencing remorse for things we've done wrong is one thing: This is a desirable human emotion, without which we would all be career criminals. Wallowing in guilt is another. This serves no purpose except to punish ourselves for our wrongs, real or imagined. Contrary to popular belief, prolonged guilt does not prevent future misdeeds. In fact, many people experience this as sufficient punishment to justify repeating the behavior. We contribute to our own emotional healing when we forgive ourselves, just as we do when we forgive others.

On resentment:

Resentment is not effective as punishment for the other person. The only person who suffers from my resentment is myself, as I harbor these toxic emotions in my body and soul.

Resentment is not effective as an antidote for pain. Being resentful enables us to put up emotional walls, giving us the illusion that we are then protected from hurt. In reality, this creates more pain, as the relationship deteriorates, distance builds up, and a painful breakup becomes inevitable.

It is misleading to justify resentment by making a judgment about the other person. Rather than just say, "I don't like what you did, it hurt me, and I would like you not to do that again," we say things like "Anybody with any brains would know not to do that, so you either don't care for me at all or you have no brains. Which is it?" Or, "Everyone knows you can't do that in a relationship." These assessments take you away from the simple truth: *You don't like the behavior.* Your partner is trapped in a no-win, with only one choice, to defend herself. As a result, the cycle of hurt is perpetuated and resolution becomes impossible.

One additional step, and one that is often overlooked, is to make room for the request for an apology. Many believe, and you may, that your partner should know exactly what he did that hurt you. The reality is that what hurts one person may not cause any problem with another. The upshot is that we don't always see exactly how we've done emotional damage and so it is important to see clearly how we have, and take steps not to repeat it.

After Listening Empty, most likely your partner will make the appropriate apologies. If there's something he's missed, and it's important to you that it be acknowledged, then *ask for it.*

"There's one more thing. I'd also like an apology for rolling your eyes at me when I bring things up to you. It seems as if you're real put out with me, and that makes it hard for me to express my feelings to you."

"I can see how that's a problem, and I guess I don't always realize I'm doing it. I apologize for doing that to you."

Apologizing, forgiving, and releasing resentment renews love in a relationship. It enables you to reconnect at a basic level and to re-create yourselves as partners and teammates. Let's look at Randy and Denise's story once again to see how this process works.

After Listening Empty to Denise and Mirroring her thoughts and emotions, Randy begins the Apology and Forgiveness process:

HE: I apologize for not keeping my commitment to support you in buying your furniture that day, Denise. I realize that I hurt you, and that you felt very let down by me, and I'm truly sorry about your pain.

SHE: Thank you for acknowledging my pain, and I appreciate your heartfelt apology. It means a lot to me that you recognize how hurt I was. I do forgive you, sweetheart. Do you forgive yourself? [Supporting him in being self-caring.]

HE: Yes, I do forgive myself. I want to move past this.

SHE: Good, I'm glad you see it that way.

HE: I have something else to say. I apologize for not listening to you about your feelings, and, in fact, actually blocking you at times from expressing them. I really hate the pain that I caused you by doing that. Can you forgive me for that?

SHE: That means a lot to me for you to say that. Of course, I forgive you.

HE: Thank you. I've really been feeling bad about that. Hard as it is, I forgive myself, also.

SHE: I have something for you. I apologize for being so resentful toward you for not listening to me, and for getting even by yelling at you for other things. I apologize for not being straight and telling you what I was really angry about.

HE: It feels really good for you to acknowledge that. At times, I thought it might be connected, but I wasn't sure. I do forgive you for that, honey.

SHE: And I forgive myself.

HE: Thank you for doing this with me. You're the best, you know it? I really love you.

SHE: So are you. I love you, too.

And you can imagine what happened next. This couple was powerfully reconnected, even after some very difficult times, through the magic of full and complete communication. Once again, here is an outline of the *basic steps to conflict resolution*:

1. Manage your own anger in a healthy way.
2. Seek understanding first: Listen Well to your partner.
3. Mirror your partner's thoughts and feelings.
4. Validate your partner's feelings and perceptions.
5. Ask for Empty Listening before you speak.
6. Speak Well, using "I" statements and responsibility.
7. Ask for Mirroring.
8. Apologize for whatever you did that hurt your partner, based on what you hear from him.
9. Forgive your partner for whatever she has done.

Apology and Forgiveness: Pitfalls

These processes only work when they are practiced with heartfelt sincerity, love, honesty, and genuineness.

Don't make this into something mechanical, going through the motions because you think you're supposed to. Only when it's authentic is it healing.

Don't blend all your apologies together. Apologizing for everything is just as ineffective as apologizing for nothing. Be specific about what you're apologizing for, and take it one incident or habit at a time.

Never apologize for your own emotions. Because you can't directly *control your* feelings, there's nothing to apologize for. Always make amends for your *behavior or your attitude, both of which you have choices about,* not your emotions, about which you have little choice.

Never apologize for someone else's emotions. You can make amends for the effect that your behavior had on someone, but since you don't control his feelings, you can't apologize for that. You can say you're sorry, that you feel bad about his hurt feelings, as this is a statement of your own remorse.

If you find that you're stuck, that forgiveness is blocked, don't try to force it or fake it. Stop and consider:

Is my response connected to something in my past? Sometimes the anger you feel may be out of proportion to the present event, and that's a big clue that there's a "hook" to something much older.

Does it feel as if I'll give up too much power if I forgive? Forgiveness opens the door to vulnerability, and sometimes that seems too scary, especially if there's a long and toxic history.

Seek outside help if you can't give up the resentment. If forgiveness continues to be blocked, even after you've given yourself time to work through the feelings and you've done your anger work, get help.

Moving On

After all of these steps, you still have one more, and it is crucial to your future success: *Create a plan for dealing with the issue(s) in the future.* Because this involves both of you, each of you contributes to the plan.

You can do this through making requests and negotiating in a loving way, like these couples:

- Rene and Paul had problems with his overpowering her in arguments. She requested that he back off when she got overwhelmed, and he asked her for a signal, so she suggested a yellow flag, which became a small scarf that she carried around and would bring out and wave when the conversation became too intense for her.
- Donna and her husband Mike had very different frequency rates regarding sex. He complained that he was always initiating, while she complained that this just wasn't part of her natural behavior. One day, Donna purchased a beautiful music box, which she and Mike decided would be their signal for romance. When Donna was ready, she gave the box to Mike, signaling her interest in intimacy. Thus, she didn't have to initiate sex outwardly, something that she was very uncomfortable with, and he could feel that she was expressing her interest in him.

Negotiating Wants

One of the greatest misnomers in modern relationships is the term *needs*. It's true that we all crave certain things from our lover: to be treated with kindness and respect, to receive affection, to be listened to with compassion, and so on. To cover this ground, modern self-help literature has coined the term *emotional needs*, which has become a kind of catch-all phrase that we throw about quite a bit.

The problem with this term is that it's misleading. What we *want* in a relationship are things that we don't actually *need* from a lover. Let me explain. We need water, air, and food to live. We need shelter from the elements. These things are basic to our survival, so they are defined as true needs.

We also have social needs. Most humans don't thrive and will even deteriorate dramatically when they completely lack social contact, such as companionship, conversation, and the gentle touch of a friend. When these needs are met, we thrive, even when we have no significant partner.

What is available in a love relationship are things we *very badly want*, but they are the icing on the cake of life and not really needs, in the sense that they are not essential to survival. We don't truly need a lover, even though it's true that most people are happier when in a love relationship than when not. We don't even need sex, contrary to popular belief. There are many who lead full, productive lives of celibacy.

Therefore, when talking to a lover and asking for emotional gifts, it's important to use the word *want* rather than the word *need*, which puts a heavy burden on the listener. Saying "I need you to take me out to dinner every Friday night" sounds as if you'll die if you don't get it. Furthermore, it places the responsibility for your well-being squarely on your partner.

Saying "I would like for us to plan a date every week" states what you want, but keeps the burden of responsibility for your well-being on you. It says that you're in touch with yourself, know what you want, and are capable of asking for it, as well as able to deal with hearing the always possible no.

So, by all means, *negotiate for your wants in a relationship*. Prioritize them and *be honest about what's really important* and what's not such a big deal. "I'd like to go out dancing Friday night, but since we're going out Saturday night also, it's not that important." "I want you to kiss me when you get home at night, and that's very important to me. It tells me that you love me and are happy to see me."

Rather than "I need," use the terms "I want," "I would prefer," "I would like," and "would you." Take responsibility for the fact that your wants are unique, ask for them, and realize that you don't always get everything you want. Be willing to negotiate with respect and compassion.

Designing Behavioral Agreements

For those areas of your relationship in which you've experienced problems, having a plan for future behavior helps, one which each of you commits to following. Love is much more than feelings, it is action that demonstrates care and respect for your partner and for the relationship. It's not enough just to keep doing the same things over and over, apologizing and forgiving but making no changes.

Be creative in your new plans for loving behavior. Brainstorm various ideas until you find one that fits for you both. Here's how to brainstorm: Throw out ideas, rapid-fire, not worrying about how silly they may sound. All ideas are okay, and no one's are put down. Do this until you've exhausted yourselves, writing them all down. Then, go back and pick out the ones that seem most feasible, putting a star beside them. Choose one that you both agree is workable, and implement it.

Hot Topics

Typical areas that couples struggle about include:

Keeping time agreements. It's vitally important to the health of your relationship that you do what you say you're going to do, and that especially means arriving on time for dates with your partner. This communicates the message that you're trustworthy, and provides stability in the relationship.

Keeping other agreements. Whether time or otherwise, keeping agreements that you have made with each other builds trust and keeps your love on track.

When you go offtrack with your agreements, use the processes above to re-create the flow of love, then design new agreements, with built-in safety measures or consequences. This might mean that the one who's on time only waits for so long and, if the other doesn't show up or call, goes ahead with other plans.

Conflicting wants:

1. Physical intimacy/sexual frequency
2. Amount of time together (distance and space)
3. Amount of time spent in conversation
4. Leisure activities
5. Involvement with children
6. Involvement with other couples
7. Other friendships
8. Contact with ex-partners and ex-spouses

9. Commitment

10. Relationship boundaries, including infidelity

When you struggle over these hot topics, keep in mind that there are always going to be certain differences between you, and one person is not necessarily right or wrong but just has a different feeling or opinion on the subject than the other. There are also differences between the two genders that contribute to these conflicts, as well. For instance, women tend to be much more verbal than men, and thus want more talking time in their relationships. Men tend to need sex in order to feel love, while women tend to need love in order to feel sexual, so men might find themselves asking for more physically intimate time in their relationships.

What's important is that you respect each other's differences, and that you continually work to understand one another, validate each other, and re-create the flow of love on a day-to-day basis through the healing conversations outlined in this chapter.

While these processes may seem somewhat awkward and stilted when you first incorporate them, remember that you're exercising emotional muscles that may not have been used much in the past. Continue practicing until you feel more natural. You won't ever be 100 percent spontaneous in these processes, but you'll certainly become very competent and at ease with them. Remember that all good communication habits require ongoing training. *You'll be in training for these skills for a lifetime!* So, get used to having to work at communication, and give up the expectation that you'll ever be completely perfect at it.

Exercise

Remember the list of communication habits that don't work earlier in the chapter? You can use this list to promote your growth whether you are currently single or whether you are in a relationship by doing this simple exercise:

• Go through the list and be brutally honest about your own behavior. If you've done it, put a check mark beside it. Make a commitment to yourself to end these destructive communication habits. You can do this by catching yourself in the act and then immediately making amends, such as apologizing and listening to its effect on the other person.

• If you're in a relationship, each of you go over the list individually and separately, looking only at your own behavior.

• Talk to each other, owning up to your own errors in the past and apologizing to your partner for each one. Forgive each other wherever possible.

• Last, create a structure for how to deal with the behaviors in the future. The way to do this is for the person who has the problem to create the solution, and ask her partner for support in implementing that. Examples:

"The next time I accuse you or blame you, gently ask me to reword what I just said and I'll take that as my cue to take the 'you' out of what I'm saying."

My sweetheart and I were talking one night while he was focused on setting the VCR to tape a movie. He was turned toward the TV, and after a few minutes of this, feeling ignored, I stopped, and this conversation ensued.

ME: You're not listening to me.
HE: Yes, I am (still looking at the television).
ME: No, you're not.
HE: (Looks at me, pauses, then, in a playful tone of voice) That's not right.
ME: What's not right?
HE: (Still lighthearted) You can't tell me I'm not listening, because only I know whether I am or not. You can say, "I want you to look at me when I'm talking to you because when you're looking away I can't tell if you're really listening, and it makes me feel ignored."
ME: (Laughing) You're right, honey. (I repeat what he said, we both smile and reconnect, and the original conversation continues.)

Another example is to agree that when one of you wants to exit because the conversation is getting too heated, that you will return at a certain time to continue the talk and resolve the conflict.

Some couples agree never to go to sleep angry with one another.

Other couples have secret hand signals that they use when in public to let each other know when a boundary has been crossed.

It doesn't matter what agreement you come up with, even if it's to agree to disagree! Some couples have certain topics about which they know they'll never agree, so they have a pact to not bring them up unless it's absolutely necessary.

What's important is that you're using these communication processes to renew your love, bring you back together, and reexperience the sense of being a team, working with each other, rather than against each other. From that place of love and connection, you are empowered to create new behavioral plans that will carry your relationship forward.

12

You and Me and Commitment

♥　♥　♥

A friend of mine, whom I'll call Jason, had a conversation with me one day about his nine-year relationship with his live-in love, whom I'll call Leeanne. He shared with me some of the insights he'd had through the significant relationships he'd had with women, including his current partnership. "The good times in a relationship aren't worth a whole lot," he said. "It's when you get into the bad times, the really painful part, and you stay, and get through it, that you find yourself, and that you find the true worth of the relationship. You create something together that's just priceless." He went on to talk about how relationships bring you into contact with the same feelings you had as a child.

"Most people think that the goal in life is to avoid ever going through the pain you suffered as a child," Jason told me. "So if you start to feel bad in a relationship, you get out as quickly as you can, because you just don't want to go there and you think you're saving yourself. The real keys to heaven, as I see it now, are in stepping into those feelings, and by going through them you eventually get past them. What you find when you stay in a relationship through the bad and get to the other side is a depth and a feeling that is indescribable."

Jason then talked about how he progressed in his relationship with Leeanne from fighting over the little things, and resenting, to acceptance. "Now, the things that used to drive me up the wall, I just love about her. I know Leeanne's not perfect, but the thought of living without her gives me a feeling of total devastation. I know she's the person I'm supposed to go through life and work on my issues with."

Jason's story shows two important things about romantic love:

- How repeated practice at conflict resolution builds emotional muscle and deepens your love and connection
- How the path of commitment allows a couple to build something really worthwhile

Commitment is the foundation of any lasting love. When a couple agrees that they will stay together on more than merely a here-today-gone-tomorrow basis, they begin to build substance into their connection. When we commit, rather than each of us having one foot out the door, we plant ourselves solidly in the same room together. Now, we can discuss our issues. We have a firm basis from which to resolve conflict, express our wants and needs, and build this thing called relationship. Commitment

Creates psychological safety. It's safer to open up in a committed relationship because we have agreed that we are there for each other. We have an investment in the relationship and, therefore, in maintaining our connection. It's a sort of an emotional safety net, a way of saying that we're in this together, each taking an equal amount of risk in whatever situation may arise.

Provides stability. We're now a couple, in our own eyes and in the eyes of the people around us. Our agreement to work on the relationship together grounds us and provides us with a certain amount of predictability. We know that if we have a problem today, we'll be talking about it today or tomorrow. We also know that we'll be seeing each other on a regular basis, which also allows us to have a reasonable degree of security about our relationship.

Commitment doesn't happen overnight, and the path to it is unique for every relationship. How do you get from "just dating" to making a commitment? The answer lies in the development of an emotional bond and, most importantly, the quality of your communication. *How you speak and listen to one another will have everything to do with moving your romance to the next level.*

Commitment: Getting from Me to We

Sooner or later, every dating relationship arrives at the point of choice: Do we make a commitment to each other or do we move on? How we manage this choice, through conversation, will set the stage for either a loving, healthy connection, or for clashing needs and heartbreak.

The central task for any love relationship is getting from Me to We. In the beginning, love is a very selfish thing. Romantic highs, starry nights, and sun-kissed days give us lots of good feelings. For many, these feelings are like water in the desert, and we drink them up as if they are endless and will last forever. We freely give because we're getting so much in return and because it's all so easy. "What would you like, my love?" we ask, knowing that the answer will be something that's just as pleasurable for the giver as for the receiver.

But endless bliss is not the path of true love. Instead, it is self-knowing, development of emotional muscle, and the ability to give freely, without focusing on the return. Ultimately, it is out of the greatest self-love that we become the most loving to our partners. The development of these qualities in a relationship takes work, and only happens through the fallout of romantic love that is inevitable, and the long, difficult climb into real love.

To do this work, we must connect with someone whom we trust and who is willing to walk the path of real love with us. We must move from a selfish, ego-centered state of Me (what do I want, what do I need, what will satisfy me?) to an openhearted, riskier, yet more rewarding, state of We (what's best for our relationship?).

In dating, we can't know if we will be able to make that leap with a person we've just met or seen only a few times. Getting to know each other, discovering and uncovering our values, preferences, and goals in life helps us understand each other. We do all of this through conversation. Out of understanding either comes the realization that there's just no lasting love connection, or that there are fledgling emotional bonds being formed between ourselves and another, which are strengthened over time through our ongoing conversations and loving behavior. This is the process from Me to We: It is characterized by hundreds of interactions, countless conversations, and the development of real love.

Stages of Commitment

In the beginning, there is no commitment beyond the next date, even though there may be expectations and inferences. Once you've progressed to the Shopping Conversation, however long that takes, the next step is usually centered around the issue of exclusivity. Every relationship is unique, but the general progression in the stages of commitment goes something like this:

1. From *dates with no promise of tomorrow* you move to
2. *The Shopping Conversation*, in which you determine that you're looking for the same thing. You continue to date, and eventually you discuss
3. *Exclusivity* (preferably before becoming sexually intimate)
At first, exclusivity means that you don't date or have sex with anyone else. Eventually, this deepens into *Emotional Exclusivity*, which implies much more. This means that you focus strictly on this relationship and no longer carry on flirtations with others, nor do you consider yourself available for any other kind of romantic connection. You continue building your relationship until you move to
4. *Commitment: An agreement to work on the relationship*
Now you are more than dating partners or even lovers. This stage signifies that each of you is willing to come to the negotiating table, which enables you to begin sorting out your differences, understanding your issues together, and finding ways for both of you to be supported in the relationship.
This commitment includes:
An agreement to be honest about your feelings and where you stand with each other, even if what you have to say isn't comfortable to the listener.
An agreement to disclose if one of you realizes the other is not "the one." This means that you don't continue to be with that person, knowing that he's not right for you, just so that you won't be alone or so that you can keep your partner around while you look for someone new.
At this level, the commitment is to *participate in the relationship with a genuine effort from the heart*. You endeavor to take care of

yourself, be good to your partner, and nurture the relationship. You communicate as fully as possible, you take responsibility for your own shortcomings, and you are forgiving of your partner's. You don't go outside the boundaries of the relationship, indulging in romantic connections with others that take your energy and focus away from your partner.

You are monogamous, faithful, and loyal. You stay present to deal with conflict, and you refrain from "escape hatches," such as drinking, drugging, working compulsively, or spending too much time with friends or on hobbies, that take you away from the relationship. You don't make an abrupt departure without processing your move fully through conversations with your partner.

Commitment: No Guarantees

Notice that nowhere in commitment is there any mention of a promise for forever or a guarantee that the relationship will never end. Promises of never-ending love are impossible to make in the real world. People change, life unfolds in unpredictable directions, and even the best relationships can flounder. No one is immune from the possibility of a breakup, not even love experts and ministers. Some of the most successful relationship gurus of our time have been divorced, most of them more than once. This is because *no one, no matter how committed, loving, or competent, can guarantee lasting love*, for one simple reason. A relationship involves another person, someone with a separate will and an unpredictable agenda.

Even when people marry, the best they can do is *promise* to stay until one of them dies. But they cannot guarantee it, because no one can know what circumstances might arise in the future that could affect their ability to keep that promise. In the case of abandonment, the person who's left doesn't even get a choice about whether or not the marriage ends.

While making a commitment is never a guarantee, it is a *strong intention*, and this can be very powerful when it comes from the heart. Couples who understand what commitment is really about, and who enter it when fully ready to honor and uphold it, usually find that they are able to navigate the path of real love and forge a lasting connection.

Emotional Timetables: Yours and Mine

Because you are two different people, it's not at all unusual for one person to reach emotional readiness for commitment before the other. Often, this is the woman in the relationship, although it can be the man. Regardless of who gets there first, both people's timetables must be respected. There is no right timing for commitment. The only definite statement that can be made is that it's definitely not right until both are ready.

The process of moving from dating with no promise of tomorrow to a genuine commitment from the heart may take days, weeks, months, or years, depending on the couple, their dynamics, and the emotional timetables of each. Later, we'll look at how to discuss this important issue while maintaining respect for each other's differences in timing.

Advanced You and Me Talks: When to Bring Them Up

The process of moving to commitment involves two things:

1. An ever-strengthening emotional bond
2. You and Me Conversations on a regular basis

Building love and trust between you is vital, as this is the fuel for the conversational engine. You do this through the constant repetition of loving behavior that is dependable and that your partner can count on. You call when you say you will. You show up on time. You send cards, flowers, and love letters. You give gifts, the most important of which are your listening, and your loving support and helpfulness in times of need.

Advanced You and Me Conversations open up the dialogue that helps lead you to a commitment. When do you do this? Whenever you feel the emotional impulse to do so, you can plan this kind of conversation.

Choose a good time, as you have for all of your important conversations. Wait until you're both rested, in a good emotional place with each other, and there's plenty of time to talk without interruption.

As you have with your other You and Me talks,

Prepare yourself mentally. Remind yourself that you will be okay regardless of the outcome of this conversation. Take a strong emotional stance of self-loving.

Begin with you and what you want. What are your goals for the conversation? Realize that your best approach will be to focus primarily on *understanding where you are with each other.* As always with these conversations, beware of having an agenda (I'm going to get something from you). Wait until you're sure that you can be open to any outcome, no matter how painful.

Introduce the subject of the talk.

"I'd like just to talk about us, about our relationship and how we're feeling about it. And I'd like to explore the idea of making a commitment, just our thoughts and feelings about that."

Create emotional safety. Reassure your partner that your only goal is to get your thoughts and feelings out on the table, and that you'll be okay no matter what he has to say.

"You know, Jeffrey, one of the things I love most about our relationship is that we've always been able to tell each other what we really feel. And that's all I want right now. Please know that I can handle whatever you have to say, and that even if I don't like what I hear, I appreciate your honesty and I'll be okay with it. Please don't think you have to hold back because of my feelings."

Set the stage for your own emotions.

"I just want to remind you that I might have a reaction to what you say, and I promise to be respectful even if I'm angry or hurting."

Remember both to share and listen, following the guidelines for conversations that work. What to cover:

Your feelings for each other. Now is the time to really express what's in your heart, even if you're afraid that you won't get an equivalent response. Holding back, you're sure to stymie the process. Why would either of you want to make a commitment if you aren't sure of the other's feelings for you? Even if you've said it all before, say it again.

"I really love you, more than I've ever loved anybody else. You have become a very important part of my life. The more I get to know you, the more I realize how right you are for me and how much I want to share with you."

The possibility for a long-term relationship or marriage. This is basically letting someone know that you see him as a potential life mate, not just a casual dating partner. You're not making any guarantees or promises, but you're declaring the *potential*:

"You are someone that I can, at this point, picture myself being with for a long time. While I can't see the future, it looks wide open to me right now. If our relationship continues to develop, and things go really well, I see a potential for us to be lifetime partners. I certainly want to explore that possibility with you, if that's what you want."

This step in the conversation is one that is often overlooked because it is so scary. No one wants to feel rejected, yet if there's not clarity about this, you will almost certainly get rejected later.

There's a scene in a well-known movie of a few years back in which a woman gets word that her ex-boyfriend, whom she dated for several years, is getting married. She's upset and crying, and she says to her friend: "I realize now that all that time when he said he wasn't ready to get married, what he really meant was that he didn't want to marry me!"

Time and time again, I counsel men and women who say that they're dating someone whom they wouldn't consider as lifetime partner material. Why? Because it's better than nothing! Most people would prefer going out with someone they like and enjoy, even if not right for them, to sitting home alone. While this seems cruel, it's just the reality of today's dating world.

It's my responsibility to be clear on where my partner stands with me. I do this by being truly open to any outcome, in this and in all You and Me Conversations. I also do this by establishing emotional freedom for us both to speak our minds and hearts honestly. In the Introduction to this book, I mention that my ex-husband and I traced the breakdown of our marriage back to a significant conversation in our third month of dating. That was a You and Me Conversation in which we were deciding about being exclusive and making a commitment. Looking back, I realize now that I had an agenda of getting a commitment from him, while he was terribly afraid of hurting my feelings and losing me. Years later, he confessed to me his true feelings at that time: While he liked and enjoyed me a lot, he wasn't sure that he wanted a long-term relationship, and he really wanted to continue dating around for a while. Rather than risk a loss, we both colluded to hide the truth from ourselves and each other, going forward on a very shaky foundation.

Willingness to work on the relationship for however long we're to-gether. This step is vital to your health and well-being in a relationship. Again, you're not making any promises or guarantees, but you're declaring your willingness, and commitment, to

1. Communicate as openly and honestly as you possibly can at all times.
2. Deal with the issues that come up between you, making your genuine best effort to resolve them in a way that's a win for both if at all possible.

This step plants you firmly in the relationship, for however long it lasts. It doesn't guarantee a permanent commitment or marriage, but it sets the stage for one to occur later, if that's appropriate. It requires both of you to be your best possible selves, and to act in a way that's genuinely in both of your best interests, giving you a measure of psychological safety to be in the relationship.

Agreement to inform each other if your feelings change significantly. This is a promise, in effect, that if my feelings about you or the relationship shift, I will tell you as soon as I'm aware of that. This doesn't mean that you inform your partner of every emotional up or down that you experience, but, rather, that you are aware enough to know if you have a change of heart that affects the future of the relationship, and that you disclose that when it happens.

These agreements, about working on the relationship, and informing if feelings change significantly, establish good faith. This means that we each have our hearts in the right place. We're both dedicated to making the most sincere effort that we possibly can to have a good relationship.

The *commitment* we're aiming for, then, is to

Plant ourselves firmly in the relationship, no longer indulging in emotional or other kinds of back doors.

Do our best to create something lasting, with an eye toward a permanent future and possibly marriage.

Communicate honestly and frequently, with respect and dignity, about what's relevant to our relationship.

Endeavor to resolve the issues that come up between us.

Getting to this point in the conversation can happen many ways. Witness Nancy and John. After dating for a couple of months, Nancy asked John to help her out at a professional workshop she was leading over the weekend. This conversation ensued:

HE: I guess what you're asking is for more involvement from me, that you want me to take a bigger role in your life, get behind what you're doing.

SHE: Yes, I guess I am.

HE: I view that as a commitment of sorts.

SHE: Yes, it is.

HE: I'm not sure. I'll have to think it over.

Even though Nancy didn't like John's ambivalence, she knew the best thing to do was to wait it out. Sure enough, three days later, John called.

HE: I've thought it over, and I've decided that I'm ready to make a commitment to work on the relationship.

SHE: What does that mean?

HE: It means that even though I have other choices, I'd rather be with you, so I'm not dating anyone else. It means I'm willing to communicate and be as honest as I know how to be. I want to work on it with you, and see where it goes. I really love you.

SHE: I love you, too. And that's what I want.

The No-Exit without Process Agreement

If you want to play in the Relationship Major Leagues, you can add one more item of discussion:

Agreement not to break up without processing fully. This means that you promise each other that you won't abruptly exit the relationship, especially if you are doing it because you're angry or hurt. If one of you is considering breaking up, you agree that you'll discuss it fully before you act on it. Your commitment is to stay firmly in the relationship until everything has been said and done, with compassion and honesty. A breakup only happens when full knowledge of where you stand with each other makes it clear that a separation is in your best interest and is inevitable. For shorthand, we'll refer to this as the No-Exit Agreement.

I call this the Relationship Major Leagues because it takes a special kind of couple to have this agreement. You must both be very well developed emotionally, certain of your ability to take care of yourselves individually and together. Your emotional bank account is constantly replenished from both sides.

You must have strong intentions of building a lasting relationship, while still knowing that there are no guarantees. There must be lots of love, respect, and trust between you.

To have a No-Exit Agreement means that you are both well beyond the temptation to consider other potential partners. It also means that you have had lots of You and Me Conversations, and that you've shown enough of your true colors to each other to really know each other well. Clearly, honoring this agreement will be hard work at times. It would certainly be sufficient to have a commitment that goes up to, but doesn't include this item. So, why would you want to do this?

Having a No-Exit Agreement creates a high level of accountability. This means that you are called upon to be scrupulously honest, both with yourself and with your partner.

It also provides tremendous healing opportunities for you both. It means that you place yourselves in the position of having to deal with the emotional hot buttons that your relationship could push in both of you and giving you the chance to grow and learn from how you both react.

If I know that I can't make a quick getaway, and I get scared, I have nowhere to run, no place to hide, and so, I find that I might as well share my fears with you, my beloved. If we succeed in having a loving conversation, then we both get to experience the incredible healing power of being listened to about our deepest pains and fears.

If I get angry, and I can't just flee, then I will tell you about my grievances, clearing the air and paving the way for a better connection.

A No-Exit Agreement empowers you both to have an even better relationship in the future with a new partner, if that's what's appropriate. Even if we find that we must separate one day, we do so with our minds and hearts crystal clear. There's still grief to deal with, but not the heavy load of emotional baggage that an abrupt ending creates.

As I was writing this section, I was suddenly struck by the thought that *most marriages don't operate with an agreement like this.* Paradoxically, even though marriage is the highest commitment that two people can make, a promise to stay together for life, the reality is that most divorcing couples separate without much real communication. Normally, one person initiates the divorce, usually after thinking it over on her own and coming to a decision with little or no dialogue in the relationship. The fallout of this kind of unilateral decision-making about divorce is anger, pain, bitterness, legal battles over money, property, and children, and emotional baggage the size of steamer trunks.

Recently, I heard of one divorcing couple who, after deciding to split, went through a counseling process to complete their marriage. They discussed everything, their expectations when they married, their grievances, their hurt and loss. This is certainly not the norm and shows a high level of personal evolution. Undoubtedly, they will go forward with far less emotional baggage than the typical divorcing couple. Still, though, it was done in the usual fashion, *after* the fact of someone deciding "I'm out of here," rather than *before.*

A friend of mine, whom I'll call Terry, told me the story of his eight-year relationship with someone I'll refer to as Francine. "We were together for seven years," he told me, "and I was miserable for pretty much the last six. Finally, I said to her, 'We need to admit that We are not working.' I told her I wanted to separate [move out], but that I wanted to go to counseling with her. I'd done the abrupt departure thing before, and I wasn't going to drag that kind of emotional baggage with me again, or leave her saddled with it."

Terry and Francine spent several months in therapy, getting everything out on the table. They left no stone unturned in their efforts to face what was going on between them, and in looking for some way to resurrect their romance. When at last they decided to move on, it was with the absolute certainty that that was in both of their best interests.

Even though they didn't have a stated No-Exit Agreement, this couple lived the principle that bespoke this kind of commitment. Terry credits this process with his being able to move on to another relationship a couple of years later, one in which he's been able to make a lasting commitment.

In contrast, I can cite hundreds of stories of breakups that were abrupt, with very little real communication, and that left tremendous pain in their wake. One story that immediately comes to mind is that of Greg and Rene, who dated and lived together for a total of six years. They were discussing marriage and both knew that Rene was having difficulty committing. Suddenly, she announced that she had taken a job in another state, that they were separating, and that she wanted Greg to move out of her condo. As soon as she moved, she cut off communication, thereby aborting for Greg, and for herself, the process of understanding what happened between them. This is unilateral decision-making in the extreme, and the effect was devastating. Three years later, Greg is still picking up the emotional pieces.

The No-Exit Agreement doesn't prevent you from breaking up, any more than marriage prevents divorce. What it does do, that even marriage doesn't, if you honor it, is *require you to stay in the relationship until everything has been communicated*. I actually think that this kind of promise is even more challenging than saying you'll never leave, which is really a promise that you can't guarantee you'll keep. This is a very high level of commitment that calls for each person in the relationship to be thoroughly accountable. I can't help but wonder what might be possible for marriages if more people were able to reach this level of commitment before they spoke their vows.

A relationship must be evolved to a very high level before you can have a safe No-Exit Agreement. Obviously, this must be a relationship in which there are no issues of emotional, physical, or substance abuse. There's tremendous love and trust between you, so that you can be reasonably certain that your partner will be able to uphold the agreement. How long it takes to get to this level will vary. Some couples will be ready after dating for a year or two. Some will not be ready until after marriage. Some will never be ready, due to the unstable dynamics of their relationship. Whenever and however you approach it, do so with much discussion and exploration together, and only make this commitment when you are both really ready.

You and Me: Getting Stuck in the Conversation

As you can see, each one of these steps builds on the ones before. Your feelings for each other, if matching, give you the heart to go to the next step and discuss the possibility of a future together. If you both see the possibility of a future, then you can discuss and agree on your willingness to work on the relationship. Once you've gotten that far, it's then quite natural to agree that you will let each other know if there's a significant change of heart.

But what if you get stuck on one of the steps? Maybe one of you is in love, while the other isn't. "I love you, Mary, but I don't know if I'm *in love* with you," is a frequent statement that one person will make. Before you attempt to go to the next step in the conversation, stop and consider how you feel about what you're hearing. Talk about it, keeping your dialogue centered on this part until you are totally clear about what's being said and felt.

"How important is it to you to feel in love with me, Andrew? What does that mean to you?" Ask questions for clarification, paying attention to what's not being said as well as to the words themselves. Give feedback about what you hear, checking to see if what you're hearing is what the speaker means. "It sounds like being in love is very important to you, Andrew, and you just don't feel that way about me." "I'm hearing you say that, even though you love me, Leslie, you're not sure that you see a future . . ." Once you're certain that you understand where your partner is coming from, you have some choices to make.

Some couples go forward, knowing that one person's heart is in a different place than the other's. Helen and Bill went forward, making a commitment to work on the relationship, knowing that Helen's feelings for Bill were not equal to his for her. Bill, fully informed that Helen did not see the possibility of a permanent future, chose to take that risk. Months later, Helen's feelings had shifted and were on more equal ground to Bill's.

Others decide that the risk isn't worth it if there's not a match in all of these steps, and that's a legitimate choice as well. There is no right way to handle these conversations. The goal is understanding, and from there you make a choice, possibly taking a calculated risk, but that's always the case with relationships. From Me to We takes time and patience, and lots of these conversations may be necessary to get you there. The journey may be rough or it may be smooth, and is as unique for each relationship as our fingerprints are to us as individuals.

Me to We: Not Sure

What if you're having this conversation, and you're not sure about how you feel? Communication can easily break down, as you each fumble around in the dark, trying to make sense out of what's happening. If you aren't sure of your feelings, that usually signifies ambivalence, meaning that you feel two ways about something. "On the one hand, I love you. On the other hand, there are some things about our relationship that concern me."

Not being sure about your feelings doesn't mean that you must wait until you are sure before you talk about commitment. What's important is that you get things out on the table. If you're ambivalent, tell your lover about it. Talk about:

Your doubts and fears. Sometimes just getting the fear expressed, with someone who is listening compassionately, diminishes it considerably.

Taking your time before committing. Commitment must be genuine, from the heart, and it's important that you feel congruence, meaning that you both *know* and *feel* that this is the next right step for you.

"As much as I love you, Gary, I'm just not ready yet to make this level of commitment. It's only been a few months since my divorce, and I'm still dealing with that emotionally. I'm still afraid of making another mistake, and I want to get beyond more of that fear before I commit."

Tell your lover what you want:

"I'd like you to give me more time to adjust to single life, and just take care of myself, before I make this commitment. Let's still see each other, but maybe not quite as often, if you can handle that. I want to talk about it again in, say six months."

Close, But No Cigar

What if you can't reach a point of total agreement? Kenny wanted a commitment to work on the relationship with an eye toward the future. Sherry wanted exclusivity but couldn't see the future. They found middle ground by making an agreement to be honest and communicate, and see where the relationship would go.

Just because you're having this talk doesn't mean that you'll necessarily arrive at a point of total agreement at the same time. Emotional timetables being different, it's not at all unusual for one person to be in one place regarding the level of commitment while the other is somewhere else entirely.

Persuading Versus Allowing

When you're not completely in sync, and you're the one wanting more, it's tempting to push for more commitment than the other is ready for. *This never works, it always eventually breaks down.* Only a genuine commitment from the heart has any real substance to it and can withstand the test of time and conflicting needs two people will inevitably feel.

Carol, after dating Harry for almost three years, was ready for a commitment, but he wasn't making any moves that way. Frustrated, she sought advice from a long-married girlfriend, who told her, "The more you push for it, the farther away it seems to get. What you have to do is find a way within yourself to be truly okay with *the way it is, expecting nothing more.*" Carol worked on this attitude until, finally, she truly felt grateful for what she had, which was a very good, loving relationship. Within a couple of weeks of her emotional shift, Harry brought up the subject of commitment. As they began planning their future, it was with his heart wholly in it, giving them a powerful foundation upon which to build their long-term relationship.

You're falling into the trap of *persuasion* if you find yourself

- Trying to convince your partner about how wonderful or right commitment is

- Doing most of the talking
- Impatient with listening to where your partner is
- Resorting to manipulation, such as issuing ultimatums, crying, or threatening to either date someone else or break up

You're *allowing* when you

- Are genuinely respectful of where your partner is
- Listen to her feelings about commitment
- State what you want, then drop it
- Are grateful for the quality of the relationship that you have with your partner
- Allow plenty of time for your partner to process what you've discussed
- Have no particular agenda or timetable in mind

Commitment? Not Me

Sometimes, a You and Me Conversation uncovers the fact that you're very far apart about what you want. One of you wants a commitment, while the other wants a no-strings romance. Communication can easily break down at this point, as you retreat due to hurt feelings and thwarted expectations. It's important to hang in there at these times until you get total clarity. There are some things you might ask:

- Is this how you always want it with me, or do you see the possibility of more commitment later?
- Is this about your fear, or not being ready, or is it that you don't see me as "the one"?
- What do you want from me?

Once you are clear about where your partner is coming from, you can then make an informed decision about what's right for you.

Can't Get to We: Hang In There or Break Up?

Maybe you've had more than one You and Me Conversation. You've shared where you are, you've listened openly and patiently to your partner, you've stated what you've wanted. You've *allowed it to be the way it is*, for as long as you think you can stand it. Still, you don't have a commitment. How do you know when to persevere, and when to throw in the towel?

First of all, get clear with yourself. Doing some self-reflection about your motivations will help you decide what's best. Before you break up over the issue of commitment, stop and ask yourself a few questions:

Am I "commitment hungry"? Sometimes the focus is far too much on getting the commitment and not enough on the quality of the relationship itself. Sometimes the illusion is that getting a commitment will provide validation of self-worth or emotional security, neither of which can be obtained in any relationship, no matter how committed.

Why now? Sometimes there's a false sense of urgency in the quest for commitment, due to factors such as age, time of life, evolution in relationships of friends, or some imaginary deadline (i.e., "I've got to be in a committed relationship by the end of the year.").

Why do I want a commitment? Get clear with yourself about what you're wanting from this. If you're wanting personal growth and the opportunity to pursue the path of real love, then you're coming from an emotionally healthy place. If you're willing to take the risk that it might not last forever, and you're rock-solid in your commitment to take care of yourself, then you're ready to make a real commitment with your partner.

If you're ready for a commitment, and your partner is resisting, then there are some steps you can take before you decide to give up and move on. This process is no guarantee that you'll get the results you want, but it will help you feel that you've done all you can do, in a healthy way, to steer the relationship in that direction.

Manage any anger or resentment away from your partner. Talk to your friends, to your therapist, to a support group. Write letters and throw them away. Hit pillows and yell while no one's around.

Exercise, do gardening, go dancing, take a vacation by yourself or with friends. In short, take care of yourself and avoid the temptation to lash out at your partner in frustration.

Make sure (s)he knows what commitment means to you. Go through the steps outlined in this chapter, briefly, so that your partner knows where you're coming from, and that it's not about a guarantee or promise of forever.

"Joe, I want you to know that when we talk about commitment, it's not that I'm asking for a guarantee or a promise of forever. It's just that I want an agreement to work on the relationship together, you know, that we both put our hearts into it and give it our best, and see what the possibilities are."

Briefly share your frustration and pain with your partner. From time to time, in conversations spread out by at least a couple of weeks, tell your partner what you feel about not having a commitment, in a non-blaming way. Make it short and sweet.

"You know, Joe, I feel really hurt and disappointed sometimes that we don't have a commitment. It saddens me that we can't seem to move to that level, and I feel a loss of something special in the relationship because of that. It frustrates me that we just can't seem to get beyond whatever is in the way of that. I really love you, and a commitment with you would make me very happy."

Then, drop it! Don't drone on and on, dragging yourself and your partner into deeper levels of angst. After you've said what you have to say, drop the subject and move on to something else, something a lot lighter. The object is to *share your feelings*, not to try to manipulate him into doing something about it at this time.

Later, share what you want and why. At other times, and again, not too frequently, share your vision of what commitment would bring to the relationship.

"I really feel that we have something special, Joe, and I'd love to see it grow and flourish. It seems to me that if we made a commitment, we'd both feel a little safer to explore our thoughts and feelings, without thinking the other person is just going to run away. I want it because I believe it would help us both grow as individuals, and it would help us see if we really have something worthwhile, something lasting, or if we don't."

Then, drop it! Again, don't go on and on. Keep it short and sweet, and then move on to another topic. All you're doing is planting seeds here and there. Trust that they'll soon grow into something substantial.

Back off just a little, with notice. After you've followed the above steps for a while, tell your partner that you're taking some time for yourself. Do it in a very loving way that has a lot of self-respect and consideration for his feelings.

"You know, Joe, since you can't make up your mind about a commitment to our relationship, I feel the need to take a little bit more care of myself, just in case you decide to move on. I'd like to spend a little more time with my friends. I still love you and want to be with you, but maybe we can get together a little less often for a while so that you can really think about what you want."

Follow through on what you've said. This process does no good if you say one thing and do another. Plus, it really is important that you be self-caring at all times anyway. Give yourself and your partner a bit of a breather, and see what happens.

Practice letting go of the results. Remind yourself that what's important is the quality of your connection, not the end result. Allow the process to unfold, and be open to whatever time span it takes.

If what you're hearing through this is something like, "I'm just not sure I can do it. I'm afraid to make a commitment. I really do love you, and yes, I see the possibility of a future with you. It's me, I just have a problem with commitment," then you have reason to persist.

If, however, you hear one or more of the following, stop and reconsider before you put any more effort into the relationship:

- "I like you and enjoy being with you, but I just don't feel the way you do."
- "I'm not sure I've found the right person yet."
- "I just want to have fun. I don't even want to talk about commitment or working on a relationship."
- "I love you, but I'm not in love with you."

You and Me: Buried Treasure

Getting into this level of communication can arouse all kinds of feelings and lead to other conversations out of which we come to know and understand each other on a deeper level. Commitment is a scary topic for most of us, and is connected to past relationships and other intense associations. As we share and listen to each other in these conversations, if we allow ourselves to be truly openhearted and honest, we may uncover a surprising buried treasure, self-knowing. And, by sharing what we're uncovering about ourselves, we reveal who we are to each other, thus strengthening that emotional muscle called *intimacy*. What we discover may include

Pain from the past. Talking about commitment may bring up remembrances of times past when I gave my heart only to have it broken. This could retrigger feelings of sadness, grief, anger, and resentment, to name a few.

Fear of commitment. Because my heart has been broken before, I may suddenly feel very reluctant to take that risk again. Commitment puts me squarely in the soup, so to speak, heart on the line and vulnerable.

Pain from present relationship. Because sometimes we uncover hurt and resentments that have been stored up between us over time, I may find that I must resolve them in order for us to go forward and make a commitment.

Infidelity. Talking about commitment may uncover the fact that one of us has been considering another relationship. I may discover that you have already gone outside the boundaries that we had established in the past and been unfaithful.

And much more.

Whatever you uncover in these talks, be totally honest with yourself and with each other, thus giving you both a clear picture from which to choose what's best. Treasure what you're discovering about yourself and about your partner. Treat it with respect and care, and know that you carry this deeper awareness with you no matter what happens.

Conversational Differences

Keep in mind through these conversations that men and women tend to process information differently, and to converse in differing ways. For instance, men tend to stop talking when they experience ambivalence. Being more concrete, they tend to take the approach that it's better not to say anything until they know for sure where they stand. When they do speak, it's usually with fewer words. Women, on the other hand, are usually perfectly open to exploring all angles of their feelings, finally lighting on one after all have been discussed. You can see this difference in the way we approach shopping.

Someone recently told me that department stores plan their floor layouts based on the differences between men and women. Women, who enjoy browsing, will move all around the store, checking out all the different styles and prices before narrowing their selection to several items, which they will then try on before making a purchase. Thus, the women's items will be at the entrance, because they know that a woman will start with whatever catches her eye and browse all the way through.

Men, on the other hand, enter the store with a mission—to find and buy a particular item as quickly as possible and get out of the store—so that it doesn't matter where they place the men's items, he'll get there. Also, women buy a lot for their men, so they place his things deep in the heart of the store so that she will have to go through the women's things to get to his.

As if those differences weren't enough, then there are the relationships in which the roles are reversed. He's more emotional while she's more logical. She's more focused, while he enjoys browsing. Whatever your differences, respect them. Go into these conversations open to all kinds of pathways and outcomes. Know that both of your communication styles are right, as long as you have your hearts in the right place and a genuine dedication to understanding one another.*

---

*I highly recommend John Gray's book, *Men Are from Mars, Women Are from Venus* (New York: HarperCollins, 1992), for a very thorough understanding of the differences between men and women.

Breaking Up Is Hard to Do

Shelley, after dating for two years with no commitment, asked Warren one day if he was willing to work on their relationship, or if it was better if they moved on, to which he replied, "It's better that we move on." She had her answer, and they parted ways, though not without great sadness on both their parts.

Sometimes these conversations lead you to the undeniable realization that there's just no future together, for whatever reason. Maybe one of you just doesn't have the heart for it, or maybe you're so incompatible in some major areas that you just can't surmount your differences. Regardless of the why, you're left with the painful task of saying good-bye.

At this point, you have a choice. You can break up in one of the standard ways:

The quick getaway. Stop calling or accepting calls from your partner.

The slow cut-off. Become increasingly less available to your partner. When he calls, tell him you're very busy. When she wonders why you haven't asked her out lately, make up some poor excuse.

Force your partner into a breakup. Do something really mean or nasty, so that anyone with common sense would break up with you. "Forget" an anniversary, show up two hours late for a date, go out with someone else, cut off physical relations with no explanation. You get the idea.

Or, you can:

Break up with integrity. Obviously, I advocate this over the methods above. This means that you communicate fully with your partner before, during, and after the breakup.

Breaking up is never easy, and talking about it is even more difficult. Doing it with integrity, while often prolonging the process, allows much more emotional closure with what has happened between you both and propels you toward a better relationship in the future.

None of these guidelines are hard and fast, as every breakup is unique and as individual as the relationship itself. Generally, though, breaking up with integrity follows these basic principles and steps:

Communicate your dissatisfactions and concerns. *Before* arriving at the decision, let your partner in on the fact that you're considering breaking up, and why. Remember to take responsibility for your own feelings, and speak in a nonblaming or nonjudgmental way:

"Sara, I need to tell you that I'm not very happy with the way things have been going between us. In fact, I'm thinking about breaking up, but before I take that step, I want to talk about what's bothering me. I guess the main thing is that it doesn't seem as though you're on the same track with me. It feels like you've got one foot out the door while I'm thinking about a future with you. Let's talk about it . . ."

"Bill, it's time for us to talk about some frustrations I've got in our relationship. The biggest one is that when your daughter's around, I feel totally left out. I've found this so difficult that I'm considering breaking up. First, though, I want to talk about it and see if there's some way we can work things out."

"Kevin, I'm thinking seriously about breaking up, and I want to tell you why before I do it. Every time I've tried to have a conversation with you about our relationship, you've clammed up and refused to talk. Consequently, I have no idea where I stand with you, and this is highly disturbing to me. Before I leave, I want to give you one last chance to talk to me and tell me what's going on."

Be honest, but never vicious. It's not necessary to tell your partner that you never liked how he kissed, or that you hate her mother. Don't drag out issues that can't be resolved and that only serve to wound your partner. If you bring it up, be willing to attempt a resolution; otherwise, leave it alone.

If there's an issue that's the reason for breaking up, and you know that you're unwilling to work on it, tell your partner what it is as long as you feel that disclosure will be beneficial to him. Make sure he knows that there's nothing to be done about it as you are not willing to attempt a solution.

Make your best effort. Express yourself fully, and then listen respectfully to what your partner has to say. Stay at the negotiating table until you're *both* satisfied that there's no resolution possible.

If you haven't got the heart for the relationship, say so. Don't pussyfoot around on this issue. Your partner needs to know if there's not sufficient love to make the relationship worthwhile. Not disclosing this keeps her hanging on, hoping that when you work out your other issues, everything will be okay:

"Sally, this is no reflection on you. It's just where I am. I don't have the heart to hang in there and work on the relationship. It really feels like it's best for me to move on."

Have an apology and forgiveness process. Sit down together, and each make a list of your transgressions, and then apologize for each one. Use the guidelines from Chapter Eleven. To the degree that you're able, forgive each other, if not today, then soon. Sometimes, this process opens up new possibilities for the relationship, and you will either proceed to a more amicable breakup, or you might continue your romance with renewed heart and energy.

Acknowledge your partner. Even though you're breaking up, acknowledge your partner for all that (s)he has been and continues to be to you. You can use the guidelines from Chapter Thirteen to add this powerful process to your relationship.

Be as emotionally present as you possibly can be. As you arrive at the decision to separate, express your pain and sadness to your partner, as much as you feel emotionally safe to do so, without overpowering them.

Keep the lines of communication open. As you separate and get on with your lives, continue to dialogue with each other. This ties up the loose ends, again freeing you to move forward with greater energy and emotional freedom.

This is not an ordinary breakup, as you can see. It is an extraordinary one in that it propels you to the next level of growth. My coaching comes from the belief I hold that even breakups can be empowering to both people. It's not absolutely necessary that ending a relationship has to leave devastation and misery. Sadness, yes. Grief, of course. Some regrets, maybe. With resolution, there are still those emotions, but, in addition, there's a sense of clarity that this is the right thing to do for both people. Respect is still there, and love, even though its form will now change.

All of this is possible, through the powerful medium of communication and conversation. Remember that how you end this relationship will have everything to do with the quality of the next. Realize that the emotional muscle you build through a process like this is priceless and that you take that with you.

The Next Step: Marriage or Living Together

If you've gotten through your You and Me Conversations so far, and you're in sync, communicating fully, then your relationship will undoubtedly progress to the point of even greater choice: Do we make a lifetime commitment? This may take months or it may take years, but sooner or later, you'll probably be faced with this life-altering decision. In the next chapter, we'll explore how to discuss living together and getting married, and how to best move the relationship to the next level.

13

Wedding Bells

♥　♥　♥

Candy and Joseph are holding hands, gazing into each other's eyes. It's an enchanted evening, complete with glowing candlelight, sparkling champagne, and soft music in the background.

After dessert, Joseph pulls out a small, velvet box. He takes her hand, and says, with tears in the corners of his eyes, "I love you more than I ever dreamed I could love someone, Candy. I can't imagine my life without you. I want to share every day with you. Will you marry me?" He opens the box and there, glistening like fire and ice, sits a perfect diamond ring, which he gently slips onto her finger.

Candy, with tears streaming, can barely speak with joy, but manages to say, "Yes!" They hug and kiss and laugh. After a year and a half of blissful romance, all of their dreams are coming true.

First Comes Love, Then Comes Marriage

Joseph and Candy's story could be a typical love story, but actually it's more like a fairy tale. It would be wonderful if all relationships reached the point of lifelong commitment so smoothly and easily, but the reality is that they don't. Witness the real-life story of the following couple.

Carl and Vicki dated for two years, going out only on weekends, the last six months of which he had been seeing someone else. When Vicki got wind of his other girlfriend, she confronted Carl, and he, feeling miserable and cornered, broke off both relationships. Vicki, believing in her heart that Carl was a good man, and that what they had was worth something, forgave him, and made it clear that she'd like to continue. They did, and a year later, Carl suggested they move in together.

Living together was tough for this couple, but they were committed to resolving their differences. They fought, they made up. They loved each other fiercely, and remained honest throughout. Four years after moving in together, they were sitting in a therapist's office, talking about their relationship. Carl said something like this:

"It's been a long time, and I guess I'm ready to go to the next step. I think it's time we got hitched." The therapist knew exactly what he meant, but Vicki, not being familiar with Texas colloquialisms, was bewildered. It took her the next several seconds to realize that Carl had finally proposed! Of course, she said yes, but she added a caveat (knowing Carl well): "Let's not tell anyone for a few weeks, just in case you change your mind."

Carl and Vicki's romance is not exactly a storybook relationship, but it is a real one. It is unique and fits the personalities of the people involved, not some story line they picked up from a soap opera. Their conversations are honest and genuine, and they're not afraid to put everything out on the table. They've reached a point of acceptance of each other, loving each other for who they are, not for who they might be. They've had lots of ups and downs, but overall, they both find the relationship satisfying and worthwhile.

This is as good as it gets! *This is real love, not fairy tale romance, because it involves real people.* The path of love is unique, as individual as the people involved, and is no less valid because it doesn't match the standards set by Hollywood and the media.

The Journey of Love: Temporary or Lifelong?

When we meet and fall in love, we embark on this journey, never knowing where it will lead or how long it will last. Old nursery rhymes notwithstanding, there's no guarantee that, after love, marriage will automatically follow. Some couples manage to make the transition from blissful illusion to real love, and some don't. Some can never quite make the leap, while others are able to progress to a lifelong commitment.

Deciding if, how, and when to move to that step is a critical stage in a romantic relationship, one which, all too often, is done hurriedly or unconsciously, without the communication that's truly needed. Divorce courts are filled with couples who married too quickly, or for the wrong reasons.

There are two main reasons that marriages fail:

1. *Getting married for the wrong reason.* Some couples marry in order to get certain needs met, rather than with a full understanding of what the commitment really means and the ability to follow through with that. Typical wrong reasons to marry include:

It's time. (My age, your age, wanting children, everyone else is married, we've dated long enough, etc.)

Avoiding a breakup. We've dated for so long that breaking up would be very painful, and since neither of us wants that loss, and it feels like it's either that or get married, we'll get married.

Emotional security. If we get married, I won't have to worry about being abandoned. I want to nail everything down so I can breathe a sigh of relief and not worry so much.

Validation of self-worth. Your marrying me would prove that I'm worthwhile, that I'm truly lovable and valuable to you. It also validates that our love is real.

Infatuation. You're so beautiful, wonderful, sexy, gorgeous, handsome, etc., that I want you for my own. I've got you on a pedestal, and marrying you would prove that I'm worth something, because I landed this incredible person.

Marriage will make me and my life okay. Life looks better for married people, and I want to be one of those. My partner's love will fix whatever is wrong with me.

2. *Inability to deal with the issues that come up in marriage.* Many couples are not prepared for the reality of marriage, and thus find themselves unable to resolve conflict. They don't maintain loving behavior, and they react to fear and pain in a way that perpetuates their problems. *Most of this is due to a lack of good communication tools and the training to use them.*

The problem of marrying for the wrong reasons, or lacking the tools of communication, is so pervasive that some states are now considering legislation to make it mandatory that couples go through premarital counseling. As challenging as modern relationships are, it would make sense that couples would be signing up for this in droves. In fact, very few couples actually address their issues prior to marriage, and especially not in the office of a professional. Why?

Most people get married in a cloud of romantic fantasy. The changes that take place in the body during courtship, such as enhanced feelings of well-being brought on by an increase in the brain's chemical feel-good messengers, are so powerful that we naturally want them to last. Sitting in a therapist's office and bringing out our issues has a deflating effect, causing us to come down from the clouds and look at what we really have and what our true potential is. Who wants to do that?

The answer is, *those who are willing to forgo some of today's gratification in favor of long-term satisfaction.* Couples who wish to have a lasting relationship, and who are willing to be uncomfortable today in order to be happy tomorrow, will embrace the process of strengthening their communication skills, whether it's with a therapist, through workshops, or on their own with the help of books like this one.

The risk of this journey is that we might not make it to everlasting union. The reward is that wherever we go, it will be with love and respect, knowing that there were never any guarantees of happily-ever-after. Regardless of what happens to "us," each of us as individuals can move forward secure in the joy of having had a truly honest, openhearted, loving relationship.

Paradoxically, it's the couples who are willing to be in full communication, in a loving and respectful way, that are most likely to spend their lives together happily. It's a natural next step to move in together, and/or marry, when the quality of the relationship is so high. Through the magic of conversation, we reveal the truth of our hearts and feelings, and that leads to an increase in the level of our commitment.

You and Me: Living Together

Many couples do not consider living together a viable option, for moral and other reasons. If that's you, then this section doesn't apply to your situation and you can feel free to skip to the next.

Many couples do consider it an option, and some would actually prefer living together over marriage. If this is you, then before you talk about it, there are good reasons and not-so-good reasons to live together that are worth considering before you take action.

Like marriage, the choice to move in together is often made hastily, without much forethought, and for the wrong reasons. As a couple, it isn't wise to move in together for reasons such as

Wanting to cut down expenses. While it's true that two can generally live more cheaply than one, this isn't sufficient reason for becoming roommates. It takes a lot more than a desire to cut down on the bills for a couple to live together successfully.

For the sake of convenience. Like the first reason, this isn't enough. Living together is very challenging, and you'll need more justification than just not having to go back and forth between your separate homes to make your cohabitation a success.

As a test for marriage. Studies have shown that living together prior to marriage doesn't make it any more likely that you'll stay together if you do walk down the aisle. Yes, you'll learn more about each other, but don't assume that this is an insurance policy against divorce.

To rescue one of you financially. This is one of the worst reasons to move in together because it immediately sets up a codependent relationship that is very unhealthy. One person feels resentful, while the other feels guilty and obligated. One is up, the other is down; you no longer have a relationship between equals. It completely clouds the issues, making it impossible for you to determine your true lifetime potential. How can I tell you how I really feel, if it's negative, when you're paying my bills?

Living together is more likely to be successful when couples

- Agree that it's not a *test* for marriage, but a *step toward* marriage.
- Already have a strong commitment in place.

- Really love each other and have strong intentions of a lifetime relationship.
- Have done enough open, honest communication to be clear about where they stand with each other (lots of You and Me Conversations).
- Consciously choose living together as the next step in their relationship, and view it as a higher level of commitment.

Conversations for Living Together

Coming to the decision to live together is a conversational process just like all the others we've discussed. Early in your courtship, you would want to discuss attitudes about living together (pro or con and why).

Initially, talk about whether or not this is an option for your relationship. If you both agree that it isn't, then you're in sync. If you each have a different viewpoint as to whether you should or shouldn't, then that is something to consider and discuss. You may or may not find a middle ground. Like all other values, when you discover that you're very far apart (one is strongly against it, while the other wouldn't get married without living together first), you should stop and reconsider the relationship. If you agree that it's a viable option, then you're on the same page and the stage is set for a possible move in the future.

When do you bring up living together? As the relationship develops and depending on where you are with each other, talk about it when you feel the emotional need to do so. As with other important You and Me Conversations, choose a time when you're both in a good place emotionally, and you have plenty of uninterrupted time to talk.

Ideally, you would be clear about where you stand with each other and ready to make the decision. But, in real life, other things interfere when it comes time to move to the next level of commitment, *fear* being the number one obstacle. You don't have to be totally clear about where you are with the issue in order to go into the conversation. In fact, there's lots of value in just being willing to talk, even if you don't know where the conversation is headed.

Daryl and Robin, after dating for two years, had begun to talk about moving in together, but then the conversations seemed to stall out on his end. Robin, while they were out driving one Sunday, suggested that they look at houses. When she brought up living together, she once again could sense Daryl's reluctance to discuss it, and this conversation ensued:

SHE: I wish you would just tell me how you're feeling about it.

HE: I feel pressured, like you're ready to do it now, and that makes me feel very uncomfortable. I still get this knot in my stomach when I think about it. I'm just not ready yet.

SHE: I'm not trying to get you to do it now. In fact, I'm not ready yet, either. I guess what scares me is that you'll figure it all out in your head about what you want, and then you'll tell me. I won't get to be a part of the process with you, talking it over and coming to a decision together. Then, if I'm not ready when you are, I'm afraid you won't have the patience to let me work through my fears.

HE: (Mirrors) So, what you're saying is that you want to be a part of the process that I'm going through to be ready for this. And, you don't want me to jump ship if I get ready before you do.

SHE: Yes. I guess looking at houses is just about my wanting to be in a conversation with you. I want to hear your thoughts and feelings so I know what's coming.

HE: I understand.

When you do talk about living together, remember, it may not be in one fast, easy conversation. Most couples, like Daryl and Robin, talk about the next level of commitment in stages, a little here, a little there. These conversations tend to go better if you're not feeling too urgent, and if you can just allow them to unfold. Things to remember:

Do your mental preparation before each talk, or as soon as you see the conversation is coming up. Remind yourself that you'll be okay no matter the outcome.

Be careful that you don't carry an agenda into the conversation, that you're not trying to push so hard for what you want that you over-power your partner.

Remember the primary goal, to understand each other.

Tell your partner how much you love him/her. Offer reassurance that the relationship is your primary focus, rather than trying to get something from your partner.

Maintain an atmosphere of emotional safety. Even though you may not like what you hear, respect it as your partner's feelings that (s)he is entitled to express.

If things get tense, call a time out. You can always get back to the subject later, when you're both feeling a little calmer.

Keep the conversation fairly short. Rather than hammering away until you're both exhausted, talk about it some, then stop and go do something fun that you both enjoy.

Conversations for living together can begin in many ways and take many forms. In Daryl and Robin's case, the first conversation worked just to open the door for later talks to occur, paving the way for dialogue even though there is fear and uncertainty on both their parts.

Stay in the conversation until you reach resolution. This means that even though you may talk about it for fifteen minutes on Sunday, then for ten minutes on Wednesday three weeks later, the conversation is open-ended until you arrive at a decision. Be prepared for this to take however long it takes. Some couples talk about it a little, then drop it for months, taking it up again later.

When it's done consciously and for good reasons, much of the process of discussing living together overlaps with talks about considering marriage. If living together is a step toward marriage, then whether you acknowledge it or not, you're now opening the door for that level of commitment as well.

Conversations for Marriage: Do We or Don't We?

Contrary to popular belief, the best marriages aren't the ones with surprise proposals out of the blue. Healthy marriages are based on lots and lots of conversation between partners, long *before* the proposal is delivered. Yes, it's highly romantic to date, fall in love, and then someone, usually the guy, "pops the question" one night, complete with diamond ring and getting down on one knee. No discussion necessary, right? We met, we fell in love, it felt right, and so . . . now we're engaged!

The problem with this scenario is that marriage is a huge commitment, one that calls for an understanding about where you each come from. One person may be marrying for love, while the other is marrying for financial security or for other reasons. With little or no communication, you can imagine where a marriage like that will go. Discussing your feelings about marriage helps you understand each other better, giving you a much greater chance to create a lasting connection.

Having *conversations for marriage* means that you have the courage to talk about your feelings with each other, to express the desire to marry, and to discuss why you wish to marry. It means that if one of you is uncertain or ambivalent, you get the opportunity to express that and what it means. *Talking about marriage doesn't mean you've agreed to get married!* It paves the way for a commitment to occur at some point, if that's appropriate.

We all tend to shy away from these discussions, for the same reasons we are reluctant to bring up commitment. Men are afraid to talk about marriage because

- She'll think I'm proposing
- She won't like it if I express ambivalence
- I might get rejected
- It's easier just to figure it all out for myself, then propose

Women are afraid to bring up marriage talks because

- He'll think I'm pressuring him
- Everyone says this is the worst thing to do with a man
- If I just continue dating him and being a wonderful girlfriend, he'll automatically want to marry me and I won't have to bring it up

You can minimize a lot of these fears by setting the stage for your marriage talks with something like this:

"Martin, I'd like to talk about marriage, but please understand, *I'm not trying to get a proposal.* I just think it would be smart if we share our feelings about marriage as a possibility, and what marriage means to each of us. I really don't know for sure if that's what I want, and maybe you don't either. Talking about it might help us get clear on where our relationship is headed, if anywhere."

"We've been dating for three years, Janet, and I think it's time to put marriage on the table for discussion. *I'm not proposing* at this point, I just want to talk about it and see if we're on the same page, you know, headed in the same direction."

Once you've set the stage, there's lots to talk about (although not necessarily in one discussion):

Talk about the possibility of marriage between you. Hopefully, you've covered this more than once in your earlier You and Me Conversations, but now's the time to reiterate once again that, yes, you do see each other as marriage material. If you don't see your partner that way, say so! It's highly misleading to allow someone else to think that he is being considered for marriage, when in fact he's not.

If you have doubts about whether you've found the right person, say so. In a compassionate way, express reservations about the rightness of this relationship, even though this may be extremely difficult. Obviously, you don't want to be critical. It's not necessary to pick the other person apart. Getting your doubts out in the open often has the effect of helping you see how petty they are, or of giving you clarity that yes, indeed, you are not with a right partner.

Talk about what marriage means to you. Some people see marriage as a sacred vow, truly made only if it is for life. Others see it more like an experiment: We'll get married and see how it goes. If we like it, we'll stay together, if not, we'll get divorced. This part of your conversation is about sharing your attitudes regarding marriage with your partner. Obviously, you may have second thoughts if you realize you're miles apart in your view of what marriage is all about.

If you haven't already, discuss whether or not you want to live together before marriage. Again, you want to discover if you disagree on this issue, or if you pretty much share the same point of view.

Talk about your timetables for marriage. This part of the discussion establishes a psychological boundary, if possible. Sometimes, one person pictures dating for about a year, getting engaged, and marrying six months later, while the other sees courtship more like five years of dating and a one-year engagement. This talk is important in revealing how far apart you are in your expectations, not for imposing your time frame on someone else. Later in the chapter, we'll look at how to manage the conversation if you're not on the same timetable.

Talk about your purpose for getting married. We've saved the most important subject for last, and in the next section of the chapter we'll look more closely at this issue.

For some couples, these conversations will reveal that you're working from the same standpoint, and you'll sail forward, probably moving together and/or marrying very soon. For others, in fact for most couples, there will be differences! This is natural and normal and not something about which you should get overly concerned.

The miracle of communication and conversation is that by understanding each other and our stances, we both have the opportunity to shift our positions. Most couples get married after having a series of conversations in which they express themselves, leave it alone for a while, express more of their feelings, and leave it alone some more. Gradually, two people who begin negotiations for a life together from very different places, find common ground and are able to make a genuine commitment. While there are no guarantees on reaching the outcome you seek, know that by being patient and willing to communicate with compassion over and over again, there's every possibility of moving the relationship to marriage if that's where you'd both like it to go.

Conversations for Marriage: Mission and Purpose

Once upon a time, people married for obvious reasons, to form a family, have children, and carry on the business of life. Lots of people today marry for those same reasons, besides the fact that they love each other. Younger couples, especially, tend to marry because there's a biological push behind it. Both of their little clocks are ticking away and saying, *"It's time. You want children, don't you? You love him/her, don't you? Well, then, go ahead!"* Being in love and wanting the same things out of life, such as family and children, are basically the reasons these couples marry.

For many other couples nowadays, the reasons that used to be dictated by firm tradition don't quite apply. Maybe they've already had children in a previous marriage. Perhaps they don't feel that they need marriage in order to have children. Maybe their focus is more on career, and starting a family is second. If there's already been a marriage and divorce or two, then it gets really fuzzy.

"Why marry?" some people ask. "I'm happy enough now and I have a wonderful person whom I love deeply. I don't need marriage to make my life complete or to add anything to the relationship." *This is actually a very good question to ask, one that all couples who are considering marriage should ask themselves and each other.*

Most modern couples lack a sense of purpose in their marriage. The standard reasons they came up with for their union initially don't usually hold up over time. Once the honeymoon's over and the problems begin, they often find that marriage is not what they thought it would be. Love rises and falls, sex diminishes, and the pressures of work, bills, and mortgage payments are great. Secretly, each wonders, "Why did I get married? Is this all there is?"

If children are the primary purpose in being together, then separation is inevitable once they are grown. If love is the reason behind marriage, and we lack the tools to sustain a passionate, romantic connection, then freedom to find a new partner looks pretty good after a few years. The quest for financial security has kept more women in bad marriages than we could ever tally.

Over the years, I have frequently asked people who had been or were currently married, "Why did you get married?" I've heard all kinds of reasons, including:

- My parents liked my choice of partner
- I couldn't think of what else to do with my life at that time
- We were in love
- It was time
- I knew I had found "the one"
- He/she asked me, and I couldn't say no
- I wanted to have children
- And many others . . .

I have rarely run across a couple that has a mission and purpose for being married, and who works to keep the lines of communication regarding their relationship open on a regular basis, continually looking at whether they are fulfilling that purpose. One rare couple like this told me that they have regular talks in which they discuss their purpose: how well they're doing at being soul mates.

Many marriages fail in today's world because couples don't have a sense of purpose in their marriage and don't work actively to keep it in focus. Being in love, wanting to start a family, the desire to merge your lives together—these are all good reasons, but may not be quite enough. These things change, and as they do, couples find themselves drifting through marriage, uncertain of why they're together or even if they should be. *Creating and sustaining a lifelong relationship is so difficult in today's world, that I believe we are being challenged to discover an inspiring and lasting purpose for getting married, one that is unique to each relationship.*

When I do premarital counseling, I like to challenge my clients to talk about and create this purpose before marriage. If you are looking at moving to the next, and highest, level of commitment, now is the time to consider, and talk with your partner about, questions like the following:

Why get married? What are my personal reasons for considering this step in my life?

Why now? Why get married now, as opposed to later? Am I feeling some urgency, and if so, what is that about?

Why marry this person? Am I choosing someone because I think he/she is a right partner for me, or for other reasons?

What is our mission and purpose together?

This last question will be the toughest, and the most essential to handle. *Having a stated mission and purpose*

- Acts as a stabilizing force in the relationship and helps keep you together at the times when you are tempted to bail out
- Establishes a context, or background, against which all of your communication will occur

Mission establishes the fact that your relationship exists in the world and that your lives touch other lives, whether that's your family and children, or whether that's your friends and acquaintances, or both. *Purpose* establishes the reason (as defined by the two of you) that you are together, and sets the stage for how you behave with each other on a day-to-day basis.

To see how this works, let's look at Anne and Marvin's Mission and Purpose Statement and how it works for their relationship:

Our *mission* is to be an example of a loving relationship to those around us, inspiring them to find ways to love each other better and to be their best possible selves. Our *purpose* together is to help each other heal and grow so that we can be our best as creative individuals, able to make a difference in the world.

Anne and Marvin's *mission* tells them to be mindful of their relationship when in the company of others. They don't put each other down to their friends, nor do they behave in ways that undermine their connection. They treasure what they've built together and enjoy being a positive example for other couples.

Anne and Marvin's *purpose* tells them that their goal on a daily basis is to endeavor to understand each other and resolve their differences in as loving a way as possible. Thus, they are committed to full communication, Speaking and Listening Well to each other every day. They are both willing to go to the negotiating table whenever need be. They give each other a sanctuary from the stresses of the world, so that they can both grow to their fullest capacity as human beings. They help and support each other, freeing their energy for creativity in their work, for nurturing their children, and for whatever they do that makes a difference.

When Anne and Marvin get really angry with each other, or when they're feeling discouraged, they look again at their Mission and Purpose Statement, and are renewed in their resolve to sustain a loving relationship. They know they'll never be a perfect couple, and acknowledge that they're on a journey and in a process. They use their Mission and Purpose Statement to help get them back on track at those times when they are challenged in their relationship.

It doesn't matter whether you follow this format or not, only that you talk with your partner and that the two of you put your creative minds and hearts together, coming up with some kind of statement of your purpose in being together and what your relationship is about. As you can see, you will have to have evolved to a rather high level in the relationship in order to do this. You will have already put in many miles on the conversational highway with You and Me talks, and resolved many of your differences along the way. You will have built a great deal of love and trust between you, making the formation of a Mission and Purpose Statement the natural next step.

Good Reasons to Marry

When deciding about marriage, most people look at things such as:

- Good and bad qualities in the person
- The package: looks, age, wealth, body shape, and size
- Their chances of finding someone better

If you believe that choosing a marriage partner is like buying a car, then this method works. If a person is a commodity, then you would, of course, evaluate his worthiness as a lifetime partner by looking at criteria such as these. You would also measure that against the odds of finding a better "deal" somewhere else.

The problem with this approach is twofold:

People aren't like cars! When you take home a green car, it doesn't gradually turn into a red one. People, on the other hand, do change, so that the way they look today is not the way they will look tomorrow. One thing you can definitely count on is that as we age we will lose the looks and body shape we had in youth.

People evolve. One thing you can count on is that the way your partner behaves today is not the way he will behave ten or thirty years from now. Everyone is in a process of growth, so it doesn't work to look at a potential marriage partner as if he will always be the way he is today.

Criteria like the ones above are not bad, they just aren't good indicators of a lasting relationship. Early in the chapter, we looked at wrong reasons to marry. If you want a marriage that could actually last a lifetime, then by far the best reason to marry, and thus the number one thing to examine is

The Quality of Your Connection

How well do we resolve conflict? Your relationship is only as good as your ability to come through your darkest moments. Unfortunately, lots of couples marry while they are still on their early relationship best behavior, so they don't get to test the dark side of their connection. Being able to deal with anger and to resolve your differences is a critical indicator as to whether you will be capable lifetime partners. This is one reason that I advocate putting off marriage until you've dated long enough to get thoroughly mad at each other and discover how you're going to get through it.

How well are we able to negotiate our wants? What's important is not how often you get your way, but how often you both end up feeling satisfied with the solutions that you create together.

What is our level of self-care and relationship care? Do we do loving things for each other? Do we both make regular deposits to the emotional bank account? How well are we able to take care of ourselves as individuals while still maintaining a good, loving connection to each other?

What works and what doesn't in our relationship? Talk about both the positive and the negative in your connection (i.e., "We do really well with our communication, until we get around our families, and then we seem to fight for no good reason.")

What is our heart connection? Do we really love each other?

Is it good enough? When all has been said and done, is the good between us worth the difficulties we experience?

Once you've looked at these things for yourself and gone through these conversations, you will have a very good idea of the quality of your connection, and getting married will either be the next natural step, or you'll know you're not with a right partner. Before you marry, there's still more to talk about.

Together Forever: Myth or Possibility?

Throughout this book, I've emphasized the importance of realizing that there are no guarantees, ever, in a relationship. Marriage is no different in that regard. Because we can never predict what life will bring, and especially what our partners will do, we can never be fully certain that we can keep those vows until one of us dies.

Knowing this, however, is not justification for being only halfway committed. In order to make marriage work, married couples must have a *very strong intention* to stay together forever, and be committed to doing whatever it takes to maintain a loving connection. To get to that level of commitment means doing lots of the groundwork in your romance along the way, which is the premise for this book.

Usually when marriage is under discussion, the last thing anyone wants to address is the possibility of a divorce. Yet not talking about the reality that relationships end leaves some important groundwork undone in your commitment. Paradoxically, discussing the possible end of a relationship can create safety for staying in one. It gives you more emotional muscle, and it reinforces that you're both stable, self-caring individuals, aware of your weaknesses in the relationship and willing to work on them together.

Sam, who married his wife, Debbie, three years ago, was moved and overjoyed to hear her say to him recently, "I love you more than I ever have anyone, Sam, more than I even thought it was possible to love someone. What we have is better than I ever dreamed marriage could be. Yet, I know that if it all ended tomorrow, I would be okay and life would go on, even though it would hurt like crazy." Sam knew that what she was telling him was that their relationship had helped her become a better, stronger person, someone with a far greater capacity to love herself and to love her husband. This is a fulfillment of the true purpose of marriage: to give us both a safe place in which to become the best that we can be.

Talking about the possibility of an end helps set the stage for a strong marriage that will lead to further development of both people in it. The following are some additional premarital conversations to have with that in mind:

Talk about why you would ever leave or divorce. Most of us have a bottom line in a relationship, something that, if it happened, we would be out of there. For many, it's infidelity, although for others it's something else. Putting this out on the table prior to marriage gives each of you fair warning about the biggest emotional minefields that you will want to avoid.

Promise each other that you would be okay if it ended. This step is crucial in establishing your commitment to self-care. This says, not that it would be okay if you left, but that I wouldn't die if you did. It also reassures you that, in the event of one of your deaths, life would go on for the surviving spouse.

Talk about the No-Exit (without process) Agreement. If you don't already have this, consider it before marriage.

Deciding about marriage in this way is a *fully conscious process, focusing on the quality of our connection.* It is much more than mutual admiration, far more than powerful attraction. Rather than being commodities for each other, which we select by comparison to other models, we are soul mates, individuals who have chosen to take the journey of lifelong love together. Instead of valuing each other's looks or financial portfolios, we treasure our relationship, the way we connect and love one another on a day-to-day basis. More wealth than this no one possesses or ever will.

Getting to "I Do"

Conversations for marriage put the issue of lifetime union before both partners, and what happens after that we can't be sure. As you can see, getting to "I do" is a journey in itself. Some will make it, and some won't.

Carlene and Jerry, after dating for one year and living together for an additional two, were having conversations for marriage. At first, it appeared that they had a power struggle over whether to move to this step. As their talks unfolded, with the help of a therapist, what emerged were clashing wants. Carlene wanted more financial security so that she would be freed up from her job to take care of their future children. Thus, she kept hoping that Jerry would change career directions and raise his income more quickly. Jerry wanted her love and admiration regardless of where he was financially, and was unwilling to change career paths. Both eventually realized that they could not accept each other as they were, that what they wanted, the other could not provide. They sorrowfully left the path of lifetime relationship, separated and moved on. However, they did so with lots of conversation, kindness, and respect.

It is better to be honest enough with each other before marriage to make a powerful choice you can stand behind, than to rush through these conversations. If you both don't understand where you're coming from and make a knee-jerk decision, you may get down the aisle, but you are greatly increasing your chances of winding up, in just a matter of time, in divorce court or finding yourself unhappily married for years.

Maintaining the focus on your ultimate goal of understanding empowers you to make a right choice. What if you're pretty sure you've found a right partner, but you're on two different timetables?

Allowing Versus Pushing

Although the stories abound, Rebecca and Vic's story is a great example of conversations for marriage that worked. This couple dated for a year and a half with no significant problems. Then, Rebecca's emotional-timetable alarm clock rang. Suddenly, she was ready to move in together and marry. It never occurred to her that Vic wouldn't be in the same place, so she brought up the subject. Right away, he began backing away, saying that he wasn't ready. The power struggle was on, with Rebecca campaigning for marriage and Vic resisting.

Finally, in frustration, they sought counseling. The therapist helped Rebecca see how pushing him was actually putting off the engagement, and helped Vic see that some of his fears and apprehensions weren't as big as he thought. Rebecca made a decision to stop pushing, dropping the subject of marriage. At the same time, she resolved to keep the lines of communication wide-open. If she felt uneasy or had something to say, she didn't hesitate to approach Vic.

Meanwhile, Vic was struggling with the fact that Rebecca didn't fit his ideal image of the perfect woman, although he did love her deeply. Rebecca, rather than try to convince him that she was right for him, began a subtle campaign to educate Vic about what was important in a relationship.

She continually pointed out the good in their relationship, saying things like "Isn't it great how much fun we have together?" and "It's wonderful how well we understand each other, isn't it?" and "I really love waking up each morning with someone I know I'm going to have a good day with." She focused on the positive, on what clicked between them, reminding him of how much they had in common and how much they loved each other. From time to time she'd point out that their looks would fade as they got older, and that it was so much better to have someone with whom to connect well. Thus, Vic came to understand the true value of their relationship, leaving behind his old, misinformed quest for the perfect package. Three months after their visit to the therapist, Vic surprised Rebecca with a proposal, complete with engagement ring.

If you and your partner's emotional timetables are different, you don't have to be completely passive, waiting forever for your partner to decide. For many couples, the following things have helped nudge the process along:

First and foremost, give up trying to make it happen. Pushing for marriage will either stall the process, or it will get you a reluctant spouse, setting you up for possible affairs and/or divorce.

Respect your partner's emotional timetable. Getting resentful about the fact that (s)he isn't ready will only inhibit the flow of love between you, making your partner even less likely to want to marry you.

Be self-caring. As you would always want to do, have your own life. Don't be constantly at your partner's beck and call. Spend time with friends, take a class, get a new hobby.

Share your feelings about marriage. From time to time, tell your partner how you feel about getting married. Share your vision of what your lives could be like together, and infuse the conversation with love and inspiration. Talk about what the purpose of marriage is for you, and how and why you want to share that with your beloved:

"Sometimes I think about marriage with you, Richard, and it's because we have such a wonderful relationship. I think we complement each other well, and we give each other lots of room to grow. We're good for each other; we're better people for being together. I imagine us sharing a life together and being wonderful partners to each other. Our love is very special, and it makes me want to be with you always."

"I feel that getting married is the next step for us. We communicate

so well and we help each other be the best we can be. To me, this is
what it's all about. I think living together and creating a future would
be good for our relationship, and I'd like to do that with you, whenever you're ready. I love you very much."

"I have this wonderful vision of getting up each day with you,
sweetheart. We could have a cozy little house together, and maybe a
couple of dogs. We'd go to work each day and come home to each
other, have dinner, and go out dancing. We'd invite our friends over
and they would all be so impressed with how much we love each other
and the wonderful life we have together."

"Marriage is a sacred commitment to me, one which would really
require me to stretch in my personal growth. I think you're the perfect
person to take on that challenge with me. Together, I believe we could
both benefit from sharing a life and from finding a way to maintain
our love, which is so wonderful."

Create your own vision statement, keeping it short and sweet, and
from time to time, share it with your partner. *Then, drop it!* Just let
your words sit there, percolating. Avoid the temptation to try to get a
response or to hammer home your point.

If you feel sad that it's not happening, share that, but do so rarely.
Not dwelling on it, but being honest, occasionally tell your partner
how sad you are that it's not happening yet.

"Sometimes when I think about getting married, I get sad that we
don't seem to be moving in that direction. I imagine us sharing a life
and a family, and I feel a loss, knowing that it may never happen."

Accentuate the positive in the relationship. Like Rebecca did, remind your partner at every opportunity of the value of your love and
connection.

Open the door for your partner's feelings to be expressed. Let your
lover know that you would be happy to listen to whatever he has to
say, even if it's full of ambivalence or doubts. Make it truly emotionally
safe and you may actually succeed in getting your partner to open up.
Sometimes, being able to share doubts helps diminish them, paving
the way for a commitment:

"Sweetheart, I've told you so much about how I feel about getting
married, but I guess I haven't heard much from you. I want you to
know that it's okay to tell me whatever you feel about it, even if you

have doubts and fears. I'm ready to Listen Empty, and I promise not to use anything you say against you later. I just want to understand how you feel."

Manage your anger and resentment away from your partner. Vent your frustration about how long it's taking with your friends, your therapist, or your support group. Constantly blowing up at your partner, or manipulating through prolonged crying jags, will only emphasize the poor quality of your relationship, making it less likely that (s)he will want to marry you.

Above all, keep in mind that marriage isn't right until both people want it very much and are emotionally ready to move in that direction. If you're marriage-minded and your partner isn't, you may be tempted to leave the relationship over this issue. Before you do, refer back to Chapter 12 about hanging in there, and ask yourself:

Am I "commitment hungry"?
What is my feeling of urgency?
Why do I want marriage, and why with this person?
What is the quality of our relationship?

One client of mine, whom I'll call Samantha, was very frustrated and getting resentful about the fact that her boyfriend of four years wasn't ready to get married. Many times in the past, she had talked about the relationship, and her accounts were nothing but glowing. "This is by far the best relationship I've ever had," she said. "I know without a doubt that he loves me deeply, and he constantly tells me that he's in love with me, and that I'm 'the one.'" Yet, because she was frustrated, she had begun to secretly suspect that he perhaps didn't really see her as marriage material. She even hinted that she might end the relationship over this issue.

In our session one day, I listened to her vent her frustration. Then, I reminded her of how she had always spoken of the relationship. I asked her if she really believed he was withholding any feelings from her about how he felt about her, and she finally said that no, she didn't. I asked her if she would really prefer being alone to being with this man and not knowing when they would marry. She, of course, had to say that no, she wouldn't. Then we talked about how she might just be able to enjoy the relationship exactly as it is, rather than pushing for something more.

Three days later, I got a call from a much-happier Samantha. "Thank you so much for the things you said the other day," she told me. "After our talk, my point of view shifted, and I now feel really able just to be in the relationship and enjoy it for what it is. This is the best thing in my life, I really believe this man is my soul mate, and it would be crazy to walk away over this issue."

If you believe that the quality of your relationship is very high, and you believe that your partner really loves you, and you love him/her, then you might not want to end a good thing over this issue. One of my other clients expressed intense regret over walking away from someone with whom she shared a deep and passionate love just because he wasn't ready yet to get married. She rebounded from that into a loveless marriage from which it took her ten years to get out.

On the other hand, if you find that the quality of your romance isn't very high, or you have doubts about your love for him/her or his/her love for you, then you might question your own push for marriage. Your move toward marriage may be much more about commitment hunger than it is about joining your hearts for life in a loving relationship.

Marriage is a unique relationship in all of life. It is the only one that we choose as adults, that is legally sanctioned, and that only ends through a legal process or through death. In its highest form, marriage is the pinnacle of human relatedness. It is extremely challenging, and never more so than today. Making the choice about whom and when to marry is one that deserves your complete attention and focus, and one that calls for the exercise of all of your conversational and emotional muscle.

Marriage closes off the exits so that you have the opportunity to deal with that which frightens you the most in a relationship. You will face great challenges without being able to run away easily. It works best when it is consciously chosen, with lots of love, trust, honesty, and communication, and then fully honored for the powerful commitment that it is.

14

The Heart of Love Full Circle

♥　♥　♥

Over morning coffee, Sandy turned to Mick and said, "You know what? You are really the most thoughtful person. I noticed when I came home last night that you took out the trash, cleaned the kitchen, and picked up all the old papers. I appreciate so much how you help out around the house. Thank you, honey."

Alan gave Teresa a kiss when he came in the door, and then did a double take, stepping back to look her up and down. "Wow! What a gorgeous woman. Are you really my date tonight? Man, am I the lucky guy. You know, I really appreciate how you take the time to dress up and look really beautiful for our dates, sweetheart."

"Jeremy, I just want to acknowledge you for your raise. You worked really hard for it and you deserve that and much more. I am so proud of you."

What are these couples doing? They are expressing three of the most important things to communicate in a love relationship, and in so doing, they are filling the emotional bank account they share with loving deposits.

Love Deposits

In the beginning, when we first fall in love, it's easy to make deposits to the emotional bank account. Romantic cards, flowers, candlelit dinners, and thoughtful little gifts of appreciation all say, "Thank you for being in my life, and I appreciate who you are." It's easy to do these things in the beginning because the general theme is courtship. We're on good behavior, putting our best foot forward, and making a statement: I want you in my life. We have each other on pedestals and it's easy to thank and acknowledge someone who is so wonderful.

When these early stages of courtship pass, and we get into the rhythm of a long-term relationship, it's easy to let these thoughtful, romantic gestures fall by the wayside. Other things take priority, and we're no longer courting. Unconsciously we slip into a mind-set that says, "I have you in my life; why do I need to impress you or continue to win you over?" Ironically, we become neglectful of that which we worked so hard to obtain.

Yet, long-term successful relationships require a steady ongoing stream of romantic gestures and words of love in order to thrive. Some of the happiest couples I've met were the ones for whom these little acts of love never end. He still sends flowers and brings her little sentimental gifts. She still tucks little love notes into his suitcase when he leaves for business trips. They still go out dancing together on a regular basis and have romantic weekend getaways. And, *they regularly speak their love and appreciation of each other, making love deposits on a day-to-day basis.*

Acknowledgment, Appreciation, and Thanks

Conversation—heart-to-heart, open, honest, and vulnerable—is the most powerful healing medium we have in life. When someone is able to open up, especially about his deepest, darkest secrets and emotional pain, to a caring, empathic listener, there is a magical energy that is created and that flows from one to the other and back again. It's far more than merely talking and listening, it is *conversation*, true communication, a meeting of the hearts and souls. It is the place, not marked in time or space, but registered deep within us, where true understanding occurs.

Because of the words we've exchanged, and so much more, we now know one another more fully, and thus find that there's even more to love in ourselves and in each other than we originally saw. We are connected, bound together by an intimacy that is more valuable than any physical treasure of this earth. Some have called it *communion*, an act of sharing and fellowship. Because of it, we briefly transcend the cares of daily living. Stress and emotional pain melt away, as we are transported through this connection to a place of comfort and understanding.

The power of conversation is so great that it is the basis of all of life's healing processes: psychotherapy, confession, Twelve-Step work, coaching, and personal-growth workshops. *This healing power can be tapped into on a regular basis and will infuse a relationship with tremendous love and energy.*

Throughout this book we've looked at many ways to do this, through the magic of Listening and Speaking Well, through open, honest sharing, and through apology and forgiveness. By practicing the communication skills that enable us to resolve conflict, and even divert it before it happens, we can lift away most of the stress of being in a love relationship, free our energy, and more thoroughly enjoy our connection. By giving each other the gift of listening, we strengthen the love and trust between us more with each passing day. Maintaining that flow of love and connection once it's been achieved is the next step, and that brings us to another essential communication process, one which will help you to make a steady stream of love deposits to the emotional bank account you and your partner share.

One very powerful way to create lasting positive energy in your relationship is through *affirmation*: confirming over and over again how wonderful your romance is, and saying how much you appreciate the caring partner who is enhancing your life. There are three basic ways to do this, and while they might appear to be the same, they are actually quite different.

Acknowledgment. This is a way of noticing your partner in a positive way, of saying "I see you and who you are. I'm paying attention to the ways that you work hard and make a difference in our relationship, as well as in the world."

"Michael, I just want to acknowledge you for the outstanding job you did preparing dinner the other night. It certainly was a lot of work to make all that food for all those people, and you managed to do it without looking stressed or frayed. Everyone was delighted with the results, as I heard nothing but good comments. I really admire you for doing that."

"Julie, I want to acknowledge you for your promotion. I know you worked really hard for it, and I'm so proud of you. I think you're wonderful, so talented and so smart, and that what you do in your job is something truly outstanding."

Appreciation. This is a way of expressing gratitude for all that your partner does. It is also a way of pointing out his positive attributes, which you are, again, noticing.

"You know, Bill, I appreciate your good attitude with me, especially on those days that I drag you all over the mall trying to find the right pair of shoes. I realize it takes a lot of patience and good humor for you to do that."

"Ann, I appreciate so much those little back rubs you give me at night. It makes a huge difference in my stress levels at the end of the day. You're the best."

Thanks. Saying "thank you" directly conveys gratitude. It lets your partner know that you don't take for granted their good deeds. It acknowledges that you realize your partner has given you a gift in the relationship and that you appreciate it very much.

"Thank you for picking up the dry cleaning, honey."

"Thanks for taking out the garbage, dear."

"Thank you for cleaning up the kitchen after dinner."

"Thanks for paying for that fabulous dinner, sweetheart. I enjoyed every bite!"

Verbal Love Deposits

Speaking acknowledgment, appreciation, and thanks is a very special way to make love deposits. Often overlooked, these expressions are very powerful for a relationship, when given from the heart. Usually, a simple "thank you" is the most you'll hear anyone say in a relationship, and that's better by far than saying nothing at all.

Speaking appreciation goes one step further, in that it allows you to specifically point out that which you value in your partner and in what he does. Appreciation *reaches into* the relationship in a way that allows the other person's heart to be touched, and this is very powerful.

Acknowledgment goes another step beyond appreciation, in that it is a way of noticing the other person, of calling attention to them in a positive way. It shines the spotlight squarely on your partner, in a loving way, much like an awards ceremony marks a person's accomplishments. Acknowledgment is like a little mini award to the one you love, letting them know that their achievements have not gone unnoticed.

One of the things that little children do to develop their images of who they are is to try and get noticed in the family. So, they make up characters to play, they pretend to be animals and act like them, and they create things as an artistic expression of who they are becoming. They "perform" for their parents, and in a loving, attentive family, they will get responses like, "Wow, what a big roar you have! You are sure a scary tiger," and "You are the most beautiful fairy princess I've ever seen!" as well as "Look at how green those trees are, and that sky is so big and blue! I love those interesting little flowers you've put there. Let's hang this in the family room so we can all enjoy it."

This is very powerful affirmation to a child: Noticing him, calling attention to how special she is, and appreciating the unique little person that is in the process of becoming. If we all got that in sufficient measure as children, we would find ourselves naturally being the best we can be as adults, confident of our unique talents and abilities and using them to make a difference in the world.

The reality is that most families fall short of their central task: helping the children become *who they are*, and to be their very best at that. The pressures of running a household, making enough money to take care of life's necessities, and of having other children to nurture seem to take priority. In a family where there's pain and dysfunction, the resources are even further diminished. Therefore, most of us grew up in an environment in which we got little or no affirmation, or what we got was the agenda of the parents and not what our spirits really craved.

In a love relationship, we have the opportunity to heal from this by providing each other with the affirmation that we missed as children. This is not to say that it's our job to give partner self-esteem. That's something that is best addressed in the office of a therapist. What we're talking about here is having your relationship be a source of healing for each other, something we could all use since almost all of us missed out to some degree on being noticed and affirmed for who we are and what we do.

Acknowledgment and appreciation, when spoken from the heart, infuse a relationship with love and healing energy. These simple yet very powerful communication tools can make a bad relationship good, make a mediocre relationship great, and empower a great relationship to last for a lifetime, blissfully.

• One man I know isn't the least bit bashful about announcing to everyone present, on a regular basis, that he is married to the most beautiful woman in Dallas. She says that he still surprises her with flowers and special gifts on a regular basis. They both report, when interviewed separately, that their relationship continues to grow and get better all the time. And this is after twelve years.

• One couple acknowledged each other in front of their guests at dinner one night. He expressed his love and appreciation to her, describing her best qualities in detail. She thanked him for all that he does for her, and acknowledged his wonderful attributes in glowing detail. Everyone present was inspired.

• One couple's marriage, after about twenty years, had grown very stagnant. They were leading separate lives and had lost touch with their feelings of love for each other. One day, the husband began a campaign *simply to acknowledge his wife*. So, day after day, he noticed the little things that she did, and even the ones she overlooked, and began acknowledging and thanking her. At first, she thought he was crazy. Then, she found herself actually making an effort to do things well. Eventually, they reestablished their loving connection, all due to the healing power of affirmation.

How to Make These Deposits

Whether your romance is brand-new, or whether you've been together for years, you can use affirmation to put new life in your connection or to ensure that your love will continue to grow. Here are the basic steps to follow if you wish to incorporate these powerful communication tools into your repertoire:

The first step is **noticing**. Pay attention to and make note of what your partner does well. Notice the little things (s)he does for you. Keep a running mental list of your lover's accomplishments and good deeds.

Begin with "thank you." In many relationships, this little step has been too long overlooked. Rather than diving straight into a long speech of appreciation, start with simply thanking your partner for some of the little things (s)he does for you.

Choose a time to speak your acknowledgment and appreciation. Plan ahead, so that at dinner on Friday night, you know what to say.

Speak your appreciation. Look back over that week, noticing what you appreciate about your partner. Now tell him/her what you've noticed.

Be specific. Saying "I appreciate you" is nice, but doesn't convey much. Saying "I appreciate you for how hard you work to contribute to our income" or "I appreciate you for being so thoughtful of me by sending your maid to clean my apartment last Saturday" conveys much more. Being specific reaches into the relationship and touches your partner's heart. It says that you are attentive and caring enough to notice the details, about your partner, and about his/her contributions to you.

Speak your acknowledgment. Choose something your partner has done or point to something about them.

Be specific. Again, this is the key. "I acknowledge you for being a great person," is good, but "I want to acknowledge you for the contribution you're making to the world through your volunteer work. I'm so proud of you for putting so much heart into a cause that you believe in," is much better.

Allow your partner's response. Because so many of us haven't been acknowledged, we are often uncomfortable with it when we do receive it. It may bring up feelings of embarrassment, even though it's something for which we have secretly longed. Sometimes acknowledgment is so difficult, we even attempt to ward it off with things like, "Oh, it's nothing. I didn't do anything so special." When that happens, have some understanding for how awkward your partner may feel. Don't argue about it. You might try saying something like "I understand that you don't want to brag about yourself, but in my eyes you're wonderful, and this is my way of telling you."

The Behavior of Love

Real love is doing what works in a relationship, over and over again, never assuming that you've done enough already and now you can relax. One woman, married forty-five years, complained to her husband that he never told her he loved her, to which he replied, "I most certainly did. The day we married I told you I love you." Clearly, to him her memory of those three words spoken forty-five years ago should have been enough. This is like putting a hundred dollars into your bank account in 1950, and then expecting it to be enough to live on for the rest of your life!

Love is like anything else worth having in life: It requires regular maintenance. Affirmation, acknowledgment, and gift-giving (the maintenance of love) are needed on a daily, weekly, monthly, and yearly basis. This means paying attention to your lover, noticing the special things she does, and who he is, and then finding ways to mention what you see. It means actively looking for ways to acknowledge the one you love. It means noticing the little things that delight your lover's heart, and then giving them as surprise gifts, not just on anniversaries and special occasions, but at other times and for no reason at all.

Daily: Notice your lover's contributions to you, and thank him. Every day you have the opportunity to speak little affirmations that make a difference in the relationship.

Weekly: Have at least one date every week. Dating is not just for courtship, it is a way of celebrating your romantic connection for a lifetime. Going on dates every week insures that you have quality time together, specifically set aside to enjoy each other and do something fun. This is your opportunity to relax, put aside your cares and worries, and enjoy your relationship. When distressed couples come to see me, I usually find that they have long ago stopped dating, that they have forgotten how to make special time for each other, and so that's the first homework I give them.

Buy or create special little gifts for your lover, things which you know will make him feel special, and surprise him on your weekly dates. Bring flowers, give a back rub, cook a special dinner, make a card by hand, write a poem, sing a song, paint a painting: It doesn't matter what it is, as long as it's from the heart.

Monthly: *Have a getaway weekend every month,* if at all possible. Some couples go camping, others stay at a bed-and-breakfast once a month, others fly away to other cities, depending on financial means. This is your opportunity to have a prolonged date, away from children and responsibilities, to recharge your batteries, and to make large deposits into the emotional bank account of your relationship.

Yearly: *Always remember anniversaries*. Even though you're giving gifts and performing acts of love all along, those special occasions are important markers in a relationship that should be acknowledged. Have dinner out in your favorite restaurant, take a long vacation together, buy a special gift such as jewelry or golf clubs. Or, be creative and do something that's not the norm: Go on a hot-air balloon ride, hire someone to serenade your lover, go on a photographic safari, stay in a spa for the weekend. One man I know, paying attention and hearing his girlfriend say that she always wished she had learned to play the violin, rented an instrument and gave her some private lessons for her birthday.

Use these special-occasion times to go out of your way to affirm your partner. Prepare in advance, using the conversational tools above, and then verbally speak your appreciation and acknowledgment, being specific.

Doing What Works

A gift is only a gift when it's something that the receiver wants. It takes work and special attention to know what to give your lover. Normally, we give what we would ourselves like to receive, or we give what we think they should have, but this is a selfish stance to take in a relationship. Then, the gift is about the giver, rather than the receiver.

Pay attention to your lover. Listen and you'll find that, in countless ways, he is constantly telling you what makes him happy, what reaches into her heart and delights her soul. Then, give what you know will be joyously received.

Some people crave acknowledgment more than others. Rather than take the stance that since she knows you love her that should be enough, take the stance of a true giver. Acknowledge her, tell her she's wonderful, and how (be specific). Appreciate him, listen to him, and thank him for all that he does (be specific). Do this, not because you should, but because doing it works! Do it, not because it's expected, but because you know your lover craves these words of affirmation that will fill her heart with joy.

Do what works! Give up, now and forever, the notion that loving someone in your heart is enough. If you have a miserly mind-set about love, let it go! *Withholding that which you know would make your lover happy isn't just neglect. It's negative energy that will be perceived by your partner whether you ever admit to it or not.* One woman told me once that, even though she had told her husband countless times that she loved being kissed on the neck, he never did it, not once in ten years of marriage. That particular withholding caused her a great deal more pain than the destructive things that actively went on between them.

Love is an action verb! Be loving, do loving things, speak loving words, and you'll find that love grows by leaps and bounds. You'll fill the emotional bank account to overflowing, and when difficult times arrive, you'll find that there's plenty of energy for easily resolving the problems between you.

Exercise

Acknowledgment is an emotional muscle that, in most of us, is pretty weak. As a way of exercising that muscle, and in order to make some deposits to the emotional bank account, you can set aside time with your partner for the following process. The basic steps are:

1. Sitting quietly, with pen and paper handy, both of you (eyes closed or open) reflect back over your life together, from the day that you first met. Review the entire history of your relationship, paying particular attention to the major events:

♥ The day you met.

♥ Your first date, first kiss, first dance together, the first time you made love.

♥ Moving up your commitment level, getting engaged.

♥ The times you met each other's families and/or friends.

♥ Major career changes and/or accomplishments.

♥ Special travel and vacations together.

♥ Moving in together.

♥ Your wedding day.

♥ Buying a house together.

♥ Having children.

2. Really revel in this reflection, picturing yourselves together at those times, laughing, talking, holding hands, kissing, or whatever.

3. Now, in your reflecting, zero in on the times you've spent together on a day-to-day basis:

♥ Waking up together in the morning.

♥ Going to bed together at night.

♥ Eating meals together.

♥ Going dancing together, taking dance lessons.

♥ Exercising together.

♥ Making love.

♥ Taking care of the children.

♥ Making decisions.

♥ Laughing, crying together.

♥ Going to the movies, going out on dates.

♥ Being proud together.

4. Really take your time with this, picturing your lives together like a video playing out in your mind's eye. See yourselves, see your surroundings, smell the smells, feel the feelings.

5. When you're ready, open your eyes, put the pen to the paper, and just begin writing. Don't worry about how you write it, you can always edit later. Just let the pen flow across the paper, and write down as much as you can about:

All of the qualities that you appreciate about your lover personally. Be very specific, going into as much detail as possible. "You're caring, kind, sensitive, sweet, and loving. I appreciate your spirit, your creativity, the way you brush your hair out of your eyes when you're talking to me. I love the way you kiss, the touch of your hand, your beautiful smile. I'm touched by the way you cry at sad movies. You're handsome, courageous, and yet aren't afraid to show me your soft side. I can't get enough of the taste of your lips, and your body! I love your . . . (be specific here). You have the kindest eyes, and I appreciate the gentle way you talk to our children, and how forgiving and compassionate you are."

What your partner brings to the relationship that you appreciate. Be very specific. "You work hard on yourself and are completely committed to your own personal growth. You've taught me more about love and life than anyone I've ever known before. You bring life and energy to our relationship; I don't have to try to get you to do things with me, you're always ready to enjoy life together. You're kind, even when I don't think I deserve it. You call me on my stuff, and I love the way you stand up for yourself. You're the best lover I've ever had, better than I even dreamed you would be. You're truly my best friend. I know that you want the best for me and the best for you, always."

What you acknowledge your partner for, both big things and little things. Specifically name the things that your lover has done that you admire and appreciate. "I acknowledge you for how hard you work to juggle both a career and taking care of our home. You're an incredibly great mom and the best partner I could have ever found. I really want to acknowledge you for going back to school and getting your degree, even though it was difficult and took so much time and energy. You must be so proud. I am so proud of you for . . ."

What you want to thank your partner for. List specific things that you wish to thank your lover for, even if it overlaps with the above list. "Thank you for cooking dinner so often. Thank you for washing my car every Saturday. Thank you for taking me out every week. Thank you for that great weekend trip last month. Thank you for being a wonderful partner and for being in my life."

6. When you've both finished your lists, face each other and begin acknowledging each other. Look at some of the things on your list, and then look at your partner and tell him while looking into his eyes. Don't just read off the paper. Do it slowly, speaking each thing carefully and putting as much feeling into it as you can. Pause between

each item so your partner can absorb what you've just said, then go on to the next.

7. Take turns every so often. Make it an exchange of one acknowledging, the other receiving, then vice versa, then back to the other way.

8. When you've both run out of things to say, stop, and once again, do some reflection. After listening to your lover's acknowledgment of you, think about what he might have left out. List the things you would like to hear that haven't already been said. Then, tell each other for what you wish to be acknowledged.

Usually, this part would be left out. There's a myth that if you have to ask for it, it doesn't count or it diminishes the power of it. While it's true that asking for what you want can be overdone (never giving your partner the opportunity to think of it first), it's also true that your lover can't think of everything. Sometimes, what I most want to be acknowledged for is something that my partner has overlooked, and my reminding him is a gift. He then knows exactly what I want to hear, what will touch my heart and heal my soul the most.

"I want to be acknowledged for the time you broke up with me and I hung in there for you while you worked through some fear. I really want to be appreciated for that, because doing it was one of the hardest things I've ever done."

"I would like for you to acknowledge how far I've come in my personal growth since we've met, and even before that. I want to feel like you really understand how big it is for me to be with you in the way that I am, and that you appreciate my efforts."

You have now accomplished something that rarely occurs in a relationship: You have acknowledged each other to the bottom of your hearts and souls. If you're not headed for the bedroom right now to make love, then it's only because you're still reading this book and haven't done the exercise yet!

Conversations for a Lifetime

Now that you've learned what it takes to maintain a powerful lifetime love, use this book and the information in it as a continual reference.

Think of these exercises in the same way that you do your daily workout. Don't expect to be a world-class bodybuilder overnight or to stay in great shape without daily practice. *Aim for quality of life*, and that means practicing over and over, using the tools until they are no longer awkward and unfamiliar but are second nature.

Remember that having your heart in the right place is the most important thing in all of your relationships. Whether you're still single and looking for a partner, or whether you're thinking of marriage, you can use these tools to create a more rewarding experience of life. My wish for you is that you will find love first and foremost within yourself. From there, that you will be eventually lucky enough to have a committed partner with whom to travel the path of real love. And, in all of your relationships, that you will know the joy of conversation that creates a bridge between hearts, connecting you in the way that only humans are capable, in the way that we were meant to be with one another.